Debt, Taxes, and
Corporate Restructuring

Debt, Taxes, and Corporate Restructuring

JOHN B. SHOVEN
JOEL WALDFOGEL
editors

The Brookings Institution | Washington, D.C.

Copyright © 1990 by

THE BROOKINGS INSTITUTION

1775 Massachusetts Avenue, N.W., Washington, D.C. 20036

Library of Congress Cataloging-in-Publication data:

Debt, taxes, and corporate restructuring / John B. Shoven and Joel
  Waldfogel, editors.
     p.   cm.
  Includes index.
  ISBN 0-8157-7884-8 (cloth) — ISBN 0-8157-7883-X (paper)
  1. Consolidation and merger of corporations—United States—
Finance. 2. Consolidation and merger of corporations—
Taxation—United States. I. Shoven, John B. II. Waldfogel,
Joel, 1962–   .
  HD4028.M4D43   1990
  338.8′3′0973—dc20   90-2168
                                             CIP

9 8 7 6 5 4 3 2 1

The paper used in this publication meets the following requirements of the
American National Standard for Information Sciences—Permanence of
Paper for Printed Library Materials, ANSI Z39.48-1984.

Set in Linotron Times Roman
Composition by Harper Graphics
  Waldorf, Maryland
Printed by R.R. Donnelley and Sons, Co.
  Harrisonburg, Virginia

Foreword

DURING the 1980s the income taxation of corporations and individuals changed dramatically. The decade also witnessed a massive wave of corporate mergers and acquisitions, a sharp increase in the issuance of corporate debt, and a startling removal of large amounts of corporate equity from the marketplace. The resulting concern about the possibility of a rash of bankruptcies, and disappointment with the revenue generated by the corporate income tax, have encouraged a reexamination of the taxation of debt and equity.

The chief difference between the taxation of debt and equity is that the return on equity is taxed at both the corporate and investor levels, whereas the interest return on debt is taxed only at the investor level. Although corporate and individual tax rates both declined in the 1980s, their relative magnitude shifted, and after the 1986 tax reform the corporate rate exceeded the highest personal rate for the first time. This new pattern of tax rates has increased the relative tax advantage enjoyed by debt returns.

In this book the authors consider several important issues regarding taxation and corporate restructuring. They present evidence about the increased use of leverage throughout the economy, question the possibility of making a meaningful distinction between debt and equity, and examine one of the leading theories that attempt to explain the new corporate financial behavior. They also describe and analyze some tax reforms that could eliminate the tax preference enjoyed by debt.

This volume is the result of a conference organized by John B. Shoven that was held at the Brookings Institution in May 1989. The papers were edited by Caroline Lalire, Jack Kirshbaum, Nancy D. Davidson, and Theresa B. Walker, and were checked for factual accuracy by Roshna Kapadia and Pamela Plehn. Florence Robinson prepared the index.

Brookings gratefully acknowledges financial support for its Center for Economic Progress, sponsor of this effort, from the following: Donald S. Perkins, American Express, AT&T, Chase Manhattan Bank, Cummins

Engine, Ford Motor Company, Hewlett-Packard, Morgan Stanley, Motorola, Springs Industries, Union Carbide, Warner-Lambert, Xerox Corporation, Aetna Foundation, Ford Foundation, General Electric Foundation, Prudential Foundation, Sloan Foundation, Smith Richardson Foundation, Institute for International Economic Studies, and Alex C. Walker Education and Charitable Trust.

The views expressed here are those of the authors and should not be attributed to the trustees, officers, or staff members of the Brookings Institution.

BRUCE K. MAC LAURY
President

June 1990
Washington, D.C.

Contents

Introduction and Summary   1
John B. Shoven and Joel Waldfogel
    The Present Tax Treatment of Debt and Equity   2
    Mechanisms for Restructuring and Sources of External Finance   6
    How Much Did Leverage Increase?   7
    The Case for Reform of the Taxation of Debt and Equity   10
    Summaries of the Papers   11

Federal Policy and the Accumulation of Private Debt   21
C. Eugene Steuerle
    Trends in the Pre-1981 Era   22
    The Turnaround in the 1980s   29
    Future Trends   35
    Conclusions   36
    Comment by Jane G. Gravelle   37

Corporate Leverage and Leveraged Buyouts in the Eighties   43
Margaret M. Blair and Robert E. Litan
    Trends in Aggregate LBO Activity and Corporate Leverage   46
    Why the 1980s?   54
    Leverage and LBO Activity by Industry   63
    Conclusions and Additional Implications   78
    Comment by Robert A. Taggart, Jr.   80
    Comment by Scott Smart   85

Debt, Equity, and the Taxation of Corporate Cash Flows   91
Alan J. Auerbach
    Debt, Equity, and the U.S. Tax System   92
    The Interaction between Tax and Nontax Incentives   102
    Reforming the Taxation of Corporate Cash Flows   105
    Alternative Proposals   108
    Conclusions   126
    Comment by James M. Poterba   126
    Comment by William D. Andrews   130

Distinguishing Debt from Equity in the Junk Bond Era   135
Jeremy I. Bulow, Lawrence H. Summers, and
Victoria P. Summers
  The Blurring of the Debt-Equity Distinction   137
  Thinking about Debt-Equity Distortions   145
  What Should Be Done?   160
  Comment by David F. Bradford   166
  Comment by Martin D. Ginsburg   169

Converting Corporations to Partnerships through Leverage   173
Myron S. Scholes and Mark A. Wolfson
  The Evolution of the Tax Treatment of Debt and Equity   173
  A Simple Model of the Tax Advantages of Debt   177
  Corporate Taxation of Economic Rents versus
     Competitive Returns   179
  Retained Earnings and Dividend Policy   192
  Concluding Remarks   196
  Comment by Laurie Simon Bagwell   196
  Comment by Jeremy I. Bulow   200

Contributors   203

Index   205

Tables

John B. Shoven and Joel Waldfogel
  1. Sources of External Funds for the Nonfinancial Corporate
     Business Sector, 1978–87   7
  2. Annual Cash Distributions to Shareholders, 1977–87   8

Margaret M. Blair and Robert E. Litan
  1. Five-Year Average Payments to Capital, Twenty Industries,
     1948–87   62
  2. Three Measures of Leveraged Buyout Activity and Corporate
     Leverage, by Industry   64
  3. Industries Ranked by Return to Capital, 1980   68
  4. Industries Ranked by Average Return to Capital, 1978–87   69
  5. Industries Ranked by Rate of Decline (or Increase) in Return
     to Capital, 1972–87   70
  6. Interindustry Correlations between Measures of Leveraging
     Activity and Measures of Growth and Investment Rates   72

Contents

7. Regressions Predicting Ratios of Interest to Cash Flow,
   by Industry   75
8. Regressions Predicting Ratios of Debt to Total Assets,
   by Industry   76

Alan J. Auerbach
1. A Summary of Reform Proposals   110

Jeremy I. Bulow, Lawrence H. Summers, and Victoria P. Summers
1. The Revenue Implications of Marginal and Average
   Leveraged Buyouts   150
2. RJR's Declining Net Investment   158

Myron S. Scholes and Mark A. Wolfson
1. The Degree to Which Debt Financing Avoids Double Taxation   180

Figures

John B. Shoven and Joel Waldfogel
1. Debt-to-Asset Ratios, 1969–86   9

C. Eugene Steurle
1. Credit Market Debt in the United States, 1946–88   23
2. Changes in Net Outstanding Debt, Various Sectors, 1948–68,
   1968–81, 1981–88   26
3. Changes in Outstanding Debts and Loans, Various Sectors,
   1948–68, 1968–81, 1981–88   28
4. Debt-to-Asset Ratios, Selected Years, 1948–88   34

Margaret M. Blair and Robert E. Litan
1. Number of Mergers and Acquisitions and Leveraged Buyouts
   in All Industries, 1978–88   47
2. Number of Mergers and Acquisitions and Leveraged Buyouts
   in Manufacturing Industries, 1978–88   47
3. Value of Mergers and Acquisitions and Leveraged Buyouts
   in All Industries, 1978–88   48
4. Value of Mergers and Acquisitions and Leveraged Buyouts in
   Manufacturing Industries, 1978–88   48
5. Debt-to-Equity Ratios for the Nonfinancial Corporate Sector,
   Book Values, 1949–88   49
6. Debt-to-Equity Ratios for the Nonfinancial Corporate Sector,
   Market Values, 1949–88   49

7. Actual and Projected Interest–Cash Flow Ratios for the
   Nonfinancial Corporate Sector, 1948–87   51

8. Net New Debt and Equity Raised by Nonfinancial Corporations,
   1965–88   53

9. Return to Capital and Real Cost of Capital in the Manufacturing
   Sector, Twenty Industries, 1949–87   58

10. Return to Capital and Real Cost of Capital in the Manufacturing
    Sector, 1949–87   60

Jeremy I. Bulow, Lawrence H. Summers, and Victoria P. Summers

1. The Corporate Debt Burden in Historical Perspective, 1952–90   137

Introduction and Summary

John B. Shoven and Joel Waldfogel

THE FINANCIAL structure and behavior of American corporations has changed dramatically since 1984. Before that time corporations as a whole sold equity to American households and institutional investors; since then they have been net purchasers rather than net issuers of equity claims. Many of the largest firms in the United States were once thought to be invulnerable to hostile takeovers, but in the last five years the country has seen acquisitions involving $20 billion or more. Shareholders used to get most of their cash return through dividends, but lately they have received more than half their return from corporations buying their own shares or the shares of other companies. Many of the strongest firms in the economy used to operate with little or no debt. This structure is becoming rare. A great many companies, including some of the biggest and strongest, have dramatically increased their debt levels. Overall it appears, at least to the casual observer of U.S. financial markets, that a significant substitution of debt for equity financing is taking place. This raises three obvious questions: Why? Why now? And does it matter?

On the surface, the tax system seems to be the main factor encouraging the changes in the corporate financial structure. But the view that tax considerations alone explain the phenomenon is dubious for two reasons. First, the favorable tax treatment of interest relative to dividends has been a fixture of the tax code, at least since World War II. Why, then, did the dramatic changes appear to begin in 1984? Second, the present value of all the future tax savings generated by the increased reliance on debt often cannot account for the premium price that acquirers pay in taking over a firm.[1] Nevertheless, we believe the tax system is indeed an important element in the corporate restructuring and one worth careful consideration. Although taxes may not have been the only cause of the recent wave of

1. Alan Auerbach and David Reishus, "The Effects of Taxation on the Merger Decision," in Alan J. Auerbach, ed., *Corporate Takeovers: Causes and Consequences* (University of Chicago Press, 1988), pp. 157–83.

corporate restructuring, they have certainly encouraged leverage. Either way, corporate tax reform has the ability to discourage further restructuring. Moreover, the new corporate financial practices have important tax consequences, in the form of the revenue generated by the corporation income tax, the role of the alternative minimum corporate income tax, and the cost of capital facing corporate investments.

The five substantive papers in this volume deal with the subject of taxation and corporate restructuring. Before summarzing those papers, however, we examine several relevant issues.

We first review the current tax treatment of debt and equity. Then we briefly describe some of the mechanisms used for restructuring the financing of U.S. corporations. We also present some facts about changes in the sources of external financing for corporations in recent years.

We next look at the evidence about how much aggregate debt levels have actually increased. Analysts use different measures of leverage and equity value, and their results depend significantly on the chosen measure. This dependence is evident in one of the papers in this volume: while corporations have increased their reliance on debt financing, their share of aggregate debt securities in the economy has actually fallen. Households, unincorporated enterprises, and the government have been increasing their indebtedness at even faster rates than corporations. That, of course, does not warrant a lack of concern about the consequences of the new corporate financial structure.

Finally, we consider the case for reform of the taxation of debt and equity returns. The question immediately arises whether it is possible to distinguish between debt and equity in the modern world of sophisticated security. The current tax code is based on the ability to make such distinctions. We briefly discuss ways of reforming the current system with respect to its treatment of debt and equity, principally corporate tax integration and the introduction of a corporate cash flow tax. This section is brief, since another chapter in this volume deals with the subject in detail.

The Present Tax Treatment
of Debt and Equity

Corporations are financed by both debt holders (bondholders, note holders, and bank lenders) and equity owners. The taxation of corporate cash flows (net of depreciation) depends on whether the money is deemed to be an interest payment to debt holders or income paid to equity claimants. From a tax standpoint, the most important distinction is that interest payments to debt holders are deductible from the tax base of the corporate income tax, whereas dividend payments to equity holders are not. Insofar as cash flows are deemed interest, they escape taxation at the *corporate* level. Both interest and dividends are fully taxable at the level of the individual investor, provided the investor is a taxable entity. If equity earnings are retained in the corporation rather than paid out as dividends, then the personal tax treatment is different. Presumably the retained earnings result in an accrued capital gain for the shareholders—other things being equal, the price of the stock will rise. A tax may be ultimately payable on that capital gain, but it can be postponed until the gain is realized and may even be avoided entirely if the asset is not sold before passing through an estate. Under the 1986 Tax Reform Act, realized capital gains are fully taxable at ordinary income tax rates. Most analysts judge, however, that the combination of the deferral and escape possibilities means that the present value of taxes on accrued capital gains is about half what it would be if such accrued gains were taxed immediately.

With the current tax code, it is obvious that cash flow treated as interest is taxed more lightly than that treated as return to equity. The tax advantage given to debt financing is partly offset by the above-mentioned ability of equity holders to defer the tax on accrued capital gains until realization, which lowers the effective personal tax rate on retained earnings. However, at current marginal tax rates on corporate and personal income, debt finance has a clear advantage. For example, an investor in the 28 percent marginal tax bracket, whose effective tax rate on realized capital gains is 14 percent and who holds stock in a corporation that pays out 50 percent of its equity earnings in dividends, pays an overall tax of 48 percent on an equity investment but only 28 percent on a debt investment.[2] Consequently, for households in the top income categories, the return on cor-

2. Let t_p be the marginal personal income tax rate, t_c the corporate tax rate, t_{KG} the effective marginal rate of tax on accrued capital gains, α the fraction of equity income distributed as dividends, and T_E and T_D the total marginal taxation of equity and debt payments, then

(1) $$T_E = t_c + (1 - t_c)(\alpha t_p + (1 - \alpha)t_{KG})$$

and

(2) $$T_D = t_p$$

(3) $$T_E - T_D = t_c - t_p + (1 - t_c)(\alpha t_p + (1 - \alpha)t_{KG}).$$

As is clear from equation 3, if $t_c > t_p$, debt finance is always tax favored no matter what the effective rate on capital gains relative to the tax on ordinary income. But even if $t_c < t_p$, the tax on equity income can still be larger than the tax on debt income if α is high or the effective tax rate on capital gains is not much lower than the rate on ordinary income.

porate equity is subject to a 20 percent surtax relative to the tax on interest income. The surtax is even greater for investors in the 15 percent bracket or for tax-free investors. For the latter, the tax disadvantage of equity is the full 34 percent corporate tax rate. In general, though this analysis has included only federal taxes, consideration of state level taxation would merely widen the gap between the taxation of debt and the taxation of equity.

That equity is taxed more heavily than debt for all investors is ensured by the fact that the corporate tax rate exceeds the highest personal tax rate—indeed it would hold even if the corporate rate were somewhat lower than the personal rate (see note 2). The current relative rate structure, in which corporate taxes are higher than the highest bracket of the individual tax, first occurred in recent times with the 1986 tax reform. However, it was probably also true that all investors had a tax advantage in having their income treated as interest rather than as equity earnings in the 1980–86 period. During that time the peak personal tax rate was 50 percent and the corporate tax rate was 46 percent. Before 1980, when personal rates on ordinary income went as high as 70 percent (91 percent before 1964) and capital gains received a favorable treatment, the relation between the total taxation of the return to debt and that to equity was less clear. Under such tax rate structures some investors (those with very high personal tax rates) may have had a lower total tax rate on equity earnings than on interest income. One would expect those investors to have formed "clienteles" and to have acquired firms that paid little or no dividends—dividends have always been tax disadvantaged relative to both retained earnings and interest. But the evidence that such clienteles formed is weak.[3]

With today's tax rates, interest is clearly taxed more lightly than equity earnings for everyone, and dividends are more heavily taxed than retained earnings for all taxable investors. The general outline of the change since 1984 in corporate behavior (increased use of leverage and share repurchase programs, for instance) seems to be consistent with the changes in the tax law that took place in 1981.

3. Although there is some confirmation of the theory, Scholz found a negative correlation between an investor's personal tax rate and the dividend yield on his or her equity holdings. John Karl Scholz, "The Effect of the Relative Tax Treatment of Dividends and Capital Gains on Corporate Valuation and Behavior," Ph.D. dissertation, Stanford University, 1988. The theory of clienteles is referred to as "Miller Equilibrium," but it is largely irrelevant under the tax structure that has existed since 1980. Merton H. Miller, "Debt and Taxes," *Journal of Finance*, vol. 32 (May 1977), pp. 261–75.

With the return to debt holders clearly tax preferred, one natural question is, what determines the optimal financial structure of the firm? The traditional answer is that the tax advantage of additional debt has to be weighed against the increase in the probability of incurring bankruptcy costs that more debt can entail. Indeed, concern over increased bankruptcy probabilities seems to have been one of the main reasons policymakers have expressed concern about corporate restructuring. It is possible that the real resource costs of bankruptcy have decreased over time with such innovations as Chapter 11 of the bankruptcy code. Bankruptcy still involves large legal fees but no longer necessarily involves the liquidation of assets or the closing of facilities. Examples of important bankruptcies that entailed little disruption of the real activities of the firm include Texaco, Johns Manville, and Campeau. If bankruptcy costs have indeed declined, that may be an additional explanation for the increased use of leverage in recent years. Less reassuring, the unprecedentedly long economic recovery of the last seven years may have reduced the probability that investors assign to recession-induced declines in corporate cash flows.

Aside from the possibility of reduced bankruptcy costs and a change in the incentives, two other hypotheses seek to explain the timing of recent corporate restructuring. The first is financial innovation, in particular the development of junk bonds. Junk bond issuance has grown rapidly in the last decade, especially since 1984.[4] If the tax incentives favoring leverage existed since 1981, however, why did junk bonds have to wait until 1984? Conceivably, financial markets need some time to learn. The second hypothesis (offered by Blair and Litan in this book) is that in the 1980s firms in some industries faced investment opportunities whose returns were below the cost of capital. Substitution of debt for equity in such firms alleviates the conflict of interest between managers, who may seek to enlarge the firm, and investors, who want their return paid out to them rather than reinvested at low returns.

The timing of recent corporate restructuring activity is difficult to explain. Tax law has encouraged restructuring since at least 1981, yet restructuring activity began in earnest in 1984. If corporate financial structure responds instantly to tax incentives, then taxation, in particular the tax reform of 1981, does not explain restructuring three years later. Clearly

4. Robert A. Taggart, Jr., "The Growth of the 'Junk' Bond Market and Its Role in Financing Takeovers," in Alan J. Auerbach, ed., *Mergers and Acquisitions* (University of Chicago Press for National Bureau of Economic Research, 1988), pp. 5–24.

the structure of corporate taxation encourages leverage. Whether tax policy is the prime cause of increased leverage or simply a factor facilitating increased leverage, changes in tax policy could discourage further restructuring activity.

Mechanisms for Restructuring and Sources of External Finance

The most straightforward and traditional mechanism for a financial restructuring that replaces equity with debt would be the issuance of bonds for the explicit purpose of retiring equity. But it is difficult to attribute the historical changes in the leverage of a firm to specific financial actions, because almost all financial payments affect leverage. For example, the payment of dividends reduces equity; the use of retained earnings to repurchase stock does the same; the cash acquisition of another company decreases the aggregate amount of equity outstanding in the economy; and leveraged buyouts often dramatically increase the leverage of a firm.

Although the financial structure of a firm depends on its use of internally generated earnings as well as of external funding sources, it is instructive to look at the trends in the use of external funding. Table 1 shows the source of external funds raised from 1978 through 1987. The annual average total amount raised through external sources did not change much from 1978–83 ($70 billion) to 1984–87 ($75 billion). But the composition of that funding did change dramatically. During 1978–83 net new equity issues averaged $3.9 billion, which shows that gross equity retirements almost canceled gross new equity issues. During 1984–87 net new equity issues averaged − $78.3 billion. Since 1984 corporations have been retiring massive amounts of corporate equity, primarily through share repurchase programs and cash mergers. This behavior would not necessarily have led to a dramatic change in corporate leverage if it simply reflected a change in the way equity earnings were paid out—a replacement of dividend payments by equity retirements. That, however, is not the case, as is apparent from the second column of table 2, which shows that dividends grew steadily even while equity repurchases through cash acquisitions and share repurchases greatly increased. Dividends as a percentage of total cash distributions fell from almost 80 percent in 1977 to just under 40 percent in 1987.

Table 1. Sources of External Funds for the Nonfinancial Corporate Business Sector, 1978–87[a]

Billions of dollars

Year	Gross equity issues	Gross equity retirements	Net new equity issues (issues minus retirements)	Net new borrowing[b]	Total net funds raised in market
1978	n.a.	n.a.	−0.1	71.0	70.9
1979	n.a.	n.a.	−7.8	68.0	60.1
1980	21.1	8.2	12.9	57.8	70.7
1981	21.5	33.0	−11.5	102.1	90.7
1982	28.9	22.5	6.4	43.4	49.8
1983	40.0	16.5	23.5	54.4	77.9
1984	18.0	92.5	−74.5	170.3	95.8
1985	25.0	106.5	−81.5	132.4	50.9
1986	37.8	118.6	−80.8	173.8	93.1
1987	35.5	112.0	−76.5	136.8	60.3
Averages					
1978–83[c]	27.9	20.1	3.9	66.1	70.0
1984–87	29.1	107.4	−78.3	153.3	75.0

Source: Joint Committee on Taxation, *Federal Income Tax Aspects of Corporate Financial Structures*, Joint Committee Print, 101 Cong. 1 sess. (Government Printing Office, January 1989).

n.a. Not available.

a. Excludes farming corporations.

b. Excludes trade debt.

c. Equity issues and retirements are averaged over 1980–83.

The pattern of net new borrowing through time is the opposite. Net borrowing averaged $66 billion a year in 1978–83, but grew to an average of $153 billion in 1984–87 (see table 1). Though it is true that funds are fungible, and therefore difficult to trace, it does appear that the additional borrowing largely financed equity withdrawals rather than additional new investment.

How Much Did Leverage Increase?

Data such as those just presented have led many observers to conclude that leverage increased sharply in the United States during the 1980s. But because of the large rise in stock market prices, the *value* of equity holdings did not fall during the period. This raises the question of how one should measure leverage. The standard measures of leverage fall into three broad categories: solvency measures, such as ratios of the value of debt to the value of assets; liquidity measures, such as the ratio of interest payments to cash flow; and hybrid measures, such as the ratio of debt to income.

Such solvency measures as debt-to-asset ratios differ according to whether they are measured in book- or market-value terms. Market-value measures,

Table 2. Annual Cash Distributions to Shareholders, 1977–87
Millions of 1989 dollars

Year	Cash via acquisitions	Dividends	Share repurchases
1977	4,274	29,450	3,361
1978	7,228	32,830	3,520
1979	16,888	38,324	4,507
1980	13,081	42,619	4,961
1981	29,319	46,832	3,973
1982	26,247	50,916	8,080
1983	21,248	54,896	7,709
1984	64,244	60,266	27,444
1985	69,971	67,564	41,303
1986	74,522	77,122	41,521
1987	62,240	83,051	54,336

Source: Laurie Simon Bagwell and John B. Shoven, "Cash Distributions to Shareholders," *Journal of Economic Perspectives*, vol. 3 (Summer 1989), p. 131.

which are sensitive to the stock market's volatility, fluctuated widely from 1969 through 1986 (see figure 1) but did not rise systematically in the 1980s. Rather, rising equity values allowed the market-value debt-to-asset measures to decline on average in the 1980s. The ratio of the value of debt to the total value of the firm (at market value) averaged 0.301 between 1982 and 1986, as against 0.327 for the preceding five years. By contrast, book-value measures of debt-to-assets, which progress more smoothly over time, rose steadily between 1983 and 1986. In 1986 the book-value debt-to-asset ratio stood at 0.273, its highest level since 1977. Crudely, the ratio of debt to assets measures the relation between fixed obligations (debt) and the capacity to cover those obligations (the value of assets). If the market value of equity better reflects the corporate sector's ability to generate cash for meeting its fixed obligations, then market-value debt-to-asset ratios may be a more reasonable indicator of corporate solvency than book-value ratios.

Although market-value solvency measures held steady or declined, corporate liquidity measures, such as the ratio of interest to cash flow, rose. Some observers (including Blair and Litan) favor flow measures of liquidity, because these gauge a corporation's ability to meet its current fixed obligations. Flow measures of corporate liquidity are considered better indicators of the risk of bankruptcy than others. Corporations have devoted increasing proportions of cash flow to debt service (see Blair and Litan's figure 6). Rising interest burdens are compatible with stable debt-to-asset ratios if share values increase by more than corporate earnings. Indeed, that has happened. Whereas corporate debt growth has been matched

Figure 1. Debt-to-Asset Ratios, 1969–86

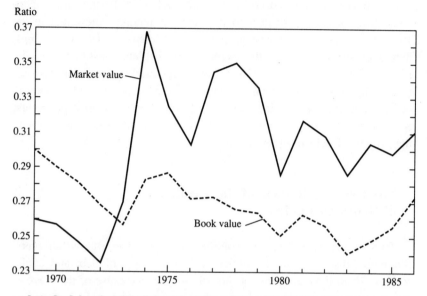

Ratio

Market value

Book value

Source: Ben S, Bernanke and John Y. Campbell, "Is There a Corporate Debt Crisis?" *Brookings Papers on Economic Activity, 1:1988*, table 4, p. 103. Market value is "Method A."

by growth in the value of corporate equity, debt growth has exceeded growth in corporate earnings. Stated another way, corporate price-earning ratios more than doubled between 1980 and 1986.[5]

According to the hybrid stock-flow measures of debt cited by Eugene Steuerle in this book (such as the ratio of corporate debt to gross national product), corporate leverage rose in the 1980s. Corporate debt stood at 30.3 percent of GNP in 1980; it reached 36.8 percent of GNP in 1987. Whether that is excessive depends on the determinants of the economy's debt-carrying capacity. If GNP is a good indicator of the corporate sector's ability to service its debt, then debt increased substantially in the 1980s. However, it is instructive to compare this growth to the growth in household and federal government debt relative to GNP. Whereas the ratio of corporate debt to GNP grew by 12 percent between 1967 and 1987, the ratios of household and federal government debt to GNP grew by 34 and 27 percent, respectively, during the same twenty-year time span.[6]

5. See Ben S. Bernanke and John Y. Campbell, "Is There a Corporate Debt Crisis?" *Brookings Papers on Economic Activity, 1:1988*, p. 111 and table 11.

6. These figures are adapted from the Joint Committee on Taxation, *Federal Income Tax Aspects of Corporate Financial Structures,* Joint Committee Print, 101 Cong. 1 sess. (Government Printing Office, January 1989).

The three kinds of leverage measures just discussed suggest different assessments of current corporate financial behavior. Rising ratios of interest to cash flow, and debt to measures of income, show that in the 1980s the corporate sector became more debt intensive. Two factors militate against the view that the increased use of debt constitutes a crisis. First, rising equity values, which have kept market-value debt-to-asset ratios relatively stable, signal stockholders' confidence about the viability of the corporate sector, including its ability to meet interest payments. Second, the growth in corporate debt has been moderate compared with the growth of debt in other sectors.

The Case for Reform of the Taxation of Debt and Equity

Two of the papers in this volume (Auerbach and Bulow-Summers-Summers) discuss possible reforms of the taxation of debt and equity returns. Even if taxation is not the sole or primary cause of the wave of corporate restructurings, it clearly plays an important role. Both papers discuss the traditional approach to the problem through an integration of the corporate and personal tax system that would eliminate the double taxation of dividends. Both also discuss a new proposal by the American Law Institute (ALI).

The key consideration in both papers, and one that has not received much attention in the policy debate, is the extent to which removing the double taxation of corporate equity conveys a windfall gain to the owners of the existing capital stock. The prices at which stockholders purchased the stocks they now hold presumably reflected—that is, were depressed by—the relatively unfavorable tax treatment of dividends. Removing that tax disadvantage through one of the traditional approaches—either by eliminating the taxation of dividends at the corporate level or providing dividend recipients a credit equal to the imputed value of the corporate tax already paid—would boost the value of their existing stock and give them a windfall they could realize without undertaking any additional saving or investment. The authors of both papers argue that such a windfall is inappropriate and unnecessary, a major drawback of the traditional proposal of a ''partnership method'' of corporate tax integration. The task they set for themselves is to design a tax system that is neutral with respect to debt and equity and encourages new investments, but one that does not create a windfall for existing capital.

The corporate taxation proposals that most nearly meet these criteria are the ALI proposal (described later in the summary of Auerbach's paper) and a corporate cash flow tax. Auerbach discusses several variants of a cash flow tax. One would disallow interest deductions from the corporate tax base but at the same time permit the complete expensing of new investments. The corporate tax would thus apply only to the excess of net cash flow over the value of outlays on new investments. For instance, if dividends and interest payments were matched by new investments of equal value (financed, perhaps, by new external financing), no tax would be currently owed. The cash flow tax would treat all financing as if it were equity but would offset the double tax with immediate investment writeoffs. Such a tax can be shown to be nondistortionary in that any project which is profitable without the tax will still be profitable after the tax.

We recognize that a cash flow tax (or a corporate tax integration scheme with provisions to offset the windfall gain to the owners of existing capital, such as the ALI proposal) is a radical change from current practice. Further study of the application of either method to financial intermediaries and to multinational corporations is necessary. Research is also needed in order to predict the revenue consequences of adopting such proposals. What can be said now is that both alternatives have the potential to remove the tax advantage for leverage and also to improve the incentives for qualified investments. We feel they clearly merit serious examination.

Summaries of the Papers

The summaries that follow do not attempt to be comprehensive, but it is hoped they will give the reader a useful preview of each paper.

Debt and Taxes

Eugene Steuerle analyzes the use of debt since World War II. He concentrates on the effect of fiscal policy—in the form of changes in government indebtedness—on debt use generally. He argues that it is misleading to examine the debt held by any one sector—say, the corporate sector—in isolation. According to Steuerle, one should also consider other sectors' demand for debt as well as the total supply of loanable funds. When Steuerle views debt in this way, he finds that the corporate sector's current use of debt is modest compared with the noncorporate and household sectors' use.

Steuerle notes that the ratio of total debt to GNP was roughly constant in the United States between 1948 and 1981; relative to GNP the federal government reduced, while the private sector increased, its debt. As the federal government paid down its World War II debt, consumers took advantage of increasingly efficient credit markets to borrow money for such things as cars and houses. The total amount of debt in the economy remained a stable 1.21 times GNP throughout 1948–81.

The extent of individual debt holdings was also affected by tax incentives. According to the theory of tax arbitrage, the higher a taxpayer's tax rate, the greater is his incentive to issue debt (borrow). Similarly, taxpayers in economic sectors facing higher tax rates are more inclined to issue debt than are those in low-rate sectors. Thus, before 1980, when the top individual rate significantly exceeded the corporate rate, high-bracket individuals had greater incentives than corporations had to issue debt. Furthermore, Steuerle says, bracket creep, which raised individuals' tax rates, increasingly made borrowing attractive to households.

After 1981 total debt in the United States began to grow relative to GNP, reaching a multiple of 1.64 by 1988. In Steuerle's view, the large debt increase in the 1980s can be explained by three factors: a turnaround in fiscal policy, financial deregulation, and an increase in tax arbitrage activity.

During the 1980s the federal government went from being a large net lender to being a large net borrower. Whereas the fiscal policy of earlier years kept interest rates low, the deficit-led surge in government borrowing in the 1980s raised real interest rates.

As a result of market pressure for higher interest rates, along with financial deregulation that eliminated interest rate ceilings, interest-bearing assets with higher returns became available. Steuerle notes that the demand for such interest-bearing assets—and the concomitant debt—grew. Increased financial intermediation occurred: between 1981 and 1988 all sectors in the economy increased both their loans and debt relative to GNP.

The use of tax arbitrage also grew during the 1980s. The simultaneous increases in borrowing and lending by different sectors of the economy were partly pure tax arbitrage. For example, tax-exempt state and local governments simultaneously increased their borrowing and lending. Since they can borrow (tax exempt) at rates below their lending rates, they can gain from such arbitrage.

Steuerle finds that the increase in the debt of noncorporate businesses, farms, and households is more noteworthy than the growth in corporate debt. But he also finds that the Tax Reform Act of 1986 has altered sectoral incentives to hold debt. The corporate income tax rate is now higher than the top individual rate, so that corporations have relatively greater incentives to borrow. He predicts that the tax law may lead to an increase in the share of total debt in the economy issued by corporations. Yet, Steuerle argues, increased corporate debt may actually reduce the total risk in the economy if the increased corporate debt replaces more risky noncorporate debt.

Leveraged Buyouts

Margaret Blair and Robert Litan attempt to explain the increase in corporate leverage and LBOs in the 1980s in the face of historically high real interest rates. Traditional thinking would lead one to believe that high interest rates mean a high cost of debt financing and that they would tend to encourage firms to use equity rather than debt. Just the opposite seems to have occurred in the 1980s; hence the need for an alternative theory.

The Blair-Litan paper starts with the Jensen free cash flow theory as a possible explanation of the 1980s developments in corporate financing.[7] The fundamental idea of this theory is that the growth-oriented objectives of management and the value-maximization objectives of shareholders may diverge for new investments, particularly at times when, or within industries where, the incremental return on new investments is below the relevant cost of capital. In those situations the investors would be better off if any available cash earnings were distributed, whereas management might still have an incentive to enlarge the firm, even at the cost of pursuing unprofitable reinvestments of earnings. One way to alleviate this conflict of interest is to substitute debt, with a fixed contractual pattern of payouts, for equity. Debt has the advantage of tying the hands of management with respect to cash distributions. And since cash payout through dividends is disadvantaged by the tax system relative to payout through interest payments, incurring debt is a doubly attractive way of forcing the firm to pay out earnings. Within this framework, debt is viewed as an alternative financial instrument for investors to hold, rather than as a claim of outsiders. Instead of discouraging the use of debt, high real interest rates may encourage it, since high interest rates (and hence a high cost of

7. Michael C. Jensen, "Agency Costs of Free Cash Flow, Corporate Finance, and Takeovers," *American Economic Review*, vol 76 (May 1986, *Papers and Proceedings, 1985*), pp. 323–29.

capital) increase the possibility that management will make unprofitable investments with internally generated cash earnings.

Blair and Litan examine different measures of leverage and choose for their analysis the ratio of interest payments to cash flow. They assert that this measure best indicates the business sector's exposure to bankruptcy. Although they find that the market-value ratio of nonfinancial debt to equity has hovered in a narrow range (between 70 and 80 percent) since the mid-1970s, the ratio of interest to cash flow has risen steadily since 1948.

The authors use two-digit SIC code manufacturing industries to look at the rise in LBO activity and leverage, the two phenomena their paper seeks to illuminate. Although both rose in the aggregate in the 1980s, the authors find no significant interindustry correlation between LBO activity and increases in their measures of leverage. This result suggests that the LBO is but one of many devices for restructuring corporations. While an LBO may help reduce the conflicts of interest between shareholders and management by increasing the use of debt, other financial policies such as share repurchase and debt-for-equity swaps may serve the same purpose in that they also liquidate equity and raise a firm's ratio of debt to equity.

The principal observable implication of Jensen's free cash flow hypothesis is that industries without profitable investment opportunities should be disbursing cash to shareholders, thereby increasing their proportionate amount of debt. Blair and Litan rank fourteen manufacturing industries by different measures of return to capital (their proxy for returns to marginal investment). They compare this ranking to rankings of LBO activity and increases in leverage and find little or no systematic relationship.

Finally, the authors test the relation between their measures of leverage and the quality of investment opportunities in a panel regression over fourteen manufacturing industries and fourteen years, 1974–87. These regressions control for real interest rates, the business cycle (through the unemployment rate), effects peculiar to particular industries, and a time trend. The authors find that investment opportunity, measured by the change in value of the capital stock, is negatively related to their smoothed measures of leverage. In other words, rapidly growing firms use less leverage. The authors interpret this finding as support for the free cash flow theory, since it contradicts the prediction of traditional finance theory that growing firms would issue a high proportion of debt. Blair and Litan conclude that their evidence provides reasonably strong support for the free cash flow hypothesis.

Corporate Tax Reform

Alan Auerbach analyzes the link between tax policy and recent corporate financial behavior. First, he examines the distortions in existing corporate taxation. Second, he describes and evaluates several major corporate tax reform proposals.

Auerbach considers three basic types of tax reform proposals: various tax integration schemes, the American Law Institute proposal, and a cash flow tax. All these reform schemes seek to alleviate the existing distortion between debt and equity. But the plans differ in their treatment of new and existing equity, in particular their treatment of the windfalls experienced by owners of existing equity.

Under full integration, the corporate tax would, in effect, be abolished, at once eliminating the tax distinctions between debt and equity and between corporate and noncorporate ownership. All equity income would be subject to the individual's personal income tax rate, as interest income now is. Full integration would produce significant windfalls for owners of existing equity as the prospective corporate income tax liabilities disappeared. Since tax liability would fall on the investor, foreign and tax-exempt shareholders would escape taxation entirely. Auerbach also describes partial integration schemes under which dividend payments would be deductible from taxable corporate income. Under partial integration, retained earnings would remain taxable at the corporate rate. Thus the tax rate facing newly contributed equity would be lower than the rate facing projects financed internally.

Like integration schemes, the ALI proposal seeks to place debt and equity on equal footing. The two-part ALI proposal also tries to avoid the windfalls brought about by integration schemes. First, as in those schemes, dividends paid on newly contributed equity would be deductible. Interest payments would remain deductible; thus the return on debt and new equity—inasmuch as it was paid out as dividends—would bear the same tax burden. Second, and more controversial, under the ALI plan distributions of equity through share repurchase—or anything other than dividends—would be taxed at 28 percent, creditable against individual tax liability on the distributions. Effectively, such distributions would be taxed at least as heavily as dividends.

The second ALI component seeks to offset the current tax advantage of share repurchase. Share repurchases pay out cash earnings to stockholders and also raise the price of the remaining stock. Under the ALI scheme stockholders, rather than facing only capital gains taxation on the amounts received in excess of the tax basis, would face taxation on the entire repurchase amount. This provision of the ALI plan would raise the minimum tax of getting old equity out of the corporation sector. Thus, insofar as prospective individual taxes were capitalized into share values, the corporate minimum tax on nondividend distributions would reduce the value of existing shares.

The ALI plan would foster a distinction between new and existing equity; dividends on new equity would be deductible from taxable corporate income, whereas dividends paid on existing equity would remain taxable at the corporate level. As in the partial integration schemes, new equity would have a lower tax burden than existing equity.

The final scheme surveyed by Auerbach is the corporate cash flow tax. This tax offers the possibility of equalizing the tax treatment of debt, new equity, and existing equity without creating windfalls for owners of existing equity. Under the corporate cash flow tax, a corporation would be taxed on its receipts less its expenditures. New investment (that is, investments after the effective date of the new tax) would qualify as a deductible expenditure. But interest payments on new debt issues would not be deductible. Under this system of taxation, the competitive portion of the return to new investment, whether financed by debt, equity, or retained earnings, would not be subject to tax. That is because the cost of new investment is deductible from corporate income immediately.[8]

The cash flow tax avoids altering the value of existing equity, since it does not change the tax treatment of that equity. First, depreciation allowances for existing assets would remain. Second, (dividend) payments to holders of existing equity, which are now taxable as corporate income, would remain taxable as corporate cash flow. Third, existing interest payments would continue to be deductible. Thus the shift to a corporate cash flow tax need not confer a windfall gain to the owners of existing equity. But most important for the question at hand, the issuance of new

8. More precisely, if investment can be expensed for tax purposes, the investor effectively realizes the tax deductions from the depreciation charges all at once, instead of having to wait until depreciation allowances gradually become available. With a 34 percent rate, the government would effectively earn 34 percent of the cost of the investment (through the expensing), but would receive 34 percent of the future cash flows through taxes. With a competitive investment, the present value of future cash flows equals cost, so a 34 percent claim on these cash flows is worth 34 percent of cost. Therefore, for competitive investments the expected present value of tax payments less the tax value of the expensing would be zero. Only the portion of the return above a competitive rate would effectively be subject to tax.

debt to replace existing equity would no longer generate a stream of tax-deductible interest payments. Thus the current tax advantage to making payouts through interest rather than dividends would be removed. Leveraged buyouts might still occur as a means of forcing management to pay out a larger proportion of capital income, but the tax system would be neutral, as it probably should be, with respect to this choice.

Distinguishing between Debt and Equity

Jeremy Bulow, Lawrence Summers, and Victoria Summers assess the effect of recent financial innovations on the taxation of corporate-source income. They argue that new debt securities—for example, pay-in-kind securities and high-yield debt—are equity masquerading as debt, or "equity in drag." Although tax-deductible junk bond finance offers "backdoor integration" (by making what amounts to an equity-like return tax deductible), the resulting corporate restructuring has, the authors argue, been of questionable benefit. They then advocate corporate tax reform that levels the debt-equity playing field by raising taxes on interest payments.

Debt has traditionally been distinguished from equity, in section 385 of the Internal Revenue Code, on the basis of five characteristics: reasonable debt-equity ratios, the seniority of debt over other obligations, the commitment to make fixed interest payments, convertibility of debt into stock, and the divergence of the interests of equity and debt holders. Bulow, Summers, and Summers argue that the debt instruments used during the 1980s violated all these statutory principles, and they conclude that the main criterion now determining a security's tax status is the issuer's designation.

One can view the development of equity-like debt securities as backdoor integration of the corporate tax. The development of high-yield debt is then a democratizing innovation that extends the availability of debt financing to investments which would otherwise be unable to secure tax-deductible debt finance. Yet one can distinguish between high-yield debt used to finance new investment and that used to replace equity. In 1988, the authors say, only 2 percent of new high-yield debt financed internal growth, whereas 40 percent was associated with LBOs.

Bulow, Summers, and Summers argue that the availability of high-yield debt gives a tax subsidy to restructuring activity, and that this subsidy has questionable merit in light of the negative externalities the authors associate with restructuring. While some authors have recently argued that

LBOs improve corporate performance and therefore benefit the Treasury, Bulow, Summers, and Summers argue that the tax *consequences* of LBOs are logically distinct from whether taxes *cause* LBOs.[9] The correct question is whether the tax system encourages a marginal LBO. Indeed, under the current tax code, leveraged transactions that would otherwise fail to break even can become profitable solely because of tax considerations.

The authors claim that the legitimacy of a tax subsidy for LBOs depends on the external consequences of these transactions rather than on their consequences for the efficiency of individual firms or transactions. Although LBOs are apparently beneficial for the firms that undertake them, third-party "stakeholders" may experience distress as a result of these transactions. Other possible negative external consequences include reduced investment and research and development spending after buyouts, as well as "reputational externalities" associated with breaches of implicit contracts. Thus the authors argue that a tax subsidy for LBO activity is misguided. They also point out that if LBOs improve efficiency, these transactions would take place without a tax subsidy. This conclusion puts the authors somewhat at odds with Blair and Litan, who believe the upsurge in leverage, forcing a payout of cash, was an appropriate way for the economy to allocate some of the cutback in national investment that was the inevitable consequence of the recent decline in national saving and the attendant rise in real interest rates.[10]

The analysis of Bulow, Summers, and Summers suggests a case for reform that would eliminate the current tax subsidy to restructuring. They distinguish between the "carrot" of reducing dividend taxation (see Auerbach's discussion of integration schemes) and the "stick" of limiting interest deductibility. The integration carrot is dismissed because the windfalls it would confer on shareholders represent lost tax revenue (as much as $40 billion) with little associated encouragement to new investment.

The authors instead endorse two "stick" approaches. The first is a disallowance of interest deductions for debt incurred to repurchase equity. This policy change would eliminate firms' incentives to replace equity with debt, but it would not adversely affect firms' incentives to invest in new capital. The second approach is the American Law Institute proposal

---

9. Bulow, Summers, and Summers take issue with the recent study by Michael Jensen, Steven Kaplan, and Laura Stiglin, "LBOs and Tax Revenues of the U.S. Treasury," *Tax Notes*, February 6, 1989, pp. 727–33.

10. Blair and Litan, however, recognize that the large decline in national saving and the associated fall in national investment was itself a highly undesirable development.

(once again, see Auerbach's paper), which would also remove the incentive for restructuring.

Avoiding Corporate-Level Taxation

Myron Scholes and Mark Wolfson look at corporations' ability to avoid corporate-level taxation. They analyze the common belief that corporate restructurings allow elimination of the corporate tax. They examine some devices reputed to eliminate corporate tax—including various types of restructuring and employee stock ownership plans (ESOPs)—and conclude that debt financing allows corporations to shield, at most, the competitive part of their return from corporate—and therefore double—taxation. Thus the backdoor integration of taxes described by Bulow, Summers, and Summers is not equivalent to full integration.

Scholes and Wolfson demonstrate the well-known tax advantages of debt. If a corporate project is financed with debt, then the returns on the project that the firm has arranged to pay out as interest escape corporate-level taxation. Only above-competitive returns are subject to corporate tax. The authors consider different devices within corporations for reducing corporate tax liability but conclude that none avoid the double taxation of above-competitive returns. Theoretically, ESOPs allow elimination of the corporate tax. They offer three tax-deductible ways for distributing corporate profits to investors: interest on ESOP loans (used to acquire ESOP shares), employee compensation, and dividends on employee-owned shares. However, the authors question the extent to which ESOPs have been undertaken for tax purposes. They suggest, instead, that the recent popularity of ESOPs is due to the voting control they give management.

Finally, Scholes and Wolfson consider whether corporate taxes are more effectively avoided if an investment is undertaken within the corporation or, after liquidation, outside the corporation. They show that the decision depends on whether the firm anticipates projects with above-competitive returns. If so, the corporation should not retain earnings. Rather, the corporation should pay a dividend, allowing the project to be undertaken outside the corporate sector. Essentially, investors can pay taxes either on the dividend now, or on the corporate project's return later, with interest. If the project has an above-normal return, then shareholders— in paying tax on that return—in effect pay above-normal interest on today's dividend tax liability. If the corporate project has normal returns, then shareholders are indifferent between the corporation's dividends and retained earnings.

Conclusion

Taken as a whole, the five papers in this volume buttress the case that (1) something can be done to restructure the taxation of the return to corporate debt and equity so as to eliminate the tax bias toward debt finance; and (2) though no technique is without some drawbacks, there are several ways to achieve this purpose without providing a windfall to existing stockholders. The magnitude and consequences of the recent move toward the increased use of debt are not quite as alarming as some people believe. But no evidence suggests that there are any national economic benefits from leverage sufficient to warrant the existence of the substantial incentives that the current tax code provides for high leverage. The papers point out, however, that in reforming business taxation one must focus on changing tax incentives as they relate to the financing of new physical investments and avoid transferring massive windfalls to the owners of existing capital.

Federal Policy and the Accumulation of Private Debt

C. Eugene Steuerle

CORPORATE DEBT is not an isolated issue. The amount of debt incurred by any one sector of the economy is related to the amount demanded by all sectors and to the amount of loanable funds these sectors supply. An increase in one entity's debt must be supplied either through a decrease in some other entity's debt or through an increase in loanable funds.

When the market for loanable funds is examined from a broad historical perspective, postwar changes in the private accumulation of debt and its allocation among sectors are dominated by a few important changes in fiscal policy, financial and monetary policy, and tax policy. Notable fiscal policy changes have included a policy that first made available significant amounts of loanable funds to the private sector and then, in the 1980s, provided the dominant demand for such funds. In financial and monetary policy, greater recognition of human capital as collateral for loans, government preferences for institutions engaged primarily in noncorporate lending, and significant reductions in the price of borrowing for individuals relative to corporations all led individuals to increase their borrowing. In addition, the removal of interest rate ceilings, plus other financial market deregulation, led to increases in the private supply of loanable funds (and in the money supply) in the 1980s. And in tax policy, a significant increase in the ability of markets to arbitrage differences in rates of return and in the tax treatment of various assets has pushed borrowing toward the sectors with the highest tax rates or with the greatest relative increases in tax rates and has encouraged lending from nontaxable and foreign sectors.

Over the last few decades there has been a dramatic shift in the United States: debt-to-asset ratios have become more even across various private

The author is indebted to Henry J. Aaron and Jane G. Gravelle for helpful comments, to John Wilson and Betsy Fogler for assistance and guidance through the Flow of Funds accounts, and to Robert Gay, Michael Jensen, and Stephen Waite for useful discussions on the restructuring being financed through corporate debt.

sectors, while the corporate sector's share of total private debt has declined. In terms of increases in private leverage, what is most notable is not growth in corporate debt, but growth in the debt of the noncorporate business sector, the farm sector, and the household sector.

Despite recent history, I would expect to see future increases in the share of debt incurred by the corporate sector. The Tax Reform Act of 1986 has adjusted incentives so that from a tax perspective the optimal borrower is now in the corporate sector, not in the noncorporate business or household sector. Moreover, noncorporate businesses now exceed the corporate sector in terms of debt-to-asset ratios and households have moved closer to the corporate sector in this regard. These noncorporate sectors may be less likely in the future to increase their shares of total debt by outbidding the corporate sector for available supplies of loanable funds.

While a future increase in corporate debt may be associated with a decline in the corporate tax base, this does not necessarily imply that the economy would suffer from greater risk. In many cases, additional corporate debt may be less risky than the noncorporate debt it replaces. An example is presented by the recent failure of some farm credit institutions and savings and loan institutions that made speculative loans to noncorporate businesses, farms, and households. By the same token, the aggregate data examined in this study reveal little about the riskiness of particular transactions such as a leveraged buyout or a real estate venture.

Finally, the tendency of different sectors of the economy to move toward greater constancy in debt-to-asset ratios may imply that financial intermediaries are channeling gross saving in ways that increasingly minimize short-term risk, rather than maximize long-term rates of return in the economy, and that provide funds for consumption rather than investment. If this is correct, future growth in the economy could actually require an increase, not a decrease, in risk taking. In that sense, the danger is not so much that the corporate sector may start to outbid the individual sector for loanable funds, but that it may copy what the individual sector has been doing for some time now: redirecting gross saving toward old assets rather than new investment.

Trends in the Pre-1981 Era

Debt seems to be a perennial issue. While much current focus has been on corporate restructuring, in earlier periods there was heightened concern about the debt of other sectors. Increases in mortgage debt have been accused of leading to a decline in investment in plant and equipment. The

Figure 1. Credit Market Debt in the United States, 1946–88

Percent of GNP

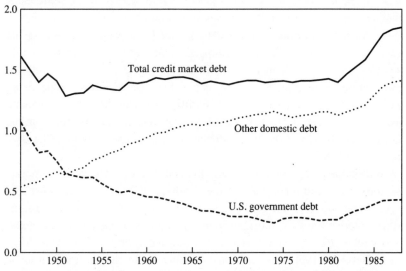

Sources: Author's calculations based on *Economic Report of the President, February 1989*; and Board of Governors of the Federal Reserve System, "Flow of Funds Accounts: Financial Assets and Liabilities," Statistical Release Z.1 (various issues), table 1.

growth of consumer credit was also alleged to reduce investment and increase consumption. Increases in government debt in the 1980s have led to problems such as a large negative balance of payments for the United States and high real interest rates that have hurt third world development. Only recently have corporate debt increases—in particular, those used to finance leveraged buyouts—been the primary focus of discussion about debt in the economy.

These movements in public concern often coincide with shifts in sectoral allocations of debt and assets. The constantly changing nature of these concerns should show that it is a mistake to try to interpret trends in leverage by looking at only one sector of the economy.

In the postwar era, the total amount of credit-market debt in the United States remained fairly constant from 1948 to about the end of 1981 (see figure 1). Possible explanations for this stable debt-to-income relationship often include some degree of risk aversion in the portfolios of individuals.[1] Regardless of explanation, this constancy in total debt was mainly the

1. Benjamin M. Friedman, "Portfolio Choice and the Debt-to-Income Relationship," *American Economic Review*, vol. 75 (May 1985, *Papers and Proceedings, 1984*), pp. 338–43.

consequence of two offsetting trends: the federal government was significantly reducing its stock of debt relative to GNP while the private sector was increasing its share. Coming out of World War II, many individuals had savings tied up in U.S. savings bonds and other government securities.[2] As the government stock of debt declined relative to GNP, the private sector converted its assets into comparable interest-bearing assets, usually savings accounts in banks and savings and loans. The government also paid interest rates that were low or negative in real terms, while rising rates of inflation often imposed a significant tax on holders of financial assets. This aided a process whereby the government could run nominal deficits yet benefit from a significant decline in the amount of its debt relative to GNP.

Within the private sector the growth in debt was led not by the corporate sector, but by the three parts of the "individual" sector—the household sector, the noncorporate business sector, and the farm sector. At the same time, interest rates for mortgages and automobile loans declined dramatically relative to the interest rate on long-term corporate debt and the prime rate. Between 1950 and 1980, for instance, auto finance rates dropped almost 9 percentage points relative to the prime rate.[3] This seems to have been mainly a supply phenomenon, led by government insurance, special preferences for savings and loan institutions and credit unions, and innovation in financial markets toward greater recognition of the value of human capital as collateral for loans.

From the end of the 1960s until the beginning of the 1980s, inflation rates continued to rise significantly. Land increased in value, while the stock market stagnated in real terms. During this period farmers and noncorporate business owners incurred significant increases in debt. Farmers began to borrow much more against increases in farmland value,

2. Savings bonds alone accounted for 22.0 percent of deposits and credit market instruments in 1948, compared with 2.5 percent in 1988. See Board of Governors of the Federal Reserve System, "Balance Sheets for the U.S. Economy, 1946–85," Statistical Release C.9 (October 1986), and "Balance Sheets for the U.S. Economy, 1949–88," Statistical Release C.9 (April 1989).

3. In 1950, for instance, the auto finance rate was 12.07 percent, while the prime rate was 1.87 percent. By 1980 the prime rate was 15.27 percent and auto finance rates 15.25 percent. Similarly, for long-term rates, in 1950 Moody's AAA bond yield was 2.62 percent and the new home mortgage yield 4.86 percent, while by 1980 the former was 11.94 percent and the latter 12.65 percent. See *Economic Report of the President, February 1990*, table C-71, p. 376; Board of Governors of the Federal Reserve System, *Federal Reserve Bulletin*, various issues, 1950–80; and, for some auto finance rates, Robert P. Shay, "Major Developments in the Market for Consumer Credit since the End of World War II," *Journal of Finance*, vol. 21 (May 1966), pp. 369–81.

although such borrowing was not reflected in investments in reproducible assets. Other noncorporate business—whose principal asset is also real estate—continued its dramatic and continual postwar trend of increasing its debt relative to assets.

Until the early 1980s, then, the individual sector—households, farms, and noncorporate businesses—effectively absorbed most of the borrowing that had formerly been done by the federal government. The corporate sector changed only modestly in its debt-to-GNP ratio.

Figures 2 and 3 demonstrate these results. The first two bars in each grouping in figure 2 show changes in net outstanding debt for different sectors of the economy during 1948–68 and 1968–81. Net outstanding debt is defined here as credit market debt less the supply of loanable funds. For these purposes, the underlying calculations attempt to "wash" through financial intermediaries. Deposits in financial intermediaries, as well as direct holdings of mortgages, government securities, and consumer credit, are regarded as the source of loanable funds for the credit-market debt. In effect, the figure provides a sectoral analysis of the loanable-funds market by showing that one sector's borrowing must be provided by another sector's lending. The U.S. government and foreign sectors are shown on a net basis.

Figure 3 breaks out gross borrowing from gross lending by the private domestic sectors for the same periods. This figure demonstrates that increases in gross borrowing, not just net borrowing, occurred primarily in the household, noncorporate business, and farm sectors. While the corporate sector's debt also tended to grow in the 1948–68 period—it too absorbed some of the debt no longer being incurred by the federal government—during 1968–81 its debt-to-GNP ratio actually declined and it competed less with the individual sectors to maintain its share of this debt.

The Tax Incentive Structure

In an inflationary economy, interest-bearing assets held directly by businesses and individuals tend to be the most heavily taxed assets. Returns from almost all other assets receive some sort of special treatment, including deferral, so that at least total nominal income—both cash flow plus change in value—is not reportable for tax purposes on a current basis. Even though the nominal interest rate equals the real interest rate plus the inflation rate, both components are fully subject to tax on a current basis.

Figure 2. Changes in Net Outstanding Debt, Various Sectors, 1948–68, 1968–81, 1981–88

Percent of GNP

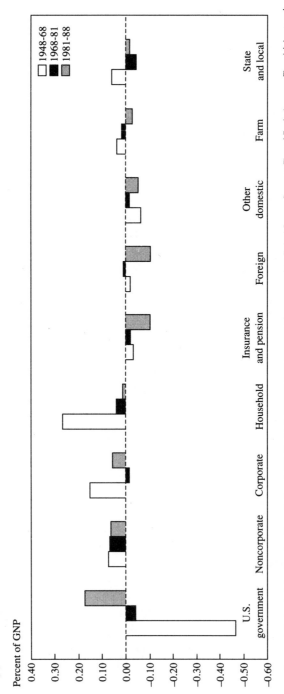

Sources: Author's calculations based on *Economic Report of the President, February 1989*; and Board of Governors of the Federal Reserve System, "Flow of Funds Accounts: Financial Assets and Liabilities," Statistical Release Z.1 (various issues), table 1, "Balance Sheets for the U.S. Economy, 1946–85," Statistical Release C.9 (October 1986), and "Balance Sheets for the U.S. Economy, 1949–88," Statistical Release C.9 (April 1989).

Under what I have labeled as normal tax arbitrage, the optimal owners of the least tax-favored assets are the lowest-rate taxpayers.[4] Correspondingly, the optimal owners of the most preferred assets are the top-rate taxpayers. When it comes to rates of payment on borrowings, the order reverses itself. The optimal debt issuers become the highest-rate taxpayers. An example makes some of this ordering intuitively obvious: with an inflation rate of 4 percent and a real rate of interest of 4 percent, the after-tax real interest rate for a taxpayer in the 50 percent bracket is 0 percent, while for a tax-exempt taxpayer it is 4 percent. The after-tax real return for a nontaxable asset, however, will be the same for the two taxpayers.

Before the 1986 tax reform, the highest-rate taxpayers were in the noncorporate sectors, where the top individual rate was greater than the corporate rate. Until 1982, when the top rate was reduced to 50 percent—still higher than the corporate rate—the top rate paid on interest income was 70 percent or greater.

Many individuals, of course, had tax rates below corporate rates. Bracket creep, however, was occurring only among individuals, not corporations. All other things being equal, this bracket creep increased the extent to which borrowing would be undertaken by individuals, not corporations. For individuals with rates below the corporate rate, bracket creep narrowed the differential in after-tax payment rates and made this part of the individual sector more competitive with the corporate sector. As a result, the individual demand curve for loanable funds was shifted upward relative to the corporate demand curve. In sum, the tax system encouraged taxpayers in the individual sector to increasingly outbid the corporate sector for the supply of loanable funds.

Supporting these tax developments was a growing level of sophistication in the tax and financial markets. As higher rates of inflation tended to increase the tax subsidy for borrowing—thereby effectively increasing the tax benefits from tax arbitrage—the markets simultaneously increased their ability to take advantage of arbitrage opportunities. It became quite profitable to borrow to purchase tax-preferred assets, including those on which inflationary and even real gains were deferred from taxation.

Among the most important assets for tax arbitrage was real estate, both buildings and land. Because most of the gain tended to be accrued over long periods of time, and not realized, significant tax arbitrage opportun-

4. C. Eugene Steuerle, *Taxes, Loans, and Inflation: How the Nation's Wealth Became Misallocated* (Brookings, 1985).

Figure 3. Changes in Outstanding Debts and Loans, Various Sectors, 1948–68, 1968–81, 1981–88

Percent of GNP

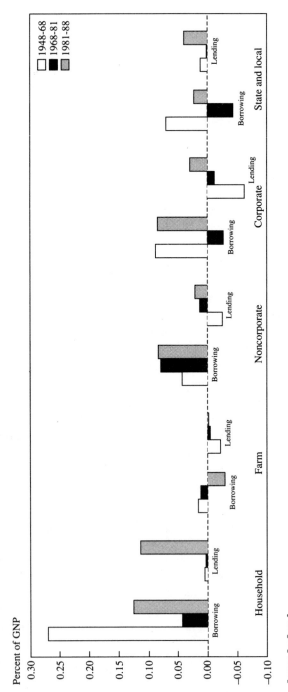

Sources: See figure 2.

ities led many to invest in real estate assets even when the returns from such investments were negative from society's viewpoint, but positive in after-tax terms.

The tax shelter market represented one portion of the market created by tax arbitrage opportunities. This market was dominated by partnership sales within the individual sector.[5] Leverage was among the most frequently used devices to gain maximum tax advantage.

A Straightforward Tale

Up until the early 1980s, then, the tale of debt allocation appears to be somewhat straightforward. Fiscal, monetary, financial institution, and tax theory can be pulled together to tell a consistent story. The supply of loanable funds tended to be somewhat inelastic relative to GNP, a variation on the theme that at least during this period there was a close relationship between money supply and income. Supply-side changes in financial institutions—in particular, the greater recognition of human capital as collateral and government-provided preferences for savings and loans and other institutions lending primarily to individuals—led to a significant decrease in the rate of interest charged individuals relative to that paid by corporations. In addition, higher tax rates decreased the price of borrowing (the after-tax real interest rate) for individuals relative to that for corporations. With a somewhat fixed supply of total loanable funds relative to GNP, it is not surprising that the private sector absorbed greater debt as fiscal policy led to significant decreases in public debt relative to GNP, or that households, noncorporate businesses, and farms—not corporations—effectively absorbed most of the debt made available by the decline in government debt.

The Turnaround in the 1980s

Beginning approximately at the end of 1981, total debt in the economy began to grow significantly relative to GNP. Between 1948 and 1981 the total amount of lending (currency and interest-bearing assets) and bor-

5. For implications for monetary policy, see Benjamin M. Friedman, "Monetary Policy without Quantity Variables," *American Economic Review*, vol. 78 (May 1988, *Papers and Proceedings, 1987*), pp. 440–45; and Robert H. Rasche, "Demand Functions for U.S. Money and Credit Measures," Econometrics and Economic Theory Paper 8718, Michigan State University, Department of Economics, 1988.

rowing (credit market debt with federal and foreign sectors treated on a net basis) had remained almost constant at about 121 percent of GNP. From 1981 to 1988, however, both increased to about 164 percent of GNP. This unexpected growth in debt was accompanied by an unexpected growth in various measures of the money supply.[6] That these events occurred simultaneously should not be surprising, given the simple equivalence between financial assets and financial liabilities.

These dramatic changes can be explained partly by a complete turn-around in fiscal policy. The federal government's rate of decline in its stock of debt relative to GNP began to decelerate in the late 1970s and then to increase significantly in the 1980s owing to large increases in federal deficits. In fact, on a net basis and measured as a percent of GNP, the government moved from being the major lender in the loanable-funds market to being the major borrower (see figure 2).

The change in fiscal policy probably also had an effect on interest rates. Interest rates had been kept low in the first two or three decades of the postwar era, not simply because inflation kept exceeding expectations, but also because of the significant decline in the government supply of interest-bearing assets (relative to income) during this period. As this decline waned and then turned into a dramatic increase in borrowing, the effect was similar to what would be caused (in traditional economic analysis) by the shifting from a period of running government surpluses to one of running government deficits.

This shift in fiscal policy should not be attributed solely to the increase in nominal deficits in the 1980s. With postwar fiscal policy for the most part having abandoned the goal of running nominal surpluses, an eventual turnaround was almost inevitable. Continual nominal deficits imply that, as a percentage of GNP, a decline in the federal debt-to-GNP ratio must approach zero over time or must increase. The turnaround in fiscal policy—as measured here by the change in federal debt-to-GNP ratio—became increasingly likely as this ratio kept moving to postwar lows. The budget deficits of the 1980s made the shift much more significant, of course, but it may also have been influenced by the decreasing availability of a fiscal dividend on the outstanding stock of government debt.

6. For numbers on the growth of partnership activity reporting negative income, the industry concentration of such income, and the extent to which high-income taxpayers were engaged in tax shelters, as measured by the presence of negative partnership income, see Lowell Dworin, "An Analysis of Partnership Activity, 1981–83," *Statistics of Income Bulletin*, vol. 5 (Spring 1986), pp. 63–74; and Susan Nelson, "Taxes Paid by High-Income Taxpayers and the Growth of Partnerships," *Statistics of Income Bulletin*, vol. 5 (Fall 1986), pp. 55–60.

As in the earlier periods, the shift was accompanied by important and simultaneous developments in the financial markets. The increasing sophistication of those engaging in transactions in those markets made it more difficult to control interest rates on selected deposits. With so-called disintermediation leading to higher interest rates for funds flowing through less regulated intermediaries, deregulation and the elimination of interest rate ceilings were soon to follow.

I alluded above to a search for an explanation of the breakdown in the relationship between money and income; this is a parallel effort to explain what is happening in the debt markets. Deregulation is sometimes cited as a major factor behind ''unexpected'' increases in .easures of the money supply. The elimination of interest rate ceilings caused an even further blurring of distinction between money and many types of interest-bearing assets, particularly checking deposits, savings accounts, and money market accounts.

On a broader basis, the allowance of higher real interest rates on interest-bearing assets should increase the demand for these assets relative to other assets. An increase in interest-bearing assets cannot occur, however, unless accompanied by an increase in debt. Hence the removal of rate ceilings should increase the amount of intermediation taking place in the loanable-funds market. In fact, in 1981–88 all sectors except the farm sector increased their amount of both loans and debts (see figure 3). Even the farm sector's figures are somewhat misleading, as the rate of decline in the value of assets such as farmland is greater than the rate of decline in debt, so that debt-to-asset ratios actually rose in this sector as well.

The Tax Incentive Structure in the 1980s

The tax structure also changed dramatically during 1981–88, but it is difficult to assess the net effect of these changes on the demand for debt. Not enought data are available to assess the effect of the Tax Reform Act of 1986, as many of its provisions were not fully implemented until 1988 or are still being phased in. The 1981–84 rate cuts did occur during this period, but for the most part they offset the rate increases of the late 1970s. These rate cuts did move the top individual rate much closer to the corporate rate and, at least in this regard, should have increased the demand of the corporate sector for debt relative to individual demand. Even here, however, speculation is difficult. Reductions in corporate tax liability toward zero, especially in the initial years of accelerated depreciation in the early 1980s, probably reduced demand for debt among those firms with low tax liabilities.

Tax arbitrage. Perhaps the most significant tax phenomenon in 1981–86 was the continued development of tax shelters. These grew substantially in number and size, while remaining predominantly in the individual sector. Increased arbitrage opportunities were made available by some of the 1981 tax changes, but there also was a more permanent adjustment to opportunities created by the movement toward higher interest rates that had begun even earlier. The increasing sophistication of markets continued to aid taxpayers in taking advantage of many tax arbitrage opportunities, not just those identified formally as tax shelters.

In the theory of normal tax arbitrage, the ideal holders of interest-bearing assets are the zero-rate taxpayers. Differences in real after-tax rates of interest between zero-rate and positive-rate taxpayers are often greatest in periods of high interest rates. If tax arbitrage is increasing, there should also be increases in the relative holdings of foreigners, pension and life insurance companies, and state and local governments. To the extent that there are increasing supplies of debt, then, it is not surprising that they should derive from increases in the interest-bearing assets held by the nontaxable sectors. This is exactly the result shown in figure 2: the dominant sources of net supply of debt in 1981–88 were foreigners and insurance and pension plans.

Pure tax arbitrage was also occurring during this period. Some of the simultaneous increase in both borrowing and lending within the same sector (figure 3) involves nothing more than lending to oneself and reaping the tax advantages. For instance, state and local government borrowing increased significantly in 1981–88, but such borrowing was matched by an increase in lending. Tax arbitrage gains were substantial since tax-exempt rates on the debt of this sector are much lower than the taxable rate received on loanable funds. Similarly, the expansion of opportunities for individual retirement accounts (IRAs) between 1981 and 1986 often involved households essentially lending to themselves, say, by making a deposit in an IRA and later taking out a loan that otherwise would have been unnecessary.

The corporate income tax. Whether the 1981–88 period or the entire postwar period is examined, corporations maintained fairly significant equity-to-debt ratios despite the double taxation of corporate income. Relative to other sectors, corporations were modest in their debt financing. A corporate income tax, of course, does encourage new financing to take place through bonds rather than equity. Most equity financing, however, comes through retained earnings rather than new issues of equity. Under at least one theory, the "new theory of dividends," it is no more worthwhile today than tomorrow to pay a toll charge to pass income outside the corporate sector.[7] In this case, the corporate tax would have little effect on decisions to finance through retained earnings.

Other studies emphasize the ability of corporations to avoid this toll charge through purchases of stock, whereby a portion of the redemption is nontaxable and the purchases may be made from nontaxable sectors.[8] As I have emphasized throughout this chapter, moreover, financial intermediaries have become increasingly sophisticated in taking advantage of arbitrage opportunities, regardless of legal changes in tax incentives. Although past trends do not support the notion that the corporate tax has led to significant increases in corporate debt ratios, it would be incorrect to assert that the corporate tax will not be a major factor in the future. Corporate equity issues, while small during most of the postwar era, fell to quite negative levels of −$74 billion to −$131 billion annually during 1984–88, implying corporations' increased sophistication in finding means of avoiding the double taxation of their income.[9] The Tax Reform Act of 1986 also affected relative incentives, as will be discussed below.

Debt-to-Asset Ratios

Figure 4 summarizes sectoral changes in debt over the postwar era by showing the debt-to-asset ratios of the various sectors. Keep in mind that asset growth is much higher in the corporate and household sectors. Slow asset growth and fast debt growth both contributed to the extensive increase in the debt-to-asset ratios of the noncorporate business and farm sectors. Whereas in the early postwar era debt was heavily concentrated in the corporate sector, other sectors later moved much closer to the corporate sector in terms of debt-to-asset ratios. The corporate sector again stands out as being relatively modest in its increase in debt.

If risk were to be measured by increases in debt relative to assets, concern could well turn to the noncorporate business sector. This sector

7. David F. Bradford, "The Incidence and Allocation Effects of a Tax on Corporate Distributions," *Journal of Public Economics*, vol. 15 (February 1981), pp. 1–22; and Alan J. Auerbach, "Taxes, Firm Financial Policy, and the Cost of Capital: An Empirical Analysis," *Journal of Public Economics*, vol. 23 (February–March 1984), pp. 27–57.

8. See, for example, John B. Shoven, "The Tax Consequences of Share Repurchases and Other Non-dividend Cash Payments to Equity Owners," in Lawrence H. Summers, ed., *Tax Policy and the Economy*, vol. 1 (Cambridge, Mass.: National Bureau of Economic Research and MIT Press Journals, 1987), pp. 29–55.

9. Board of Governors, "Balance Sheets for the U.S. Economy, 1949–88."

Figure 4. Debt-to-Asset Ratios, Selected Years, 1948–88

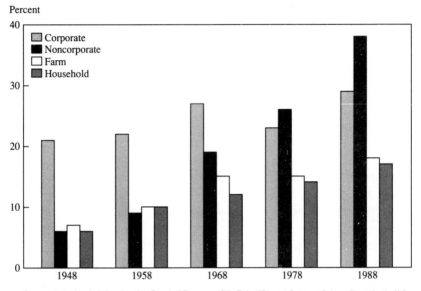

Percent

Sources: Author's calculations based on Board of Governors of the Federal Reserve System, "Balance Sheets for the U.S. Economy, 1946–85," Statistical Release C.9 (October 1986), and "Balance Sheets for the U.S. Economy, 1949–88," Statistical Release C.9 (April 1989).

has experienced the greatest increase in leverage in the postwar era, with debt rising from 6 percent of assets in 1948 to 38 percent by 1988. The recent failure of many savings and loan institutions is a warning that lending to the individual sector can easily be as risky as lending to the corporate sector.

A Less Straightforward Story

Unlike the pattern in the period preceding the 1980s, the growth in both debt and loanable funds in 1981–88 needs a more complex explanation. This period is dominated by three factors: a complete turnaround in fiscal policy, as measured by changes in federal debt relative to GNP; the deregulation of financial markets; and the increasing sophistication of financial markets in taking advantage of both financial and tax arbitrage opportunities, as reflected in the great tax shelter boom that lasted until 1986.

With higher real interest rates and deregulation of financial institutions, the total demand for interest-bearing assets increased, and reallocations of portfolios created a much larger supply of funds to be borrowed. All sectors share in these changed opportunities by increasing both their borrowing and their lending (right bars in figure 3). The noncorporate business sector continued to dominate the corporate sector in terms of rates of increase in borrowing, especially when measured relative to assets (figure 4). Net lending, however, clearly came from the most tax-advantaged sectors: foreign and pension and life insurance companies (figure 2). Corporations began to increase their debt relative to assets during this period, but at about the same rate as other sectors. For the postwar period as a whole, however, corporations maintained growth rates in debt-to-asset ratios well behind those of the individual sector.

Future Trends

Because noncorporate businesses now exceed the corporate sector in terms of debt-to-asset ratios and households have moved closer to the corporate sector, the individual sector may be less likely in the future to increase its share of total debt by outbidding the corporate sector for available supplies of loanable funds. Proposed reform of savings institutions may also reduce any bias in the system toward individual over corporate lending. Even without this reform, the debt of the noncorporate business sector is so high relative to other sectors that some stabilization or even decline would not be surprising.

There is at least one major reason to believe that the corporate sector will increase its share of total debt in the future. (This would be in contrast to its behavior in most of the postwar era, where it has often been a relative laggard.) The Tax Reform Act of 1986 changed the relative demand functions for debt by making the corporate top rate higher than the individual rate. Under the theory of normal tax arbitrage, corporations now have become the optimal borrowers.

Of course, the reduction of tax rates should make equity less expensive relative to debt and should reduce the demand for debt by all taxpayers. The reduction in demand is greater for the individual and noncorporate sectors than it is for the corporate sector. This implies that the corporate sector will move to own a larger share of debt in any case. If the supply of loanable funds again stabilizes with respect to GNP, the corporate debt-to-GNP ratio will also rise.

An increase in corporate debt could come about in a variety of ways. The corporate sector cannot simply incur more debt without doing something with the funds. It could continue recent trends by repurchasing more stock. It could also move into assets that formerly were held predominantly in the individual sectors, particularly real estate. In fact, another aspect of tax reform—passive loss rules and minimum taxes—moves ideal ownership of leveraged assets with low or negative realized returns, but positive total returns including capital gains, toward entities with significant amounts of capital income from other sources. Parts of the corporate sector are prime candidates.

By the same token, ideal ownership of equity assets, especially those that do not yield more sheltered income, has moved toward the noncorporate business sector, whose tax rate is now lower than the corporate sector's. Even under the new theory of dividends, it is now worthwhile to pay the maximum 28 percent dividend toll charge in order to move assets out of the corporate sector, where they face a 34 percent tax rate on future returns.

While increases in corporate debt could be associated with declines in the corporate tax base, risk in the economy could go down as easily as up.[10] Corporate debt may be less risky than some of the noncorporate debt that it replaces. Recent failures of some savings and loans and farm credit institutions only serve to highlight this point. By the same token, aggregate data tell little about the overall riskiness of particular transactions.[11]

Conclusions

The amount of debt incurred by any one sector cannot be understood simply by examining that sector's own demand for debt or its response to one particular policy. In fact, the market for loanable funds as a whole must be examined, as the demand for debt in one sector is a function of the demand for debt by other sectors, as well as the supply of such debt. These demand and supply functions in turn can be understood only through examination of broad fiscal, financial and monetary, and tax policies.

10. Paulus and Gay would argue that much recent corporate restructuring was also a means by which producers became more competitive. See John D. Paulus and Robert S. Gay, "Is America Helping Herself? Corporate Restructuring and Global Competitiveness," *World Economic Outlook, 1987* (New York: Morgan Stanley and Co., 1987).

11. The revenue question needs to be separated from the question of risk. Leveraged buyouts, for instance, may be among the more revenue-raising ways in which equity is transferred out of the corporate sector. Unlike leveraged buyouts, selective share repurchase allow sellers of corporate equity to sort themselves out by tax rates, with sellers more likely to come from lower tax brackets or nontaxable institutions. Jensen, Kaplan, and Stiglin argue that recent transactions may have increased revenues to the Treasury. See Michael C. Jensen, Stephen N. Kaplan, and Laura Stiglin, "Effects of LBOs on Tax Revenues of the U.S. Treasury," *Tax Notes*, February 6, 1989, pp. 727–33.

Changes in fiscal policy, increased access of individuals to loans, the removal of interest rate ceilings on interest-bearing assets, the increasing sophistication of arbitragers in tax and financial markets, and differences between tax rates for individuals and corporations explain a good deal of the changes in postwar debt incurred by all sectors in the economy.

The data on growth in outstanding private debt show that the increased leverage of the noncorporate business, household, and farm sectors is more likely to draw attention than the increased leverage of the corporate sector. Nonetheless, the Tax Reform Act of 1986 changed relative incentives, and the corporate sector is likely to absorb a greater share of debt in the future.

Policies affecting debt cannot be examined in isolation. Depending upon what happens in all sectors of the economy, attempts to maintain or increase the corporate tax base could either add to or subtract from overall risk in the economy. By the same token, even if some types of transactions such as leveraged buyouts were curtailed, this might have little effect on the future aggregate debt of the corporate sector. Corporations have become the optimal holders of debt from a tax standpoint. Attempts to shut one door to corporate integration may have little effect when movement through other doors is aided by increasingly sophisticated financial markets.

Comment by Jane G. Gravelle

Eugene Steuerle's paper takes a broad look at the influence of federal policy on the accumulation and allocation of debt in the postwar period. He begins, appropriately, with the premise that one cannot explain past trends in corporate debt—or predict future ones—without considering the demands for and supplies of debt in other sectors. These supplies and demands are, in turn, influenced both by private market developments and by broad federal policies. These policies include increases or decreases in federal debt, the regulatory environment, and the tax environment.

For most of the postwar period, until the 1980s, Steuerle presents a fairly satisfactory and cohesive story of trends in debt. Corporate-sector debt-to-asset ratios have remained relatively constant over the postwar period. The falling relative level of public debt has been absorbed primarily by the noncorporate sector, leaving aggregate economywide debt-to-GNP ratios relatively fixed and having little effect on the corporate sector. These changes could be explained without reference to tax motivations. The reduction in the wartime debt released loanable funds to the public. Assuming that portfolio preferences of asset holders did not shift a great deal, there should have been an increase in debt in the private sector in general. Yet the corporate sector absorbed very little of this debt. These funds were instead absorbed by the noncorporate sector, through borrowing by households, farms, and noncorporate businesses. Federal regulations and other programs tended to favor institutions that lend to the noncorporate sector. Moreover, private market developments made credit more accessible to individual borrowers. These trends could explain why these funds were absorbed by the noncorporate sector, leaving the corporate sector little affected.

Steuerle also suggests that the tax environment played a role in diverting funds to the noncorporate sector as inflation pushed individuals into higher marginal tax brackets. Since interest is subject to full taxation and is the least tax-preferred source of income, a movement toward higher tax rates should have increased individual borrowing relative to corporate borrowing.

His explanation of trends in debt up until the 1980s seems plausible, although, as noted below, the role of taxes may be interpreted differently. It is perhaps not surprising that his explanation of trends in the 1980s is less satisfactory, given the many puzzling aspects of that period. During the 1980s federal debt began to grow; this time, however, it was accompanied by a total growth in the debt share of all sectors in the economy, although noncorporate business debt grew faster than corporate debt. Steuerle's explanation for these events seems to turn, in part, on tax motivations. He notes that the dominant sources of supplies of debt are the nontaxed sectors—pension and life insurance companies and foreigners. These sources are influenced by tax arbitrage, since nontaxed sectors are the optimal holders of debt.

It is not easy to explain what happened in the 1980s, given the mystery of falling private savings rates. But it seems doubtful that tax arbitrage is the primary explanation. The increasing fluidity of international capital markets, along with foreigners' apparent preference for investment in the United States in the form of debt instruments, explains a great deal of the rise in aggregate national debt and the sustained growth in noncorporate debt even as public debt grew. This preference for debt by foreign investors has a long history: foreign investment in the United States has always been dominated by debt instruments and passive investments.

Pension and insurance reserves increased their supplies of debt relative to GNP as well. This growth may reflect the increased funding requirements adopted in 1974, with compliance spread over many years. It may also reflect contributions to individual retirement accounts, which may indeed be cases of pure tax arbitrage.

If foreign investment and pension and insurance assets grew for reasons other than tax motivations, their increasing role in providing debt may merely reflect their increasing importance as a supplier of capital in the market in general. One could, therefore, explain some of the trends in size and allocation without reference to tax motivations. I am not persuaded, in fact, that tax motivations played an important role.

Consider first the period up until the 1980s. It is true that during this time, particularly in the later years, inflation-induced bracket creep increased the marginal tax rates of individuals, but did not affect the rate of corporations. Other things being equal, these effects would have shifted debt from the corporate to the noncorporate sector. This increase in marginal tax rates was offset, however, by a number of tax cuts, including substantial ones in 1962 and 1963. Nevertheless, according to the Joint Committee on Taxation, the average marginal tax rate rose from about 22 percent in 1965 to about 31 percent in 1980.[12] The top marginal tax rate of corporations dropped slightly from 48 percent to 46 percent.

Although the marginal individual tax rate rose particularly as a result of the increased inflation rates of the 1970s, the corporate tax rate was higher than the average marginal individual tax rate in both the 1970s and 1980s. Inflation also magnified the benefits of debt finance, and this magnification was greater the higher the marginal tax rate. As a simple illustration, if the pretax real interest rate is fixed at 6 percent and the inflation rate is 2 percent, the after-tax cost of interest at a 48 percent statutory tax rate is 2.16 percent [$(0.06 + 0.02) \times (1 - 0.48) - 0.02$], while the after-tax cost for a 22 percent tax rate is 4.24 percent. The corporate after-tax cost is about half the individual cost. If inflation rises to 6 percent, the corporate tax rate drops to 46 percent, and the individual rate rises to 31 percent, the after-tax cost for the corporate sector is 0.48 percent and for the individual, 2.28 percent. Thus the corporate after-tax cost is about 20 percent of the individual cost. Thus inflation produced two offsetting trends: it drove up the average marginal tax rate, but also

12. Joint Committee on Taxation, *Background and Issues Relating to Individual Income Tax Reductions*, Joint Committee Print, 97 Cong. 1 sess. (Government Printing Office, 1981), p. 23.

increased the advantage of debt finance for the higher marginal tax rates, which included both high-rate individuals and corporations. It is not at all clear that in the aggregate this effect of inflation would have shifted debt from the corporate to the individual sector as a whole, although it did make debt more attractive to high-rate individuals.

Nor it is clear that tax arbitrage is that important in the noncorporate sector. Estimates supplied by the U.S. Treasury's Office of Tax Analysis indicate that the average marginal tax rates on interest income and non-corporate business profits are quite similar (28.5 percent versus 29.6 percent under 1980 law). It is true that marginal tax rates on corporate equity income are much higher—39 percent for dividends. However, this difference may derive more from the willingness of higher-income indi-viduals to invest their portfolios in riskier corporate stock. In any case, if arbitrage is going on, it appears much more likely to involve a choice between passive investments—corporate stock and debt—than between direct investments and debt. Such a result should not be surprising, as one would expect debt-equity ratios in noncorporate business to be driven more by nontax factors, such as the limited amount of the owner's re-sources, prospects for growth, and the availability of loanable funds. That is, tax motivations would seem to be much less important in influencing the debt-to-asset ratios in the noncorporate sector than in the corporate sector. Indeed, it seems possible that tax factors were encouraging more corporate debt through higher inflation rates, although this effect might have been offset because other factors attracting debt to the noncorporate sector were more powerful.

If one looks at the 1980s with this framework in mind, it would appear that tax changes probably had little effect on noncorporate debt but could have played a role in the increase in corporate debt. Corporate equity may have become less attractive as tax arbitrage possibilities decreased because of reductions in the top rate and overall reductions in marginal tax rates. However, the lower inflation rates of the 1980s would have worked in the opposite direction, perhaps with greater force. Thus tax motivations do not result in a satisfactory explanation of the increase in corporate debt over this period.

An examination of a more continuous series of corporate debt-to-asset ratios shows that the ratio rate rose during the 1960s (particularly late in the decade), dropped during the 1970s, and then rose again in the 1980s. It is very difficult to explain this behavior in terms of tax motivations. Both increases occurred during periods of a growing economy, a rising stock market, and a surge of corporate reorganization. Perhaps these relationships will help explain the past and predict the future.

Steuerle predicts corporate debt-to-asset ratios are likely to rise in the future, again because of tax arbitrage. He suggests that the noncorporate sector is less likely to increase its share of total debt, which has risen quite markedly over a long period. Moreover, he suggests that the reform of savings and loan institutions will divert funds from the individual to the corporate sector. He also suggests that the Tax Reform Act of 1986, by making the corporate top rate higher than the individual rate, will shift debt toward the higher-taxed corporate sector.

It is not clear to me that the Tax Reform Act shifted tax incentives in favor of more corporate borrowing, as Steuerle suggests. It is true that the top marginal tax rate on corporations is now above the top individual marginal tax rate. However, marginal tax rates fell more in the corporate sector than among individuals, which should actually tilt the preference for debt away from the corporate sector. In addition, the Tax Reform Act introduced a major reduction in the advantage of debt finance for corporations, at least to the extent that debt is incurred by repurchasing stock. The full taxation of capital gains considerably increases the toll charge to stockholders of replacing debt with equity relative to the tax advantage of deducting interest. Stockholders, including those who might have never sold their assets at all, will pay the full capital gains tax when stocks are repurchased, and this up-front cost will considerably offset the long-run gains from deductibility of interest by the corporation. These debt-to-asset ratios might increase, of course, if corporations begin to replace individuals as owners of rental real estate, using debt finance to acquire these properties. But it is not at all clear that the Tax Reform Act increased the preference for corporate debt relative to noncorporate debt. Thus it seems unlikely that tax changes will motivate greater acquisition of debt.

If nontax forces dominate, it is difficult to predict the future course of debt. If the growth of public debt slows or reverses, debt will be released to the private sector and, as Steuerle points out, it may be difficult for noncorporate debt-to-asset ratios to increase much more. This change might sustain higher corporate debt-to-asset ratios or increase them. Foreign investment in the United States may well contract in the future (particularly if the federal deficit falls), or shift toward more equity finance. The growth in private pension and insurance assets may slow (particularly to the extent this growth reflected the full funding requirements enacted in 1974). The private savings rate may recover and displace foreign investment (primarily in the form of debt instruments) with a mix of debt and equity. Moreover, the economy may simply be experiencing a cycle in corporate debt: economic growth, increases in the stock market, and merger activity may run their course, and corporate debt-to-asset ratios, now at a peak, may turn back down.

The most important point Steuerle makes is that an aggregate supply and demand framework must be used to explain and predict corporate debt-to-asset ratios. Aggregate supply and demand can be influenced by many factors, taxes simply being one of them. I find it difficult to see a strong influence of taxes on debt-to-asset ratios that follows the pattern of changes in the relative advantages over time. This may be because there were offsetting influences that can be sorted out only through statistical analysis, or it may be that tax advantages are not very important compared with other forces.

These observations do lead to some tax policy implications. One is that altering the tax environment might not do very much to alter corporate debt-to-asset ratios. Nor is it clear that increases in corporate debt induced by other factors, particularly those arising from corporate reorganizations, should be a major revenue concern. With full taxation of capital gains, the present value of revenue lost from replacing debt with equity through stock repurchase may be largely offset by the up-front capital gains tax paid. Similarly, an increase in corporate debt because corporations move into real estate may be relatively small if the corporation replaces individuals who are heavily leveraged as owners. Rather, it seems that changes in the tax environment should be motivated by the goals of desirable tax policy—equity, efficiency, and simplicity—rather than ad hoc responses to changes in debt ratios.

Corporate Leverage and Leveraged Buyouts in the Eighties

Margaret M. Blair and Robert E. Litan

THE SIGNIFICANT increases in leverage and leveraged buy-out (LBO) activity in the corporate sector in the United States in the 1980s have generated much controversy and confusion. The policy disputes center on whether these forms of corporate restructuring are beneficial or detrimental to the economy and, if detrimental, how they can be reversed. A key mystery is why leverage and LBO activity seem to have exploded in the last several years.

At least two factors make the recent trends particularly perplexing. First, high real interest rates made debt financing relatively expensive in the 1980s compared with historical costs. Benjamin Friedman has argued that the increase in interest rates should have encouraged corporations to make greater use of equity relative to debt.[1] The increase in corporate leverage in the 1980s seems to contradict this proposition.

Second, the bias toward debt financing built into the income tax code for over seven decades—through the deductibility of interest but not of dividends—was not significantly strengthened during the 1980s. The 1986 Tax Reform Act had offsetting effects. On the one hand, the legislation greatly reduced the marginal tax rate on corporate income, thus reducing the spread between the after-tax cost of equity and the after-tax cost of debt to the corporation. On the other hand, it eliminated the preferential treatment of capital gains income and thereby reduced one advantage of equity over debt for investors. The net effect of these changes, combined with the reduction in maximum tax rate on personal income, may have been to tip the balance of tax incentives for individual investors in favor of holding debt instruments rather than equity instruments. But it increased

---

1. See Benjamin M. Friedman, "Implications of Government Deficits for Interest Rates, Equity Returns, and Corporate Financing," in Benjamin M. Friedman, ed., *Financing Corporate Capital Formation* (University of Chicago Press, 1986), pp. 67–89.

the relative cost to investors of the transactions involved in converting equity to debt.[2]

We attempt in this paper to explain the rush to leverage in the 1980s. We begin by outlining the aggregate trends in leverage and LBO activity. Measured by three of four commonly used statistics, leverage in the corporate sector as a whole increased significantly in the 1980s; the shift in corporate financing patterns at the margin was even more dramatic, as corporations withdrew equity from the market in unprecedented quantities. LBOs, a major mechanism by which this transition was effected, were almost nonexistent before 1980. But they emerged as an important new phenomenon in the 1980s, growing particularly fast after 1983. Although it might seem obvious that LBO activity has contributed to the growing use of leverage in the aggregate economy, we found to our surprise that the empirical connection between LBOs and leverage is somewhat tenuous. On an industry by industry basis, our measures of LBO activity are, in fact, uncorrelated with one of our measures of change in leverage and only weakly correlated with another measure. We offer some thoughts about what this finding may mean.

Michael Jensen and his collaborators have argued that LBOs in particular, as well as other forms of corporate restructuring that greatly increase the use of debt by the firm, are mechanisms by which equity in firms is concentrated in the hands of corporate managers, thereby increasing the incentives managers have to manage their firms in the most efficient possible way. This reduces the "agency costs," or the costs of monitoring the managers. There is evidence to support this view. By itself, however, this "agency costs" model does not explain why debt and LBO activity should have jumped so markedly in the 1980s.

Jensen has argued further that agency costs are more likely to be a serious problem for firms that are generating more cash from existing operations than they can profitably redeploy into new investment projects. The idea that such "free cash flow," or a dearth of attractive investment opportunities that is its counterpart, may be driving the growth in leverage and leveraging transactions is explored in the second section. Shareholders' incentives to force cash out of their corporations should depend on the relation between available returns on new corporate investment and the opportunity cost of capital. If shareholders can earn high real returns on relatively safe debt securities, as they were able to do throughout most

2. For a fuller discussion of why changes in the tax laws had no effect on leveraged buyouts in particular, see Jane G. Gravelle, "Tax Aspects of Leveraged Buyouts," Congressional Research Service, Washington, 1989.

of the 1980s, they will be less willing to trust corporate managers with the cash generated by their businesses unless potential equity returns on new investment projects have also risen. But as we will show, the returns to capital in the corporate sector as a whole, and for manufacturing in particular, were on a downward trend for several decades before the 1980s, hitting forty-year lows in many industries in 1982.

In the face of declining returns, the extraordinary increase in real interest rates early in the decade should have drastically reduced incentives for new investment and increased the benefit to shareholders of corporate strategies that stress high current payout, even at the expense of long-term investment. Leveraged buyouts and other restructurings that increase corporate debt may be explained as mechanisms for institutionalizing such strategies.

In our third section we use industry data, primarily from the manufacturing sector, to test the free cash flow theory, including our hypothesis that high real interest rates in the 1980s made both leverage and LBOs especially attractive. Most of the results of our statistical tests are consistent with these hypotheses. However, measurement problems turn out to be troublesome, and some of our findings are sensitive to how leverage is measured.

At the same time, we also test a competing view about the source of increasing leverage and LBO activity in the 1980s: that both were made possible by, and have been responses to, the financial innovations surrounding the development of a "junk bond" market. Although such innovations cannot be denied, the claim that they caused the current wave of LBO activity or the surge in the use of debt does not help to explain the timing of these phenomena. Why then did these innovations arise in the 1980s? With the possible exception of certain arbitrage techniques that require the use of very high-speed computers, most financial market innovations have not involved previously unknown scientific or technological knowledge, and hence could have been used earlier if they were profitable or attractive for other reasons. In particular, high-yield junk bonds have existed for decades. In the 1980s, however, financial entrepreneurs promoted them, and investors accepted them, for use in a far wider range of applications. The statistical test we construct suggests that financial innovations in the credit market are not the principal reason for recent leverage and LBO trends.

We conclude by noting several implications of our results for future trends in leverage and corporate restructuring and for explaining how investment responds to movements in real interest rates.

Trends in Aggregate LBO Activity
and Corporate Leverage

Since the LBO phenomenon is quite recent, historical data tracking LBO activity are necessarily limited. We use here a data base compiled by Morgan Stanley, Inc., that includes all LBOs and mergers and acquisitions valued over $35 million (in 1988 dollars) since 1978. In this section we refer to the aggregates; later, we use the industry breakdowns.

Figures 1 and 2 indicate that by number of transactions both mergers and acquisitions and LBOs in all industries and for manufacturing firms in particular have trended upward throughout the last decade. Figures 3 and 4 illustrate the same trend measured by transaction value. Measured both ways, the data show an upward shift in the rate of growth in 1983, but this shift is particularly sharp for the dollar volume data. Measured this way, LBOs have grown from less than 2 percent of all takeover activity to more than 15 percent of such activity in the last three years.

Measurements of corporate leverage are more complicated. One traditional approach is to compare a firm's debt to its equity, on the theory that higher debt-to-equity ratios indicate greater exposure to bankruptcy. Figure 5 shows that when the value of equity is computed by valuing assets at either their historical costs or their replacement values, the debt-equity ratio for the nonfinancial corporate sector as a whole has been on an upward trend throughout much of the postwar period. The ratio hit a local peak in 1973 and then moved downward throughout the 1970s. The sharp rise in the ratio since 1982, accompanying the surge in LBOs, mergers, and acquisitions, suggests that these transactions may have helped to drive aggregate corporate debt-equity ratios to new highs. Still, as of the end of 1988, debt ratios based on either historical cost or replacement value were roughly in line with where those ratios would be if they had continued to climb along their trends set before 1973.

Figure 6 illustrates a much different pattern, where the debt-equity ratio is calculated by using the market value of equity. This ratio followed a downward trend until 1973–74, when stock prices fell and the ratio more than doubled. Since then the ratio has fluctuated within a band below the peak years and above the pre-1973 range but, unlike the book-value debt-equity ratio, with no upward trend.[3]

3. Ben Bernanke and John Campbell found similar results through 1986 in their analysis of firms in the Compustat data base, using estimated market values for *both* debt and equity. See Ben S. Bernanke and John Y. Campbell, "Is There a Corporate Debt Crisis?" *Brookings Papers on Economic Activity, 1:1988,* pp. 83–125. (Hereafter *BPEA.*)

Figure 1. Number of Mergers and Acquisitions and Leveraged Buyouts in All Industries, 1978–88[a]

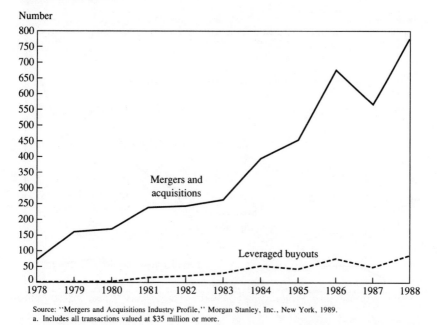

Number

Source: "Mergers and Acquisitions Industry Profile," Morgan Stanley, Inc., New York, 1989.
a. Includes all transactions valued at $35 million or more.

Figure 2. Number of Mergers and Acquisitions and Leveraged Buyouts in Manufacturing Industries, 1978–88[a]

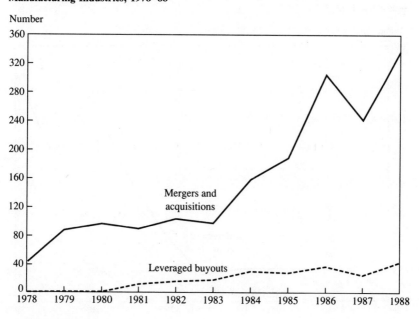

Number

Source: See figure 1.
a. Includes all transactions valued at $35 million or more.

Figure 3. Value of Mergers and Acquisitions and Leveraged Buyouts in All Industries, 1978–88ᵃ

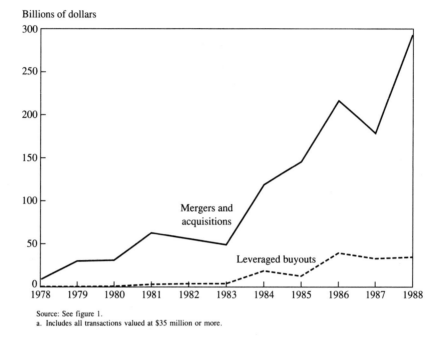

Billions of dollars

Source: See figure 1.
a. Includes all transactions valued at $35 million or more.

Figure 4. Value of Mergers and Acquisitions and Leveraged Buyouts in Manufacturing Industries, 1978–88ᵃ

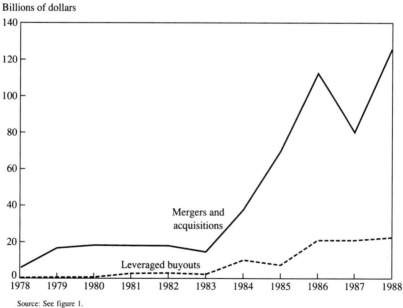

Billions of dollars

Source: See figure 1.
a. Includes all transactions valued at $35 million or more.

Figure 5. Debt-to-Equity Ratios for the Nonfinancial Corporate Sector, Book Values, 1949–88

Debt–equity ratio

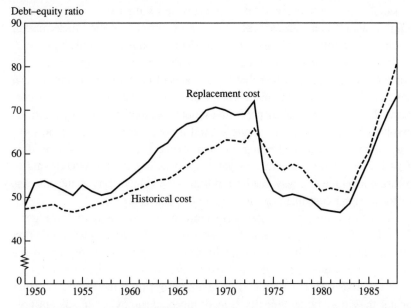

Source: Board of Governors of the Federal Reserve System, "Balance Sheets for the U.S. Economy, 1949–88," Statistical Release C.9 (April 1989).

Figure 6. Debt-to Equity Ratios for the Nonfinancial Corporate Sector, Market Values, 1949–88

Debt–equity ratio

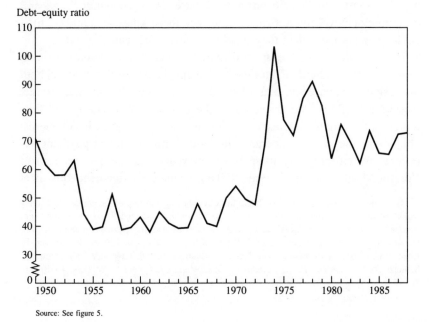

Source: See figure 5.

It is far from clear, however, whether such solvency-based measures as the debt-equity ratio are the appropriate indicators of leverage. That is especially true when the ratios are measured with the market value of equity, which can vary sharply in a short period, as the stock market crashes of October 1987 and October 1989 demonstrated only too well.

Those who express concern about corporate leverage do so primarily, if not exclusively, out of a fear that higher rates of corporate bankruptcies can have adverse macroeconomic consequences. In particular, a wave of corporate bankruptcies could depress investment spending not only by the firms involved but also by their suppliers. And a poor business climate, in turn, may depress consumer spending, as more workers fear the loss of their jobs. To the extent these concerns are valid, analysts presumably would want to measure leverage in a way that best indicates the vulnerability of the business sector to significant increases in the rate of bankruptcy.[4]

With this criterion, a potentially more useful indicator of leverage is the ratio of interest payments to cash flow. This ratio focuses attention on the degree to which leverage imposes constraints on the operating policies and strategic decisions of firms. It may also be the most relevant ratio for assessing the riskiness of leverage during a recession. Whether or not they may be technically forced into bankruptcy, even solvent borrowers may have to cut back investment spending and employment significantly if because of a sudden drop in their cash flow they have to reduce their cash holdings or liquidate fixed assets to make interest payments on existing debts. Accordingly, in the event of a downturn in general economic activity, many firms would face these kinds of liquidity difficulties much sooner than they would actually experience insolvency.

Figure 7 illustrates the upward march of the ratio of interest to cash flow (or ''interest burden'') for the nonfinancial business sector throughout the postwar era, based on data collected in the National Income and Product Accounts (NIPA). One drawback to the NIPA interest data is that they represent the sum the interest corporations actually pay in cash and interest obligations they merely accrue. The latter form of interest payment has become increasingly important in recent years with the proliferation of ''original issue discount'' bonds (OIDs), or the corporate debt equivalent

4. There is no clear consensus that a large increase in the rate of corporate bankruptcy would necessarily deepen any overall economic downturn triggered for other reasons. For contrasting views on this subject, see the comments of Benjamin M. Friedman and Lawrence H. Summers on the Bernanke-Campbell paper, *BPEA, 1:1988*, pp. 126–36; and Robert E. Litan, ''The Risks of Recession,'' in Robert E. Litan, Robert Z. Lawrence, and Charles L. Schultze, eds., *American Living Standards: Threats and Challenges* (Brookings, 1988), pp. 86–92.

Figure 7. Actual and Projected Interest–Cash Flow Ratios for the Nonfinancial Corporate Sector, 1948–87[a]

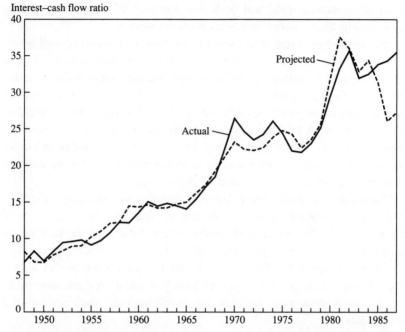

Sources: For actual ratios, National Income and Product Accounts; for projected ratios, authors' compilations (see note 6 in the text for explanation).

a. Projected path for 1981–87 shows what the ratios would have been based on historical behavior.

of zero-coupon government bonds. Because OIDs require no cash outlays for interest until the underlying obligations mature, they do not carry the risk of illiquidity associated with bonds and other debts that require interest to be paid in cash on a regular basis. According to data compiled by Morgan Stanley, however, OIDs still constitute only about 6 percent of all outstanding corporate debt obligations.[5] Thus the interest–cash flow ratios calculated from the NIPA data can still be useful indicators of the bankruptcy risks faced by corporate borrowers.

With this in mind, it is noteworthy that, unlike the book-value debt-equity ratios, which fell through much of the 1970s and only began to rise again steeply beginning in 1983, the interest burden ratio calculated from the NIPA data began climbing steeply in the late 1970s and hit a peak in 1982, when

5. More specifically, as of the first quarter of 1989, original issue discount (OID) obligations totaled $29 billion. Debt and preferred stock with interest and dividends paid "in kind," or "PIK" instruments, totaled another $8 billion. By comparison, at the end of 1988, according to the Federal Reserve's flow of funds data, there were $462 billion in outstanding corporate bonds.

nominal interest rates crested and cash flows were driven down by recession. The ratio fell the following year but has since risen steadily. Although the level of the ratio in 1987 was no higher than in 1982, it was at a postwar peak despite five years of steady economic expansion.

Since 1984 the ratio of interest to cash flow has remained well above the levels that one would have expected from historical patterns. Figure 7 also depicts a projected ratio based on a statistical regression covering the 1948 through 1980 period relating the interest–cash flow ratio to movements in long-term nominal interest rates (measured by the yield on bonds rated AAA by Moody's) and the dividend-price ratio for Standard and Poor's 500. Other things being equal, the interest burden of corporations should vary positively with short-run movements in the nominal interest rate, which the estimated regression confirms.

Movements in stock yields, however, could have conflicting effects on the corporate interest burden: the relation between the two variables could be negative to the extent stock prices influence the debt capacity of the corporate sector (that is, high stock prices imply low dividend-price ratios but high debt capacity), but positive to the extent the stock market reflects the influence of the economic cycle on cash flow and interest rate movements (that is, high stock prices signal strong cash flows that reduce interest–cash flow ratios).

If stock prices can be taken as indicators of the prospects for investment and growth, the free cash flow theory of leverage would also imply a positive relationship, since, according to this theory, firms that have low growth prospects, and hence that have a low stock price relative to their current yield, should be the firms that are being leveraged up to enforce the payout of cash flow. (This final argument, however, may be applicable only to the mass financial restructuring process that got under way in the corporate sector in the 1980s.)

In fact, the estimated equation reveals a highly statistically significant negative relationship between the interest–cash flow ratio and the dividend-price ratio.[6] Figure 7 illustrates that the projected interest burden

6. The actual equation is:

$$ICF = 6.48 + 2.56MOODY - 0.98DP,$$
$$= (5.44) \quad (25.05) \quad (-4.45)$$
$$\text{adj. } R^2 = 0.96$$

where *ICF* represents the interest–cash flow ratio; *MOODY* the interest rate on ten-year corporate bonds rated AAA by Moody's; and *DP* the dividend-price ratio for Standard and Poor's 500. This equation outperformed similar equations with a time trend or with the unemployment rate on the right-hand side rather than the dividend-price ratio.

Figure 8. Net New Debt and Equity Raised by Nonfinancial Corporations, 1965–88

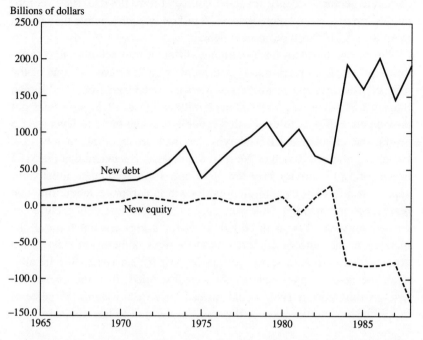

Billions of dollars

ratio based on the historical relationship to interest rates and stock yields underpredicted the interest burden ratio by a large margin from 1984 through 1987, or precisely those years in which the controversy surrounding the buildup of corporate debt was so evident.

Although measures of overall leverage are not wildly different from their long-run trend, two other measures illustrate a marked departure after 1984 in the marginal financing behavior of corporations. These measures are the total net new equity and net new debt issued by nonfinancial corporations each year. Figure 8 shows that before 1980 the corporate sector typically issued only a small amount of new equity each year, rarely withdrew equity, and issued new debt as needed to finance investment projects that exceeded its net internally available funds. In 1981 nonfinancial corporations as a whole withdrew a sizable amount of equity for the first time in decades. Then in 1982 and 1983, as the stock market began a long climb, firms issued a significant amount of new equity again, using the proceeds to reduce the required amount of new debt. With stock prices rising and interest rates high, this behavior is exactly what traditional finance theories would predict. The puzzle is that, beginning in 1984, the corporate sector suddenly reversed course. From 1984 to 1989, corporations, on net, retired more than $676 billion in equity, while they issued more than $1,070 billion in new debt.

The corporate sector has used many different transactions and restructuring programs to retire equity and increase its leverage, but one of the most conspicuous and controversial ways has been the LBO. The Morgan Stanley LBO data base extends back only as far as 1978, so it does not provide enough data to establish a reliable baseline trend in leverage for testing the effect that LBO activity has had on the trend in leverage. However, Stephen Roach of Morgan Stanley has calculated that the $167 billion of LBO activity between 1978 and 1988 accounted directly for approximately 14 percent of the total growth in corporate debt during that period.[7] More broadly, Goldman Sachs estimated that debt incurred in connection with all types of corporate restructurings accounted for all the increase in the ratio of corporate debt to gross domestic product in the nonfinancial corporate sector during the past fifteen years. Specifically, if all the restructuring-related debt were excluded, then the 66 percent level of this ratio in 1988 would instead have been roughly 55 percent, or no higher than the level of that ratio in the mid-to-late 1970s.[8]

Why the 1980s?

What accounts for the extraordinary increases in both aggregate corporate debt and corporate restructuring activity in the 1980s? Indeed, how are these two phenomena related, and are they driven by the same things? The free cash flow theory articulated by Jensen provides a starting place for thinking about these questions.[9]

Jensen has argued that the widely held corporation is fundamentally flawed as an organizational form because it separates ownership from control and thereby introduces distortions in the incentives facing managers. Because managers do not own all the stock of the firm, they do not bear the full risk or suffer the full consequences of their decisions. That creates a potential conflict of interest for the managers because the

7. Stephen S. Roach, "Living with Corporate Debt," *Economic Perspectives* (Morgan Stanley), November 1988.

8. Goldman Sachs Economic Research Group, "Debt without Disaster," *Financial Market Perspectives* (New York, December 1988–January 1989), p. 4.

9. See Michael C. Jensen, "Agency Costs of Free Cash Flow, Corporate Finance, and Takeovers," *American Economic Review*, vol. 76 (May 1986, *Papers and Proceedings, 1985*), pp. 323–29.

policies and investment decisions that maximize value for the shareholders may be different from those that best serve the managers' own interests.[10]

The potential for conflict of interest inherent in the corporate form imposes so-called agency costs on shareholders. These are, in essence, the costs of monitoring the performance of managers. Jensen and his colleagues have argued that an active "market for corporate control" reduces these agency costs because the threat of takeover helps to discipline managers. They have further argued that leveraged buyouts and other forms of corporate restructuring can reduce agency costs by reducing the outstanding equity and concentrating it in the hands of the management team itself. That realigns the incentives of managers and encourages them to adopt policies that maximize the value of the firm.

This line of reasoning has great appeal as an explanation for LBOs, although not necessarily for marginal changes in corporate capital structure. Moreover, it does not explain why the conflict of interest issue suddenly came to a head in the last decade. The corporate form has thrived for more than a century.[11] Before 1979 hostile takeovers, leveraged buyouts, and other contentious control-related transactions were extremely rare. Yet, as we showed earlier, these transactions came to represent at least 15 to 20 percent of all merger and acquisition activity in the 1980s.

One explanation for the sudden rise of LBO activity and corporate control contests relates to the fact that conflict of interest on the part of corporate managers is unlikely to be a serious or widespread problem for firms that are growing rapidly and have a long list of attractive investment opportunities.[12] If managers are motivated by the desire to build and run large organizations, or if they are motivated by the money, prestige, and perquisites that typically go with running large organizations, they will

10. Adolf A. Berle and Gardiner C. Means made this same argument almost sixty years ago in *The Modern Corporation and Private Property* (New York: Commerce Clearing House, 1932).

11. Indeed, most economic historians regard the corporation as one of the most important organizational innovations of the late nineteenth century. The liquidity provided by spreading ownership over a large body of investors who can freely buy and sell a firm's securities made it possible to marshal vastly larger amounts of resources for productive activity than could be assembled by individual owner-entrepreneurs. At the same time, it greatly expanded the pool of talent that could be drawn on to manage those resources, since top executives no longer needed to have sufficient personal wealth to own the entire firm. See, for example, Alfred D. Chandler, Jr., *The Visible Hand: The Managerial Revolution in American Business* (Belknap Press of Harvard University Press, 1977).

12. The following arguments are condensed from Margaret M. Blair, "'Free Cash Flow' and the Rise in Contests for Corporate Control," Brookings Discussion Papers in Economics, April 1989.

want to retain and reinvest the cash flow generated by their firm to take advantage of as many investment opportunities as possible. That, of course, is exactly what shareholders will want managers to do as long as the investment opportunities available to the firm can provide a return to shareholders higher than their opportunity cost. Hence a firm that is growing rapidly and profitably is unlikely to have a significant conflict of interest problem.

However, as firms mature, markets become exhausted, or the investment climate deteriorates for any other reason, managers' desire to retain and reinvest the firm's cash flow may come into conflict with shareholders' desires to achieve the highest possible return from their investment. Hence, as Jensen has argued, the agency costs of monitoring managers may be higher when firms have free cash flow, or cash flow in excess of that needed for investment in positive net-present-value projects. This ''agency costs of free cash flow'' theory implies an underlying theory of optimal capital structure in which the value-maximizing (or agency cost–minimizing) shares of debt and equity in the capital structure of a given firm are endogenous functions of the relation between investment opportunities and the amount of cash flow being generated by the firm that could be reinvested. [13]

From time to time, individual firms in any industry may find that they have exhausted their markets and that further investment in their existing business will only pull down average returns. Or whole industries may mature as demand for the goods produced by those industries stops growing (tobacco), access to resources or new markets is cut off (oil exploration), or the cost of developing, testing, and marketing new products soars relative to the revenues that can be expected from making and selling those new products (food processing

13. Unfortunately, discussions of free cash flow theory are often confused by a lack of consistency in the definitions of cash flow. When the goal of discussion is to focus attention on the degree of discretion managers have in the decisions they make about corporate spending, the appropriate definition of cash flow is after-tax corporate profits plus depreciation. In other words, it is the cash being generated that is not legally committed to being paid out. ''Free cash flow,'' then, is the portion of that cash flow which cannot be reinvested profitably. If purely financial transactions can be used to alter the proportions of debt and equity capital in a firm, thereby changing the amount of interest and taxes that must be paid out in each period, cash flow, so defined, becomes an endogenous function of the capital structure of the firm. In this paper we want to consider the reverse relationship, that is, the role that cash flow and investment opportunities play in determining the capital structure of the firm. For this purpose, we must have some definition of cash flow that is exogenous to the capital structure of the firm. Hence, later in this paper, we define cash flow as the sum of pretax operating profits, interest payments, and depreciation.

and pharmaceuticals). All four industries cited as examples have substantial assets in place that continue to generate large profits. These industries have also been subject to intense LBO, hostile takeover, and other restructuring activity in recent years.

Besides industry-specific factors that might drive down the marginal return from new investment for groups of firms (without necessarily hurting their average return on existing assets), a general increase in the opportunity cost of capital will reduce the number of attractive investment projects for firms in all sectors of the economy at the same time. Such an increase occurred in the first few years of the 1980s, when real interest rates soared to previously unseen levels. Although there can be some debate about how real interest rates should be measured, there can be little question that throughout the 1980s the real rate of return on debt instruments exceeded the returns on such instruments for any single year in the postwar era. Meanwhile, the net pretax rate of return to capital at the beginning of the decade in many industries was lower than it was at any other time in the previous thirty years.

Figure 9 illustrates the squeeze between the net return on capital and the cost of capital in the 1980s as it affected the manufacturing sector as a whole. The net return on capital is measured as the sum of interest payments plus (pretax) profits (in current dollars), divided by the current-dollar value of net capital invested. Pretax profits are used rather than after-tax profits because, within broad limits, the amount of taxes paid by firms depends on the proportions of the return to capital that take the form of interest, dividends, or capital gains.[14] The difference between pretax returns to capital and the pretax opportunity cost of capital is a rough measure of economic profits earned from the productive activity of manufacturing firms that are available for payment to the holders of risk capital or to the government in the form of taxes.

To evaluate investments, corporate finance specialists often use complex measures of the cost of capital that usually take the form of real

14. Interest payments and pretax profits are from the Department of Commerce. We took data on factor payments by industry and summed them over all manufacturing industries. The value of capital stock is computed from a new data series developed by the Commerce Department that provides estimates of the net (current dollar) value of plant and equipment by industry. To the plant and equipment data were added estimates of the (current dollar) value of inventories (using Commerce data when available, and extrapolating from available data to fill in missing years), and an estimate of the value of land holdings for each industry (estimated using Compustat data for land values relative to value of plant and equipment, by industry). The industry-specific totals for value of invested capital were then summed over all industries in the manufacturing sector.

Figure 9. Return to Capital and Real Cost of Capital in the Manufacturing Sector, Twenty Industries, 1949–87ᵃ

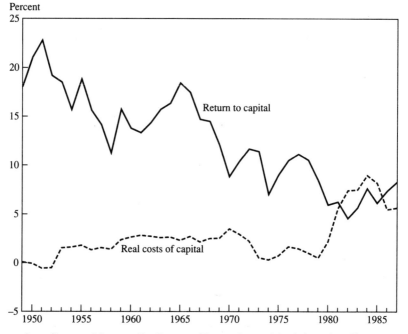

Sources: Return to capital constructed from Department of Commerce data on capital stocks, inventories, and factor payments, and estimates of land values constructed from Compustat data. Real cost of capital equals nominal rate on Moody's AAA-rated bonds minus three-year moving average of percentage changes in personal consumption expenditure index.
   a. Standard industrial classification 20–39.

interest rates adjusted for business and financial risk, for taxes, and for differences between the cost of debt-financed capital and the cost of equity-financed capital. Although such measures are useful and appropriate in certain contexts, they are extremely sensitive to the assumptions made about marginal tax brackets, factors that influence risk, and methods of measuring risk.[15] To minimize the complexity and potential arbitrariness of such measures of the cost of capital, we use (in figure 9 and in the regression analysis presented later), a simplistic measure—the nominal rate on Moody's AAA corporate bonds, minus a three-year lagged moving average of the inflation rate, measured as the annual percentage change in the personal consumption expenditure index. This measure can be regarded as the opportunity cost to investors of putting their funds into

15. See Richard Brealy and Stewart Myers, *Principles of Corporate Finance* (McGraw-Hill, 1984), chap. 19, for examples of relatively simple formulas for computing firm-specific capital costs.

risky investments in new plant and equipment rather than into relatively safe corporate bonds.

By this measure, the real (pretax) cost of capital has historically moved in a range from about 0 to about 3 percent. In 1980, however, it began climbing, hitting a peak of more than 8 percent in 1984. At no time since 1981 has this measure of the real cost of capital fallen below 5 percent. Meanwhile the average (pretax) return to capital in the manufacturing sector bottomed out at about 4 percent in 1982 and stayed well below 10 percent throughout the decade. Figure 10 presents the same return to capital data broken out into durable goods and nondurable goods manufacturing. This figure shows that the most dramatic declines in returns was in durable goods and that the lowest level of returns was reached in this sector as well.

Although the returns on existing capital stocks have varied from industry to industry, the data plotted in figures 9 and 10 suggest that many manufacturing firms faced an extremely bleak climate for new investment in the last decade. Table 1 provides a more detailed industry-by-industry breakout of the return to capital, averaged over five-year intervals since 1948, for industries that make up the manufacturing sector. The long-run declining trend as well as the low levels in the 1980s is evident for nearly every industry. The data presented in the table suggest that in many sectors of the economy the return that managers could expect to earn on new investment has probably been quite low for a number of years.[16]

Management specialists have long used the phrase "cash cow" to refer to businesses that are producing high current cash flows but that have few attractive investment opportunities. The phrase is intended to imply that these businesses should be "milked" for their cash. In other words, the appropriate strategy for managing such firms is to disinvest over time, redeploying the cash being generated by the firm to other uses. A leveraged buyout or other transaction that drastically alters a firm's capital structure toward the use of debt is an effective mechanism for instituting and enforcing such a strategy on a whole firm.

The free cash flow theory, therefore, assigns a different kind of role for debt from that traditionally ascribed to it. In particular, whereas finance

16. These numbers are indicative only. Low average returns do not necessarily imply low marginal returns, or vice versa. Note, for example, the very high average returns in the tobacco industry in recent years. Clearly the high returns on existing assets in that industry should not be taken as indicative of high returns on marginal investment. Nonetheless, the declining trend in many industries suggests that the marginal returns on new investment may have been lower than the average returns for some time.

Figure 10. Return to Capital and Real Cost of Capital in the Manufacturing Sector, 1949–87

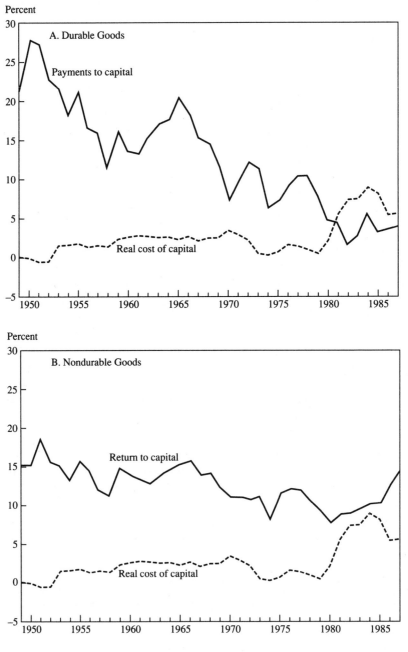

Sources: See figure 9.

theorists have viewed debt primarily as one form in which to raise new capital for investment, in recent years many firms have issued debt as a *replacement* for equity in their capital structure. As suggested earlier, this fact distinguishes corporate financing behavior in the 1980s most clearly from behavior in previous decades.[17] Indeed, Goldman Sachs estimated that 75 percent of the reduction in corporate equity by corporations from 1984 through 1988 was debt financed.[18]

When used in large amounts to replace equity, debt can perform four functions for firms: it guarantees a high, fixed payout to investors (creditors); it provides a way to get cash out of the firm at a lower (after-tax) cost than by paying dividends; it commits the firm to reordering its priorities and changing its internal management style to emphasize current cash flows at the expense of long-term investment, and provides managers with the stick they need (the threat of bankruptcy) to enforce this new management style; and it realigns the incentives of managers in a way that encourages them to maximize share value rather than to pursue growth for its own sake. Although these consequences of debt constrain managers in ways that would be undesirable for rapidly growing firms with many attractive investment opportunities, they may be appropriate for firms that are "cash cows" or those that were turned into cash cows by the surge in real interest rates of the 1980s.

If this line of analysis is correct, it suggests that a combination of high real interest rates and low returns on new investment in many industries in the 1980s could have shifted the optimal (value-maximizing) debt-equity ratios for many firms, triggering a round of corporate financial restructuring toward heavier use of debt. Although the theory is still quite primitive and details remain to be worked out, it seems to predict that restructuring activity will be most intense for those firms or industries in which the relationship between the amount of cash flow being generated and the demand for new investment has shifted most dramatically. It is less clear whether the theory predicts that small changes in cash flows or in the investment climate will lead to marginal changes in capital structure. Given the uncertainties in forecasting both cash flow and investment needs, it seems likely that firms will not try to fine tune their capital structures in response to small fluctuations in cash flow or investment needs, or both.

17. Leveraged buyouts and debt for equity swaps are two obvious kinds of transactions in which debt is issued as a replacement for equity. But that also happens in debt-financed takeovers, since the equity of the target firm is replaced by debt instruments of the acquiring firm.

18. Goldman Sachs, "Debt without Disaster," p. 5.

Table 1. Five-Year Average Return to Capital, Twenty Industries, 1948–87

SIC	Industry	1948–52	1953–57	1958–62	1963–67	1968–72	1973–77	1978–82	1983–87
20	Food and kindred products	12.6	12.4	13.7	14.3	12.2	11.0	9.3	10.8
21	Tobacco products	10.5	15.8	19.6	20.9	26.2	20.9	25.4	33.1
22	Textile mill products	14.7	6.6	9.9	14.1	10.8	8.2	6.4	7.7
23	Apparel and related products	22.0	19.6	19.2	20.1	19.2	16.6	17.8	19.8
24	Lumber and related products	37.2	24.7	20.3	25.6	20.6	18.3	10.4	11.6
25	Furniture and fixtures	24.3	22.4	18.7	24.1	17.3	10.5	13.1	16.7
26	Paper and allied products	23.8	20.0	14.4	13.3	9.8	10.9	8.0	8.0
27	Printing and publishing products	31.6	31.4	26.3	29.8	23.6	21.7	20.7	21.6
28	Chemical and allied products	24.1	20.6	20.5	20.3	14.6	13.2	7.8	9.2
29	Petroleum and coal products	4.9	–1.8	–8.7	–5.5	–4.7	0.2	2.8	10.9
30	Rubber and plastic products	21.6	19.0	16.5	13.3	11.3	7.2	6.2	10.7
31	Leather and leather products	25.1	22.8	18.2	24.4	16.9	16.7	21.2	11.7
32	Stone, clay, and glass	24.7	26.3	18.5	14.6	10.2	8.5	6.0	9.6
33	Primary metals	18.3	14.8	8.5	10.4	3.9	5.1	2.9	–0.4
34	Fabricated metal products	24.3	15.4	11.5	15.9	11.7	12.2	10.7	9.8
35	Machinery, except electrical	22.4	16.6	13.6	18.9	12.9	11.0	9.5	1.4
36	Electrical machinery	20.3	17.2	17.2	19.5	12.2	7.2	7.3	1.7
37	Transportation equipment	31.5	24.7	16.3	23.8	11.9	6.0	–2.9	3.3
38	Instruments and related products	16.4	21.9	20.5	24.6	24.4	13.7	11.4	1.8
39	Miscellaneous	27.1	16.9	19.8	18.0	18.3	18.0	15.7	12.5

Sources: Payments to capital computed from Department of Commerce data on capital stocks and factor payments by industry. Capital stock figures grossed up to include the value of land holdings by industry, estimated from Compustat data.

Nonetheless, if we are correct, we would expect to find that, as the restructuring process progresses, leverage is used most heavily in those industries that exhibit two qualities: consistent, predictable, and relatively high levels of cash flow, assuring firms in these industries that they can service the higher levels of debt; and low demand for new investment. In the next section we test one aspect of the first characteristic by asking whether the industries that have undergone the most significant increases in leverage are also the industries with the most stable cash flows. The presence of the second characteristic is harder to test, since there is no way to measure directly the marginal return to new investment. We settle with a test of whether the use of leverage in fourteen industries can be predicted as a function of several variables intended to serve as a proxy for the demand for new investment in those industries.

Leverage and LBO Activity by Industry

The increases in leverage and LBO activity have not been uniform across all industries. Table 2 presents three measures of these trends for manufacturing industries by two-digit standard industrial classification (SIC) codes. LBO activity is measured for the period 1978–88. The aggregate dollar volume of LBO activity for each industry is scaled by the value of capital stock at the end of the period. As shown in the table, LBO activity was most intense in the stone, clay, and glass products industry (SIC 32); textile mill products (SIC 22); and food and kindred products, including tobacco (SIC 20).

The table also presents data for two measures of leverage, drawn from the *Quarterly Financial Reports* published by the Bureau of the Census, for both 1978 and 1988.[19] As measured by the unemployment rate, the

19. The *Quarterly Financial Report* (*QFR*) series provides quarterly income statement and balance sheet information for manufacturing industries at roughly the two-digit standard industrial classification (SIC) level. The *QFR* provides data on a few nonmanufacturing industries as well, but these are broadly defined, and matching them to industry data from other sources proved a difficult problem. Despite the aggregation problems, *QFR* data were chosen because they are built up from firm-level data (rather than establishment-level data), which is necessary for looking at problems involving corporate capital structure. The *QFR* also includes information on privately held firms as well as publicly traded firms. That is important because it ensures that firms will not drop out of the sample if they are taken private in a leveraged buyout.

From the fourth quarter of 1973 (the earliest date when all the data are reported under the same definitions) until the third quarter of 1980, the *QFR* reports income statement and balance sheet information for all firms regardless of size. Beginning in the fourth quarter of 1980, the *QFR* reports the full set of balance sheet and income statement information

Table 2. Three Measures of Leveraged Buyout Activity and Corporate Leverage, by Industry

SIC	Industry	LBO volume/ capital stock, 1978–88	Interest/cash flow			Debt/total assets		
			1978	1988	Change, 1978–88	1978	1988	Change, 1978–88
20	Food and kindred products	.105	.159	.233	.074	.500	.623	.122
22	Textile mill products	.154	.108	.259	.151	.558	.638	.080
26	Paper and allied products	.059	.165	.145	−.019	.474	.533	.059
27	Printing and publishing products	.078	.093	.212	.119	.481	.571	.090
28	Chemicals and allied products	.015	.142	.235	.093	.462	.560	.098
29	Petroleum and coal products	.000	.122	.204	.082	.417	.633	.215
30	Rubber and miscellaneous products	.043	.215	.274	.059	.516	.653	.137
32	Stone, clay, and glass products	.245	.114	.319	.205	.461	.663	.202
33	Primary metal industries	.030	.183	.269	.086	.523	.686	.163
34	Fabricated metal products	.070	.132	.315	.183	.505	.607	.101
35	Machinery, except electrical	.057	.135	.267	.132	.449	.474	.026
36	Electrical and electronic equipment	.074	.102	.224	.122	.509	.534	.025
37	Transportation equipment	.039	.105	.207	.103	.524	.629	.105
38	Instruments and related products	.055	.085	.275	.190	.371	.534	.164

Sources: LBO volume from Morgan Stanley, Inc.; capital stock from Department of Commerce tapes; interest/cash flow and debt/total assets are authors' calculations of data from the *Quarterly Financial Report* (Department of Commerce, various issues).

pace of general economic activity was similar in the two years that bracket our data on LBOs, so broad macroeconomic effects that would be expected to influence leverage or cash flow were probably similar in those two years. The table indicates that, by either measure, nearly every industry experienced an increase in leverage during the decade, although the magnitude of the changes is considerably different, even within the same industry, when measured differently. When leverage is measured by the ratio of interest to cash flow,[20] the three manufacturing industries that recorded the largest absolute increases in leverage from 1978 to 1988 were stone, clay, and glass; instruments and related products (SIC 38); and fabricated metal products (SIC 34). However, when leverage is measured by the ratio of debt to total assets (measured at book value), the three industries recording the largest increases in leverage between 1978 and 1988 were petroleum and coal products (SIC 29), which recorded no LBOs; stone, clay, and glass; and instruments and related products.[21]

As was true at the aggregate level, the different ways of measuring the movement toward leverage by industry produce different answers to the question of how highly leveraged a sector of the economy really is, but at this level of disaggregation the differences become striking. In fact, on the basis of a simple measure of the interindustry correlations among the three indicators of leveraged restructuring in table 2, the LBO rate by industry is positively correlated with changes in interest–cash flow ratios, but this correlation is not strong. Meanwhile, the change in debt-to-asset ratios is not significantly correlated with either of the other measures. These facts were surprising to us. One possible explanation for the weakness of the interindustry correlation among measures of leveraging activity

---

only for those firms with assets of more than $25 million, and a truncated list of variables for all firms. In preparing this paper, we included data for only the firms larger than $25 million since the fourth quarter of 1980, but for all firms before then.

20. Like the NIPA (National Income and Product Accounts) interest data, the interest payments reported in the *QFR* also include accrued interest and thus do not show the risks of illiquidity as accurately as we would like. The interest payments reported in the *QFR* are reported on a line labeled "Interest, etc." in a catchall category combining various extraordinary expenses. In an effort to determine how significant the noninterest component of this catchall expense category is, we computed the ratio of "Interest, etc." to total liabilities for each industry. In no industry did the computed results materially exceed prevailing interest rates for the 1973–87 period, suggesting that the noninterest component of the "Interest, etc." category was very small.

21. Bernanke and Campbell, "Is There a Corporate Debt Crisis?" found that the industries which experienced the largest increases in their five-year average debt-asset ratios from 1969–74 to 1981–86 were petroleum and natural gas extraction (SIC 13), mining (SIC 10), petroleum refining (SIC 29), paper (SIC 26), stone, clay, and glass (SIC 32), and laboratory equipment (SIC 38).

is simply the small sample size. With only fourteen industries, a special situation or measurement problem in one or two industries can easily reduce the measured correlation to the point where it is no longer significant.

It is also likely that the connection between leveraged buyouts and increases in leverage in various industries is more complex than it might at first seem. Leveraged buyouts were only one kind of transaction used in the 1980s to restructure corporations and increase the payout to shareholders. Other devices included debt-financed stock repurchases, debt-financed takeovers, and restructurings that are specific to certain industries, such as the use of limited partnerships in the oil industry. Leveraged buyouts may be appropriate for some industries, whereas other types of transactions may work better in other industries. Moreover, while debt-financed takeovers often increase the debt levels of the acquiring firm, they may produce a decrease in the average debt levels in the industry of the target firm, whose shareholders are bought out and creditors paid off. If the acquiring firm is in a different industry from the target firm, such transactions may increase the degree of leverage in the corporate sector as a whole, but the measured effect on specific industries may be misleading. This suggests, at the least, that LBO activity is a very noisy measure of the trend toward increasing leverage.

Measurements of changes in the ratio of debt to total assets are also likely to be noisy because of significant errors in measuring the value of total assets. The data we use measure debt and total assets at book value, which is the only measure available for samples that include nonpublic companies. As we observed in looking at the aggregate data on leverage, book-value measures can deviate widely from measures based on market values. The meaning of this measure can also vary widely from industry to industry because of accounting conventions or variations in the degree of capital intensity or the nature of the capital stock used in different industries. In the rest of this paper, we report results using all three measures of leveraging activity. But because of the limitations of the debt–total assets ratio and LBO rate measures, we feel that our tests which use interest–cash flow ratios are probably more reliable.

The argument that debt is being used as a mechanism to force the payout of free cash flow suggests that, regardless of the form of the restructuring, the industries in which the shift to leverage has been most dramatic should be the industries in which investment opportunities have weakened the most relative to cash flows. Testing this hypothesis is a difficult problem. Although cash flow can be measured directly, the attractiveness of any given investment project is a function of the difference between the return that can be earned on that project and the opportunity cost to the firm of the funds used for the project. On a project-by-project basis, firms try to estimate these net returns, but in the aggregate there is no direct measure of the marginal return to new investment, and therefore no direct way to measure "investment opportunities."

The return to existing capital by industry, as calculated and presented in table 1, provides a useful starting place. Although this variable may be an indicator of the attractiveness of new investment, it may, by itself, be misleading. Moreover, it also contains information about current returns, which are a significant component of cash flow. Since we cannot effectively separate out the information about current cash flows from the information about investment opportunities, this variable must be interpreted cautiously as a test of the free cash flow theory.

Nonetheless, it is useful to look at the return-to-capital characteristics of industries being refinanced with debt. One way to do so is to rank the industries by measures of return to capital and compare those rankings to the industries' rankings by measures of leveraging activity. Table 3 ranks industries by their return to capital in 1980, table 4 by their 1978–87 average return to capital, and table 5 by their fifteen-year rate of change in the return to capital. The three tables also show whether each industry ranked among the top five industries by any of five different measures of leveraging activity. These are the change from 1978 to 1988 in the interest–cash flow ratio; the change from 1978 to 1988 in the debt–total assets ratio; the level of the interest–cash flow ratio in 1988; the level of the debt–total assets ratio in 1988; and the LBO rate.

Table 3 suggests that the industries which underwent significant leveraging activity during the last decade, or ended the decade highly leveraged, tended to be those with the lowest return to capital in 1980. Table 4 suggests some tendency for industries that ranked high by our measures of leveraging activity to be clustered in the middle of the rankings by average return to capital over the decade. And table 5 suggests that these same active leveragers tended to have slower rates of decline (a few even had increases) in their return to capital over the period since the early 1970s than had other industries in our sample.

If the free cash flow theory is correct, leverage would be used in response to low or falling returns on new investment, but by inducing managers to be more efficient, that leverage could also lead to improved returns on existing assets. Our simple industry rankings yield results that are consistent with this theory, although by themselves they do not provide

Table 3. Industries Ranked by Return to Capital, 1980

SIC	Industry	Return to capital, 1980	Top five by interest/cash flow (change 1978–88)	Top five by debt/total assets (change 1978–88)	Top five by interest/cash flow, 1988	Top five by debt/total assets, 1988	Top five by leveraged buyout rate
37	Transportation equipment	−0.0749					
29	Petroleum refining	0.0094		X	X	X	
33	Primary metals	0.0310		X	X	X	
30	Rubber and plastic products	0.0343		X	X	X	
32	Stone, clay, and glass	0.0525	X	X	X	X	X
22	Textile mill products	0.0557	X			X	X
28	Chemicals and allied products	0.0611					
26	Paper and allied products	0.0713					
36	Electrical and electronic equipment	0.0746					X
35	Machinery, except electrical	0.0913	X				
20	Food and tobacco	0.1032					X
34	Fabricated metal products	0.1075	X		X		
38	Instruments and related products	0.1131	X	X	X		
27	Printing and publishing	0.1955	X				X

Source: Based on tables 1 and 2.

Table 4. Industries Ranked by Average Return to Capital, 1978–87

SIC	Industry	Average return to capital, 1978–87	Top five by interest/cash flow (change 1978–88)	Top five by debt/total assets (change 1978–88)	Top five by interest/cash flow, 1988	Top five by debt/total assets, 1988	Top five by leveraged buyout rate
37	Transportation equipment	0.0016					
33	Primary metals	0.0126		X	X	X	
36	Electrical and electronic equipment	0.0458	X				X
35	Machinery, except electrical	0.0551	X				
38	Instruments and related products	0.0665	X	X	X		
29	Petroleum refining	0.0688		X		X	
22	Textile mill products	0.0706	X			X	X
32	Stone, clay, and glass	0.0786	X	X	X	X	X
26	Paper and allied products	0.0806					
30	Rubber and plastic products	0.0848		X	X	X	
28	Chemicals and allied products	0.0853					
34	Fabricated metal products	0.1030	X		X		
20	Food and tobacco	0.1217					X
27	Printing and publishing	0.2121					X

Source: Based on tables 1 and 2.

Table 5. Industries Ranked by Rate of Decline (or Increase) in Return to Capital, 1972–87

SIC	Industry	DELTA[a]	Top five by interest/cash flow (change 1978–88)	Top five by debt/total assets (change 1978–88)	Top five by interest/cash flow, 1988	Top five by debt/total assets, 1988	Top five by leveraged buyout rate
38	Instruments and related products	−.0125	X	X	X		
35	Machinery, except electrical	−.0088	X				
36	Electrical and electronic equipment	−.0063					X
37	Transportation equipment	−.0056					
33	Primary metals	−.0051		X	X	X	
28	Chemicals and allied products	−.0039					
26	Paper and allied products	−.0023					
34	Fabricated metal products	−.0021	X		X		
27	Printing and publishing	−.0007				X	X
22	Textile mill products	−.0003	X				X
32	Stone, clay, and glass	−.0000	X	X	X	X	X
20	Food and tobacco	.0018					X
30	Rubber and plastics	.0021		X	X	X	
29	Petroleum refining	.0115		X		X	

Source: Based on tables 1 and 2.
a. DELTA is the estimated coefficient on the time trend in a regression of return to capital on time, 1972–87.

enough information to allow us to disentangle cause and effect relationships.

A closer look at certain industries is revealing, however. Stone, clay, and glass (SIC 32) is the only industry that ranks in the top five by all five leverage measures. This industry started the decade with a return to capital that had been on a steady downward trend for about thirty years, bottoming out near zero in 1982. Since then, this decline has been reversed. At the end of 1987 the return to capital in this industry was at its highest level since 1965. Similar, though less dramatic, stories can be told for the primary metals industry (SIC 33), the rubber and plastics industry (SIC 30), and the textile mill products industry (SIC 22), all three of which rank high by three of our five measures of leveraging activity. The return on capital in rubber and plastics bottomed out in 1980 and then improved almost to the levels of the mid-1960s. The return on capital in primary metals trended downward throughout the postwar period, collapsing to levels below zero in 1982 and 1983, but since then has begun to edge back up. And returns in the textiles industry collapsed between 1977 and 1982 but have generally been improving since 1982.

The instruments and related products industry (SIC 38) also ranks high by three out of five of our leverage measures. Unlike the previous examples, however, this industry had a relatively high return to capital in 1980. Even so, it may fit the free cash flow theory. Of the fourteen industries we looked at, it had the steepest rate of decline in return to capital between 1972 and 1987, suggesting that new investment has probably not provided an attractive use for cash flow during this period.

Petroleum refining is also an interesting case. Our data show that this industry had no LBOs during the last decade, but it had the largest measured increase in the ratio of debt to total assets (starting from a relatively low debt level). Petroleum refining has historically had one of the lowest returns to capital among manufacturing industries—indeed, negative returns through much of the 1950s and 1960s. This pattern has occurred largely because integrated oil companies used the downstream end of their business to move products to market as fast as possible in order to generate higher returns on the upstream (crude oil production) end of their business, where the tax advantages were greater. With OPEC's (Organization of Petroleum Exporting Countries') restrictions on oil production in the early 1970s and the collapse of oil prices in the early 1980s, the old strategy of sacrificing returns on the downstream end of the business to enhance returns upstream no longer made sense. Oil companies stopped adding

Table 6. Interindustry Correlations between Measures of Leveraging Activity and
Measures of Growth and Investment Rates

Item	Interest/cash flow (change 1978–88)	Debt/assets (change 1978–88)	LBOs (1978–88)/ assets (1987)
Net investment/capital stock (avg. 1978–87)	−0.4986[a]	0.0143	−0.1894
Gross investment/cash flow (avg. 1978–87)	−0.1622	0.0758	−0.2836
Growth rate of capital stock (avg. 1978–87)	−0.0650	−0.4857[a]	−0.2432
Net investment/capital stock (change since 1982)[b]	−0.2786	−0.1314	−0.1382
Gross investment/cash flow (change since 1982)[b]	−0.0256	−0.1038	−0.1678
Growth rate of capital stock (change since 1982)[b]	−0.1263	−0.5716[a]	0.0951

Sources: Based on data from *Quarterly Financial Reports*, Morgan Stanley, and Department of Commerce tapes.
a. Significant at 90 percent level or better.
b. Difference between average rate, 1982–87, and average rate, 1972–81.

new refining capacity in the late 1970s, and returns have been rising since
then. But rising returns have been associated with reduced new investment,
suggesting that, at least in the last ten years, oil refining has been a classic
"cash cow" industry.

Another implication of the free cash flow theory is that leveraged
restructurings should be concentrated in industries that are growing relatively slowly or even declining. We computed six measures of the degree
to which the industries in our sample were investing and growing over
the relevant period. The first three are the ratio of net (after depreciation)
investment to the value of the capital stock, averaged over the period 1978
through 1987; the ratio of gross investment to cash flow, averaged over
the same period; and the growth rate of the capital stock, averaged over
the same period. The second three are variations on these three ratios.
Each ratio was computed for each year from 1972 through 1987, then
averaged separately over the periods 1972–81 and 1982–87. The difference between the average ratio in the later period and the average ratio
in the earlier period then provides an indicator of the change in growth
or investment rates for an industry since 1982.

Table 6 reports the measured interindustry correlations among three of
our measures of leveraging activity and the six measures of growth and
investment. If new debt were being used primarily to finance increased
investment or growth, we would expect these correlations to be positive.
In fact, nearly all our measured correlations are negative (although only
a few are high enough to be significantly different from zero at conven-

tional significance levels). This finding is consistent with the theory that leverage is being used to restructure slow-growth industries.

This preliminary examination of the data suggests some connection between low returns to capital, low rates of investment, and increases in leverage, but the links are far from airtight. To test the hypothesis that the use of leverage is associated with low levels of attractive investment opportunities in a more formal way, we use regression techniques to measure the relationship between two measures of leverage (interest to cash flow, and debt to total assets), over time and across industries, and three different variables that are indicators of the state of investment opportunities. These are the rate of growth of the capital stock by industry in each year $(GCAP)$;[22] annual industrywide ratios of stock prices to long-term earnings (PE);[23] and the real interest rate (IR).[24] $GCAP$ is a measure of the amount of new investment in an industry in a given year relative to assets in place, and to the extent that it is a reasonable proxy for investment opportunities in that industry, the free cash flow theory predicts that the coefficient on $GCAP$ should be negative in a regression predicting the use of leverage in each industry each year. But the coefficient on $GCAP$ might be negative in regressions on interest to cash flow for another reason. Interest–cash flow will be unusually high when cash flow is low, and vice versa. If actual investment in any year is constrained by available cash flow,[25] investment (and hence $GCAP$) will tend to be low in years when cash flow is low, producing a negative relationship between $GCAP$ and interest–cash flow that is due to capital market imperfections rather than free cash flow. This problem does not affect regressions on debt to total assets, however.

PE has the advantage of being a forward-looking variable because the stock price of a firm should reflect not only the value of current earnings but also the market's expectations about future growth of those earnings. If the value of a firm's stock is based on an expectation that the firm will

22. Measured as the percentage change from time $t - 1$ to time t in the (current dollar) value of capital invested in an industry.

23. Measured as the ratio of the total value at time t (end of each calendar year) of all outstanding stock of firms in a given industry that are listed on Compustat, to the total value of net earnings of those firms averaged over the years $t, t - 1$, and $t - 2$.

24. IR is the rate on Moody's AAA rated bonds minus a three-year lagged moving average of inflation, measured as the annual percentage change in the personal consumption expenditure (PCE) index.

25. Steven M. Fazzari, R. Glenn Hubbard, and Bruce C. Petersen argue that such capital market constraints are especially important for younger, rapidly growing firms that pay very low dividends. See "Financing Constraints and Corporate Investment," *BPEA, 1:1988*, pp. 141–95.

continue to generate earnings at about its current level, rather than an expectation that the firm's earnings will be growing, its ratio of price to a measure of recent earnings will be low, while firms that the market believes will be growing rapidly will have high ratios of price to recent earnings. We use an industry aggregate price-earnings ratio as an indicator of the market's expectations about growth (and hence investment opportunities) in that industry. The free cash flow theory predicts that leverage will be used most heavily in the slow-growth industries, with low PE ratios. Hence we predict a negative coefficient on PE.

The real interest rate is a measure of the opportunity cost of capital, which influences the availability of attractive investment opportunities by setting a minimum rate of return (hurdle rate) new investments must meet. When the opportunity cost of capital is high, investment opportunities will be limited, and the free cash flow theory predicts that firms will be leveraged up as a way of forcing them to cut back on investment expenditures. This relationship is not the only one at work, however. In the short run, at least, high nominal rates of interest will tend to drive up the numerator of the interest–cash flow ratio, at least to the extent that firms are financed with rate-sensitive debt. Insofar as our measures of real interest rates are correlated with nominal rates, this correlation will also lead to a positive relationship between IR and interest–cash flow.

Traditional corporate finance theory, however, predicts that firms will substitute away from debt toward equity when real interest rates rise, leading to a negative coefficient on IR in regressions predicting debt to total assets. Hence the predicted sign on IR is positive in regressions predicting interest–cash flow, but the sign in the debt–total asset regressions depends on whether the substitution effect or the free cash flow adjustment effect dominates.

Because gross cash flow, which is the scaling variable in one of our measures of leverage, is subject to considerable cyclical fluctuation, we also include the unemployment rate ($UNEM$) as a predictor to capture these purely cyclical movements. The sign on $UNEM$ should be positive, since high levels of $UNEM$ should be associated with low levels of cash flow, and hence high measured interest–cash flow ratios. For consistency, we also include this variable in the debt–total asset regressions.

Finally, the data on aggregate levels of leverage reported earlier suggest there may be a secular trend in the use of leverage that is operating independently of these other factors. To capture this effect, we also include a time trend (T) in the regressions.

Table 7. Regressions Predicting Ratios of Interest to Cash Flow, by Industry[a]

Variable	Model 1	Model 2	Model 3
Growth rate of capital stock (GCAP)	−0.3796	...	−0.3702
	(−3.635)		(−3.684)
Industrywide price-earnings ratio (PE)	...	−0.1412	−0.1381
		(−3.868)	(−3.913)
Real interest rate (IR)	0.9119	0.4307	0.8561
	(2.349)	(1.171)	(2.291)
Unemployment rate (UNEM)	−0.6150	0.5796	−0.5241
	(−1.342)	(1.728)	(−1.188)
Time trend (T)	0.2583	0.9803	0.3269
	(0.896)	(4.427)	(1.176)
Adjusted R^2	0.6007	0.6044	0.6304
Number of observations	196	196	196

Sources: Authors' calculations using data from Department of Commerce and Compustat tapes, Moody's AAA, and Data Resources, Inc.

a. Measure of cash flow used in denominator is a three-year centered moving average of annual cash flow by industry. All models include fixed effects, or separate industry intercepts. The numbers in parentheses are t-statistics.

In its still primitive state, our theory does not provide any insight into the structural form of the postulated relationships. So we estimate a simple linear model on a panel of data with fourteen observations (1974–87) on each of the fourteen manufacturing industries (the same industries used in tables 3–6) for which we could match data on leverage, growth rate of invested capital, and industry price-earnings ratios. The dependent variables are the industrywide interest–cash flow ratios, and the industrywide debt–total asset ratios for each year. Results for the first are reported in table 7 and results for the second in table 8.[26]

Our results are, for the most part, consistent with important predictions of the free cash flow theory. The first column of both tables reports the

26. The interest–cash flow ratio was constructed using a three-year centered moving average of cash flow in the denominator to smooth out some of the short-term gyrations in this variable. Since the hypothesis we are testing attempts to explain how firms may be altering their capital structure in response to their perception of the long-run outlook for cash flow and investment in their industries, we are concerned with shifts in leverage relative to some measure of long-run cash flows, not cyclical changes that may occur from year to year as cash flows fluctuate. This procedure mitigates, but does not eliminate, the problem (just described) that the sign of the coefficient on GCAP might be a consequence of capital market imperfections that make investment sensitive to cash flow, rather than adjustments to capital structure driven by free cash flow. The other leverage variable is measured as current-year debt to current-year assets, and hence is unaffected by these issues.

Table 8. Regressions Predicting Ratios of Debt to Total Assets, by Industry[a]

	Model		
Variable	1	2	3
Growth rate of capital stock (GCAP)	−0.1787	. . .	−0.1750
	(−2.421)		(−2.394)
Industrywide price-earnings	. . .	−0.0560	−0.0546
ratio (PE)		(−2.154)	(−2.125)
Real interest rate (IR)	−0.1185	−0.3417	−0.1405
	(−0.432)	(−1.304)	(0.517)
Unemployment rate (UNEM)	−1.5692	−1.0115	−1.5333
	(−4.845)	(−4.233)	(−4.775)
Time trend (T)	0.6107	0.9468	0.6379
	(2.996)	(6.000)	(3.154)
Adjusted R^2	0.6776	0.6755	0.6839
Number of observations	196	196	196

Sources: Same as table 7.
a. Debt and total assets measured at book value. All models include fixed effects, or separate industry intercepts. The numbers in parentheses are t-statistics.

results of regressions including *GCAP* but not *PE*; the second columns report results including *PE* but not *GCAP*; and the third columns report results including both indicators of investment opportunities. Although these two variables were intended to play similar roles in the regression, they apparently are not competing with each other—neither coefficient is affected much by the addition of the other variable, and the fit of the regression as a whole is improved when both variables are included. This suggests that they are each providing independent information about the state of investment opportunities. The signs on both are negative and statistically significant, as predicted by the theory.

The estimated coefficient on *IR* in table 7 has the predicted positive sign and is strongly significant when *GCAP* is included in the regressions. The sign on *IR* is negative (though not significant) in the debt–total assets regressions (table 8), suggesting that, on the whole, the tendency of firms to try to substitute away from debt when real interest rates are high may outweigh the free cash flow effects, at least during the period covered by our sample.

Contrary to our predictions, the estimated coefficient on *UNEM* is negative (though not statistically significant) in the regressions on interest–cash flow, except when *GCAP* is left out. The unemployment rate apparently captures the predicted cyclical effects on cash flow only when it is acting as a proxy for the growth rate of the capital stock. When *GCAP* is included, or when cyclical effects on cash flow are not an issue, as in the debt–total asset regressions, *UNEM* has a negative effect on leverage. That suggests there is still a strong tendency for firms to work to reduce the pressure of high debt loads when the economy is weak and unemployment is high.

As predicted, the coefficient on T (the time trend) comes in positive in both the debt–cash flow regressions and the interest–cash flow regressions. Interestingly, these coefficients are not strongly significant in the interest–cash flow regressions that include *GCAP*. Apparently the specific exogenous variables we have used in this regression are explaining most of the movement over time in the "interest burden."

Although the coefficients are not reported, dummy variables for each industry were included in the regressions to allow for industry-specific differences in leverage that are not picked up by either *GCAP* or *PE*. When we leave these dummy variables out of the debt–total asset regressions, our equation explains only about 22 to 26 percent of the variation in leverage over time and across industries. With the dummy variables in, we explain about 68 percent of the variation in leverage. This suggests that most of the prediction work is actually being done by unexplained industry-specific factors. In the interest–cash flow regressions, by contrast, most of the prediction work is being performed by the variables we are highlighting. Equations that include the dummy variables explain up to 63 percent of the variation in leverage; equations that leave them out still explain about 50 percent.

Our findings are far from definitive, and many questions remain unanswered,[27] but on the whole our results provide support for the free cash flow–poor investment opportunities theory of leveraged restructuring. Our regression results using the interest–cash flow measure of leverage are especially encouraging for this theory, and, for several reasons just discussed, we also feel they are probably more reliable.

---

27. It should be noted, for example, that the results are sensitive to certain specification issues. A number of variations on the model were estimated in which current-year data (rather than three-year moving averages) were used in the denominator of interest–cash flow, and in the denominator of the price-earnings ratio. In addition, an earnings-price ratio was tested in an effort to circumvent potential problems caused by the fact that price-earnings is nonmonotonic in earnings. Finally, the ratio of debt to cash flow was tested as a dependent variable. The finding of a negative (and significant) coefficient on *GCAP* was robust to all these variations, but the coefficients on *PE* and *IR* seemed to be sensitive to such changes. The most puzzling finding was that, when earnings-price (*EP*) was substituted for price-earnings, the estimated coefficient on *EP* was nearly always negative and usually significant. We frankly cannot explain why leverage would be negatively related both to *PE* and to its inverse, *EP*.

Finally, some researchers have suggested that the leveraging up of the corporate sector is simply a response to the development of new financing techniques, and that the interindustry differences in the extent to which firms have taken advantage of these new techniques reflect differences in the stability of cash flows that can be used to service the new debt. We find no evidence to support this view. Using quarterly data on cash flows by industry from 1973:4 to 1988:3 from the *Quarterly Financial Reports*, we estimated exponential time trends in cash flow for each industry and then computed the percentage deviation of actual cash flow in each quarter from predicted cash flow. Then we measured the relative stability of cash flow by industry as the standard deviation of these errors (the extent to which quarterly cash flows varied from trend) over time. For the fourteen industries for which we had matching data, we found positive (though not statistically significant) correlations between this measure of cash flow stability and measures of the change in debt to total assets or interest to cash flow from 1978 to 1987. This suggests, if anything, that increases in leverage have been greatest in industries with somewhat less stable cash flows.

Conclusions and Additional Implications

Our results provide new evidence to support the free cash flow explanation for the rise in corporate leverage and restructuring activity. At the industry level, leverage is inversely correlated with proxies for investment opportunities, a result that the theory predicts. Perhaps more important, some evidence suggests that the significant rise in real interest rates in the 1980s, which should have greatly reduced net returns on investment in many industries, may have contributed to the timing of the increases in leverage and corporate restructuring observed in the 1980s.

If this latter hypothesis is correct, it has several important implications. First, corporations are likely to continue to pursue leverage-based financial strategies unless real interest rates come down and the opportunities for new investment improve dramatically. Put another way, if high levels of corporate leverage are in fact being used to restrain investment in industries with low returns relative to the cost of capital, aggregate leverage levels will fall only if the marginal gross returns on investment rise or real interest rates decline.

Second, even if real interest rates remain roughly where they are now but do not rise, we would expect the pace of corporate restructuring activity to level off and perhaps decline. Although we did not explicitly include a mechanism for a lagged response to interest changes in our model, it most likely takes some time, perhaps two or three years, for balance sheets to respond fully to perceived increases in the long-run level of real interest rates. Accordingly, given the relative stability of real rates over the past two or three years, the part of the motivation for LBO and related restructuring activity that has been a response to interest rate movements has probably disappeared. Of course, if our analysis is correct, firms will continue to be leveraged up in response to downward shifts in rates of return on investment in their particular industries. Thus it would not be surprising to see restructuring move to these sectors and away from those where much restructuring has already occurred. But economywide levels of restructuring activity are unlikely to increase as long as real interest rates remain roughly where they are now.

Finally, our theory has potentially far-reaching implications for understanding how investment responds to changes in interest rates. For some time economists have been split in their views about the determinants of business investment generally.[28] In brief, "neoclassical" theorists argue that investment responds to changes in interest rates, or in more refined versions, to changes in the cost of capital (usually measured as a weighted average of the costs of debt and equity). Advocates of the "accelerator" model assert that current-year investment responds to prior changes in the level of output. And still other economists point to the importance of corporate cash flow to investment, on the theory that the cheapest source of investment funds is cash internally generated by ongoing operations.

The free cash flow theory of optimal capital structure, as we have outlined it, links up elements of two of those theories of investment by arguing that the optimal level of new investment is a function of real interest rates, but that actual investment may depend heavily on cash flow. When interest rates change radically, optimal and actual investment levels may diverge widely for institutional reasons, and massive institutional adjustments may be required to bring actual investment and management strategies by firms into line with those that would maximize the value of the firms in the new interest rate environment. By cutting the net returns from future investment projects, for example, an increase in interest rates reduces the benefit to shareholders of having corporate managers retain cash flow within the firm and reinvest it. The institutional response—in

---

28. For a summary of the conflicting theories, see Barry P. Bosworth, *Tax Incentives and Economic Growth* (Brookings, 1984), pp. 98–109.

this case, the leveraging up of the firm—serves to constrain managers from overinvesting and to enforce a short-term management style on the firms, consistent with value-maximization in the face of a high "discount rate" for new investment.

Critics of LBOs, debt-financed takeovers, and other restructuring transactions help provide circumstantial support for this line of argument. Perhaps the most vigorously voiced objection to LBOs and higher levels of debt is that they force corporations to focus on the short run and thus to reduce investment and research and development activities. Although there is growing evidence that firms which have been the object of LBOs are not normally major R&D performers, the limited studies that have been made of the effects of LBOs are consistent with this criticism.[29]

Our analysis, too, suggests that firms which have substantially increased their leverage, especially by replacing equity with debt, are already in slow-growing industries and will probably experience a further drop in investment. The effects of higher leverage on investment spending is an important question for future research. Assuming that our hypothesis about the effects of interest rates on leverage is correct, this research should help produce a much clearer picture of the institutional mechanisms that translate changes in interest rates into effects on investment.

Comment by Robert A. Taggart, Jr.

During the 1970s and 1980s the pace of innovation in capital markets around the world was startling. The rise of such developments as leveraged buyouts, junk bond financing, leveraged recapitalizations, master limited partnerships, and employee stock ownership plans changed the face of corporate finance and even the nature of the corporate form itself. Many market participants, observers, and regulators have been distressed by the

29. For a summary of these studies, see William F. Long and David J. Ravenscraft, "The Record of LBO Performance," paper presented to a Conference on Corporate Governance, Salomon Brothers Center for the Study of Financial Institutions, May 22–23, 1989. The sole exception is a study by Kohlberg Kravis Roberts which purports to show that in current dollars firms taken private by KKR have increased their investment and R&D. Long and Ravenscraft describe in their paper a number of serious flaws in the KKR study. See also Frank R. Lichtenberg and Donald Siegel, "The Effects of Leveraged Buyouts on Productivity and Related Aspects of Firm Behavior," Working Paper 3022 (Cambridge, Mass.: National Bureau of Economic Research, June 1989).

rapidly changing standards of prudent financial behavior. They have predicted impending disaster and have called for new laws and regulations to limit what they perceive as widespread financial excess. Others have extolled the ability of these innovations to cut through outmoded financial constraints, improve the incentives of different corporate constituencies, and enhance the ability of American industry to compete in world markets.

Unfortunately, these policy debates have had the benefit of only limited empirical evidence. Substantial research has been conducted on securities market reactions to corporate restructuring transactions, but as yet little evidence has been accumulated on the underlying determinants of these transactions. Margaret Blair and Robert Litan have augmented this body of evidence in their empirical study of corporate debt financing and leveraged buyout activity during the period 1974–87. Their paper is interesting and imaginative and contributes useful insights to the ongoing debate about corporate restructuring. They focus on the timing of this activity and conclude that the 1980s witnessed a combination of high real interest rates and low returns to tangible capital, resulting in a less favorable climate for investment in many industries; the industries whose investment climate has been least favorable have tended to make greater use of debt financing, perhaps as a means of forcing the payout of free cash flow to investors; and debt-based restructuring can take on many forms, and thus the connection between high industry debt issuance and high leveraged buyout activity is tenuous. Their paper thus assigns a key role to investment opportunities as a determinant of both the timing and scope of financial restructuring and argues, in support of Jensen's free cash flow theory, that debt can help align the investment incentives of corporate managers and shareholders.

My comments are primarily suggestions for further research. Possibly, more can be done to resolve whether the 1980s saw a true departure from previous corporate financing behavior or whether financing determinants that have always been present were simply configured in a different way. Since current policy discussion has raised the possibility that the 1980s were really different, the period would seem to offer a good opportunity to test the explanatory power of existing corporate capital structure theories. The three theories that have received the most attention in recent years are the static trade-off theory, the pecking order theory, and the free cash flow theory.[30] The static trade-off theory emphasizes the trade-off

30. The static trade-off and pecking order theories are described in Stewart C. Myers, "The Capital Structure Puzzle," *Journal of Finance*, vol. 39 (July 1984), pp. 575–92. A

between the costs and benefits of debt financing relative to equity. On the benefit side the tax deductibility of interest has received the most attention, whereas the primary costs are those of financial distress and of resolving conflicts of interest between bondholders and shareholders. The pecking order theory emphasizes the dynamic interaction between investment opportunities and internal funds. It asserts that informational asymmetries between managers and investors will lead to a hierarchy of fund sources, in which internal funds are used first, debt is used next until the company's debt capacity is exhausted, and external equity is used only as a last resort. Finally, the free cash flow theory emphasizes debt's ability to discipline management. Since debt service charges commit the firm to pay out a certain share of its annual cash flow to bondholders, it limits management's ability to reinvest funds in marginal projects.

Blair and Litan find an inverse relationship, across industries and through time, between the attractiveness of investment opportunities and the amount of debt financing. They interpret this evidence as consistent with the free cash flow theory, since debt's ability to limit any managerial tendencies toward overinvestment will be most valuable when investment opportunities are least favorable.

Their finding would, indeed, appear to be bad news for the pecking order theory. That theory does not contemplate poor investments by management and predicts that debt financing will fall when investment opportunities shrink relative to internal funds. Blair and Litan's finding in turn raises the possibility that the pecking order theory works well in a favorable investment climate, but less well when investment opportunities dry up. During most of the postwar period, the proportion of corporate debt financing and the availability of internal funds relative to investment needs have moved inversely, as the pecking order theory would predict.[31] During the 1980s, however, debt proportions were high despite a ready availability of internal funds, and the difference is apparently accounted for by the substantial shrinkage in the equity base of many corporations through stock repurchases, mergers, and other restructuring transactions. Thus the 1980s may ultimately shed new light on the relation between corporate capital structure and investment opportunities.

---

recent discussion of the free cash flow theory can be found in Michael C. Jensen, "The Free Cash Flow Theory of Takeovers: A Financial Perspective on Mergers and Acquisitions and the Economy," in Lynn E. Browne and Eric S. Rosengren, eds., *The Merger Boom*, Proceedings of Conference Series N 31 (Federal Reserve Bank of Boston, October 1987).

31. See Robert A. Taggart, Jr., "Corporate Financing: Too Much Debt?" *Financial Analysts Journal*, vol. 42 (May–June 1986), pp. 35–42.

But whether Blair and Litan's findings can distinguish sharply between the free cash flow and static trade-off theories is less clear. There are some reasons to believe that during the 1980s the benefits of debt financing may have increased at the same time as its costs decreased. As Scholes and Wolfson argue elsewhere in this volume, for example, the large reduction in top personal tax rates in 1981 may have enhanced the net tax advantage to corporate debt. Moreover, though different provisions push in opposite directions, a case can be made that the net effect of the Tax Reform Act of 1986 has been to increase the benefit of corporate debt financing.[32] On the cost side of the equation, it is also possible that some of the financial innovations that became prominent in the 1980s served to reduce the costs of financial distress, thus increasing corporate debt capacity. Such innovations include revolving underwriting facilities, zero-coupon and pay-in-kind debentures, and the strip financing techniques that have often accompanied leveraged buyouts.[33] In addition, the very decline in investment opportunities that Blair and Litan cite as favoring the free cash flow theory could also tend to increase debt capacity under the static trade-off theory. As Myers has argued, assets in place support more debt than future growth opportunities.[34] Hence, insofar as a greater proportion of the market values of U.S. corporations in the 1980s has consisted of existing assets rather than anticipated investment opportunities, debt capacity may have increased.

The fact that it may not discriminate precisely between these capital structure theories does not make Blair and Litan's work less interesting, nor does it detract from the emphasis they place on the causal role of investment opportunities. Nevertheless, a useful goal for additional research would be to try to sharpen the picture. That might be accomplished through further disaggregation as to firm type and through extension of the analysis to different time periods.

One type of disaggregation could be aimed at the cost of capital measure. The AAA corporate bond rate currently used captures certain economywide and sectoral features, but it does not reflect the risk characteristics

32. For details of this argument, see Merton H. Miller, "The Modigliani-Miller Propositions after Thirty Years," *Journal of Economic Perspectives*, vol. 2 (Fall 1988), pp. 99–120. For an opposing viewpoint, see Franco Modigliani, "MM—Past, Present, and Future," *Journal of Economic Perspectives*, vol. 2 (Fall 1988), pp. 149–58.

33. This argument is made in Michael C. Jensen, "Active Investors, LBOs, and the Privatization of Bankruptcy," *Continental Bank Journal of Applied Corporate Finance*, vol. 2 (Spring 1989), pp. 35–44.

34. See Stewart C. Myers, "Determinants of Corporate Borrowing," *Journal of Financial Economics*, vol. 5 (November 1977), pp. 147–75.

of individual industries or firms. Capturing these risk characteristics would sharpen the picture in two ways. First, it might give a clearer view of the investment opportunities facing each industry (this is captured implicitly, to some extent, in the authors' price-earnings ratio variable). Second, it might allow a more precise separation of individual firm or industry risk factors from economywide changes in the cost of capital. These risk factors are in turn important because, under most versions of the static trade-off theory, they should be negatively, rather than positively, related to a firm's use of debt financing. The authors have tried to capture these risk factors in their standard deviation of cash flow around its time trend, but such factors have proved notoriously difficult to pin down in empirical work.[35] An alternative approach would be to work with a multifactor arbitrage pricing theory model, which might allow some distinction between economywide and industry factors.[36]

A second type of disaggregation could be aimed at individual firms. The free cash flow theory would seem ideally suited to explaining the behavior of firms that undergo large financial restructurings, as opposed to marginal changes in financing proportions. It would thus be interesting to know whether a lack of favorable investment opportunities is associated with a high incidence of restructuring transactions in addition to the high debt ratios that the authors found. The authors had only limited success in relating debt financing to leveraged buyout activity, but perhaps a broader definition of restructuring might be more successful. If so, that might be interpreted as further evidence in favor of the free cash flow theory. Such evidence would be consistent with the static trade-off theory, however, only if adjustment costs are sufficiently large that optimal financing adjustments occur in large jumps.

Finally, it would be useful to extend the analysis to other time periods. If the authors' analysis is run in reverse, periods of favorable investment opportunities should be associated with low debt financing, since investors will prefer that firms' cash flows be reinvested rather than paid out. Casual comparison of the authors' figures 5 and 6, however, suggests that corporate debt issuance rose rather steadily in the 1950s and 1960s despite a favorable investment climate. That would

35. Sheridan Titman and Roberto Wessels discuss some of the associated empirical difficulties in "The Determinants of Capital Structure Choice," *Journal of Finance*, vol. 43 (March 1988), pp. 1–19.

36. See Dorothy H. Bower, Richard S. Bower, and Dennis E. Logue, "Arbitrage Pricing Theory and Utility Stock Returns," *Journal of Finance*, vol. 39 (September 1984), pp. 1041–54, for details on using the arbitrage pricing theory for cost of capital estimation.

seem to be worth more detailed investigation. One possibility is that a threshold effect is at work, whereby investment opportunities must become very unfavorable to trigger debt-financed restructuring transactions. At other times, the pecking order theory may be perfectly capable of explaining corporate financing behavior.

In summary, I think the authors have made a valuable contribution by calling attention to the potential links between corporate investment opportunities and financing proportions. These links afford new insights into the striking financial transactions of the 1980s, and I encourage the authors to continue and expand this line of research.

Comment by Scott Smart

Margaret Blair and Robert Litan raise a number of interesting questions in their paper, but they are primarily concerned with exploring the relationship between the corporate sector's use of debt financing and leveraged buyouts. That LBOs and other kinds of acquisitions increased dramatically in the 1980s is widely accepted. The extent to which debt levels in the corporate sector are abnormally high is more difficult to establish empirically, and economists disagree about the significance of higher leverage on corporate balance sheets. However, the existence and importance of a corporate debt crisis have been discussed at length by Bernanke and Campbell and others.[37] Thus my comments focus on the positive question of what determines the relationship (if any relationship exists) between corporate leverage and LBO activity. I also address some normative questions raised in the paper.

Blair and Litan highlight the empirical puzzle that many conventional measures of corporate leverage have created during a period in which real interest rates have been at historically high levels. If the tax advantages of debt relative to equity financing have not changed, then this shift in corporate balance sheets seems to contradict the principle that firms seek to raise funds at minimum cost. The authors point out that Jensen's free cash flow theory explains why firms might issue more debt under these circumstances. Because the opportunity cost of capital is high, marginal

37. Ben S. Bernanke and John Y. Campbell, "Is There a Corporate Debt Crisis?" *BPEA, 1:1988*, pp. 83–125.

investment projects are not profitable. Agency costs are particularly severe in this environment, since managers undertake investment projects with negative net present values. LBOs offer a solution to this dilemma for two reasons. First, higher interest payments force managers to deliver cash to investors, limiting the opportunities for managers to make unprofitable investments. Second, increased leverage gives managers greater incentive to maximize firm value, either because of the greater threat of bankruptcy or because managers hold a larger fraction of the outstanding shares after the buyout. Thus higher interest rates (possibly in combination with other industry- or firm-specific factors) bring about an increase, not a decline, in corporate leverage.

Before commenting on the authors' empirical methods and results, I want to draw attention to another puzzle that their paper does not address. The authors present data showing that returns to capital were at very low levels in the 1980s. They interpret this as evidence that investment opportunities for at least some segments of the corporate sector were poor. That result, combined with the rise in real interest rates during the same period, might explain the sudden explosion in LBOs in the 1980s. However, if investment opportunities in the corporate sector have been so dismal, how does one explain the stock market boom? If the rate at which investors discount corporate cash flows was high during this period, then the rise in equity values could be interpreted as a fairly strong statement that the outlook for corporate investment was anything but bleak. There could be other explanations for the boom, but it does call into question the authors' interpretation of the returns to capital data.

Testing Jensen's theory is problematic because accurate estimates either of the cost of capital for firms or of marginal investment opportunities are difficult to obtain. Blair and Litan recognize that their measure of the cost of capital—the nominal rate on Moody's AAA corporate bonds, less a moving average of inflation—is imperfect. No adjustments for risk, taxes, and so on are attempted. Of particular importance for their analysis is that there is absolutely no variation in their cost of capital across firms or industries. Jensen's theory predicts that debt will rise in firms or industries where the "free cash flow squeeze" (high cost of capital and low investment opportunities) is especially severe. Blair and Litan capture interindustry differences only from their proxies for marginal investment opportunities. This may partly explain why they find it difficult to establish a strong correlation between LBO activity and leverage (see table 2). Correlation coefficients between LBO volume and proxies for investment opportunities are also disappointing (none of the coefficients in the last column of table 6 are significant).

Although their evidence to support the free cash flow theory as an explanation for LBOs is weak, the authors find more encouraging results when they broaden the scope of their tests to include increases in leverage from all types of corporate restructuring. Accordingly, they introduce alternative measures of leverage and find negative correlations between these variables and their proxies for marginal investment returns. They explore these relationships further by ranking industries according to payments to capital (measured in three ways) and leveraging activity (measured in five ways). Unfortunately, the industries that "fit" the theory vary depending on which measures are used. The lesson from these results may not be that leverage and return to capital are negatively correlated, but rather that the authors' measures of leverage and return are not accurate.

Finally, the authors use regression techniques to test the free cash flow theory. They find that changes in industry capital stocks and price-earnings ratios are negatively related to two measures of leverage: the ratio of interest to cash flow and the ratio of debt to total assets. The decision to use these variables reflects a concern about the risks of a liquidity crisis, a point to which I return later. Blair and Litan interpret a negative coefficient on $GCAP$ as evidence to support the free cash flow theory, subject to the caveat that a spurious negative coefficient might result from capital constraints. The second proxy for investment opportunities in their regressions, industry price-earnings (PE) ratios, also enters with a negative coefficient. These ratios might also serve as a proxy for debt capacity (that is, industries with rising stock prices can issue more debt), but the coefficient should be positive if the debt capacity effect dominates. That the PE coefficient is negative and significant in their regressions would seem to strengthen their case. Alternatively, suppose that interindustry variations in PE ratios are capturing differences in capitalization rates not accounted for by the simple interest rate variable. If an industry's PE ratio is high because the capitalization rate is low, then firms in that industry might be expected to shift toward more equity in their capital structure. This provides an alternative interpretation of a negative coefficient on PE in the authors' regressions. In a similar vein, they note that higher interest rates would tend to increase the denominator of the interest–cash flow ratio. If it is costly for firms to adjust their capital structure in the short run, then a positive coefficient on IR (assuming a stable term structure) could mean that firms are incurring higher interest payments as they roll over short-term debt. In short, though the results of the regressions are roughly consistent with the free cash flow theory, several alternative interpretations also fit the data.

In an attempt to refute one alternative hypothesis (namely, financial innovation) for the increase in corporate leverage, the authors estimate measures of cash flow stability by industry and test for a positive correlation with their measures of leverage. However, it is not necessarily true that financial innovations should be adopted in industries with the most stable cash flows. A standard model of optimal capital structure (weighing costs of bankruptcy against tax benefits of debt) would predict higher levels of debt in firms with more predictable cash flows. Whether financial innovations should follow the same pattern depends on the type of innovation one has in mind. Jensen has suggested that firms using junk bonds to increase leverage are less likely to make "mistakes" that reduce the value of the firm as an ongoing concern below its liquidation value. In the event of bankruptcy, bondholders force managers to abandon unprofitable investment projects relatively quickly and substantial assets remain in the firm. Bondholders renegotiate the terms of their contract with the firm, and normal operations resume without liquidation. According to this interpretation, higher than predicted liquidity ratios (see figure 6) are not particularly worrisome because the consequences of a liquidity "crisis" are not severe.

Blair and Litan offer several conclusions. First, they argue that corporate leverage is not likely to fall without a drop in interest rates. If Jensen's theory is correct, then a drop in interest rates should lead to a lower pace of corporate restructuring of the LBO variety, but firms that have bright investment prospects (even when interest rates are high) might add more debt to their balance sheets as interest rates fall. Thus the net effect is ambiguous. Second, they predict that corporate restructuring will diminish in the corporate sector as a whole even if interest rates do not fall. In addition, restructuring should spread to new industries. Both of these predictions are consistent with financial innovation. The pace of implementation of many kinds of innovation rises at first and then falls. Similarly, innovation typically takes time to spread from one industry to another. It is reasonable to assume that financial innovations could be adopted more rapidly than new production techniques, for example, but court decisions, uncertainty surrounding future tax treatment of interest earned by junk bonds, and other things could slow the adoption of new financing methods.

The authors do not offer any normative conclusions, but they argue that their results support the position that LBOs force managers to sacrifice long-term investment in favor of immediate cash flows. The problem with this conclusion is that their data are not restricted to LBO firms. The dependent variables in the regressions measure industrywide leverage. Even if most of the change in leverage is a result of corporate restructuring, one must make a significant leap to draw inferences about LBOs from these data. LBOs represent only one type of restructuring. Recent studies by Lichtenberg and Siegel and Kaplan provide evidence that contradicts this conclusion.[38] Lichtenberg and Siegel found that plants involved in LBOs experienced higher productivity growth than other plants in the same industry. They also found that the average research and development intensity of LBO firms increased as much from 1978 to 1986 as did the average research intensity of all firms in their sample. Kaplan's results show that LBO firms earn substantially higher returns after the buyout. He argues that these gains are largely attributable to improved managerial incentives.

In summary, Blair and Litan present evidence consistent with Jensen's free cash flow theory. They argue that the coincidence of high interest rates and poor investment opportunities in the 1980s may explain the timing of the recent boom in corporate restructuring. Their tests do not rule out competing hypotheses, however, partly because of the limitations of their data and partly because Jensen's theory does not provide the researcher with a specific econometric specification. There is likely to be considerable intraindustry variation in leveraging activity in general, and LBO transactions in particular. Thus using firm-level data might allow one to estimate the correlation between LBO activity and other variables, such as the firm's cost of capital, more precisely. Testing Jensen's theory with firm-level data would still be a difficult task for two reasons. First, obtaining precise estimates for the cost of capital and marginal investment opportunities for individual firms is extremely difficult. Second, Jensen's theory does not predict what kind of restructuring will take place in a firm with free cash flow. Undoubtedly many factors influence the outcome of a contest for corporate control (such as LBO, hostile takeover, share repurchase). An adequate test of Jensen's theory should control for these other factors. Thus the verdict on the validity and empirical significance of the free cash flow theory awaits further theoretical and empirical research.

38. Even if higher leverage focuses the attention of managers on short-term cash flows, it is not clear that this is inefficient. See Lichtenberg and Siegel, "Effects of Leveraged Buyouts on Productivity"; and Steven Kaplan, "Management Buyouts: Evidence on Post-Buyout Operating Changes," *Journal of Financial Economics*, forthcoming. The authors of these studies argue that firms taken private in LBOs operate more efficiently after the buyout.

Debt, Equity, and the Taxation of Corporate Cash Flows

Alan J. Auerbach

IN THE LATE 1980s the United States experienced unprecedented financial changes. To many observers, the most disturbing event was the sharp increase in the use of borrowed money to retire corporate equity through leveraged buyouts, debt-financed cash takeovers, and direct repurchases of shares by the corporations themselves. The magnitude of this activity is indeed sobering. After being positive in most years before 1984 (equaling $23.5 billion in 1983, for example), corporate equity issues (net of retirements) fell to approximately −$80 billion annually during the period 1984–87, and dropped again to −$131 billion in 1988.[1] Though many have attributed this sharp shift from equity to debt to changes in tax policy, particularly the reduction in individual tax rates by the Tax Reform Act of 1986, the causal link is weak. Indeed, as argued later, the changes introduced in 1986, taken together, may very well have reduced the incentives to *substitute* debt for equity in corporate balance sheets.

Tax incentives have long existed for corporations to issue debt instead of equity and, in some cases, to substitute debt for existing equity. The recent phenomenon may simply represent, in part, an increasing sophistication and awareness among corporate managers about the tax advantages of debt and how to benefit from them. As financial innovations have blurred the real distinctions between debt and equity, the nontax costs to borrowing that limited leverage in the past may have declined. Thus even if tax incentives to borrow have not increased, the need to eliminate those that remain may have grown.

I am grateful to Albert Ando, William D. Andrews, Roger Gordon, Jane Gravelle, Joseph A. Pechman, James B. Poterba, David Shakow, John B. Shoven, Joel Waldfogel, and several conference participants for comments and suggestions; and to the Brookings Institution and the Institute for Law and Economics at the University of Pennsylvania for financial support.

1. Board of Governors of the Federal Reserve System, "Balance Sheets for the U.S. Economy, 1949–88," Statistical Release C.9 (April 1989).

The tax incentive for corporations to borrow is essentially attributable to the classical system of income taxation, which taxes corporations and their owners as separate entities. The resulting double taxation of corporate earnings causes income on debt and equity to face different total rates of tax when corporate and individual taxes are combined. An apparent solution to this problem is to integrate corporate and individual taxes, which would remove the distinct corporate-level tax, and attribute the income of corporations directly to shareholders as is done in noncorporate partnerships. However, although full integration has been carefully discussed in the literature,[2] it has never been adopted by any country to reform the corporate tax. Other, more modest, partial integration schemes that focus specifically on dividends have been adopted by several countries, and in recent years still other schemes have been developed to address some of the problems encountered with both full integration and partial integration through dividend relief. Given important institutional factors and the critical distinction between tax reform and a new tax design, the choice among alternatives is not simple. The failure of any country to adopt the apparently most straightforward solution—full integration—and the different approaches taken (some countries having tried more than one) illustrate the uncertainty about the "best" integration policy.

The main purpose of this paper is to describe and evaluate several alternatives that have been proposed to alleviate the distortion between debt and equity, using as a basis several criteria helpful in measuring the economic consequences of these proposals. But first it is necessary to discuss in some detail the relevant provisions of the current U.S. tax system and how these have changed in recent years. To understand how different reform proposals might alter individual incentives, it is important to know what these incentives are. Even a detailed description of the tax system is an inadequate guide to such incentives. How the U.S. tax system influences corporate financial policy is still disputed, and these disputes influence the evaluation of changes in the tax system.

Debt, Equity, and the U.S. Tax System

Many important characteristics of the taxation of corporate-source income in the United States have applied for several years even as specific tax provisions have been changed. Among these, the most relevant for the current questions are the following:

2. See, for example, Charles E. McLure, Jr., *Must Corporate Income Be Taxed Twice?* (Brookings, 1979); and Alvin Warren, "The Relation and Integration of Individual and Corporate Income Taxes," *Harvard Law Review*, vol. 94 (February 1981), pp. 719–800.

1. the double taxation of corporate earnings used to pay dividends, once at the corporate tax rate and once at the dividend recipient's tax rate;

2. the deductibility of interest payments by corporations;

3. the taxation of capital gains of both corporations and individuals only upon realizations, and the forgiveness of individual capital gains taxes at death;

4. the progressivity of the individual tax rate structure; and

5. the use of nominal rather than real measures of income in the tax base.

This list applies to the pre-1986 and post-1986 tax systems alike. For the pre-1986 tax system, the third provision would be expanded to include the additional preference afforded capital gains through a partial exclusion of long-term gains from the tax base. However, the 1986 elimination of the capital gains rate preference did not touch the advantages of deferral and possible elimination of tax liability. Despite the narrowing of the band of marginal tax rates applicable to individual incomes beginning in 1986, a fair degree of tax rate progressivity remains within the class of investors, which includes in large numbers those effectively in the zero bracket, such as pension funds and tax-exempt organizations.

In combination, these five provisions give rise to the distortions most often associated with the corporate tax. The next few sections discuss these distortions, in particular how they have been perceived in the literature and how they have been altered by recent changes in tax policy.

The Corporate-Noncorporate Distinction

Since no second level of tax applies to unincorporated businesses, including very large partnerships, the tax treatment of corporations discourages doing business in the corporate form.[3] But this conclusion must be qualified in several ways. First, the extra level of corporate taxation applies only to the extent that the corporation is financed by equity. Second, the corporate form offers the opportunity for high-bracket equity investors to defer personal income taxes. Third, the tax incentives for existing corporations to disincorporate are smaller than those for a new business to avoid the corporate form.

3. Under the rules of Subchapter S, corporations having no more than thirty-five shareholders and a single class of stock can elect to be treated for tax purposes as unincorporated businesses. However, perhaps because of the limitation on the number of shareholders, such "S corporations" have never represented a significant share of corporate assets.

The burden of double taxation of corporate income applies only to equity. Corporations, like norcorporate businesses, deduct their interest payments. Even if corporate *equity* income faced a greater tax burden than noncorporate *equity* income, the total difference in tax burden for a corporation with a thin equity base might well be very small; the tax incentive to alter its form of organization would also be small.

Moreover, because of the progressivity of the individual tax structure, there may be (at least there may have been before 1986) equity investors who, by accumulating funds within the corporation taxed at the corporate rate (receiving little in the form of dividends and deferring the realization of capital gains), would actually enjoy a tax reduction relative to full immediate taxation at the individual tax rate. In the extreme case in which the corporation paid no dividends and the investor realized no capital gains, the corporate equity owner could achieve a total tax burden on income as low as the corporate rate, historically much lower than the highest individual tax rates.

Perhaps most important, one must distinguish new from existing corporations and, among existing corporations, new from existing equity. The decision not to incorporate differs from the decision to disincorporate. Likewise, the decision of where to invest new equity funds is different from that of what to do with equity funds already existing inside a corporation. There are additional tax reasons to preserve existing corporations and to maintain existing corporate equity within corporations.

For a new company, the only tax distinctions are prospective. For the existing company, disincorporation entails immediate tax costs as well, because of the nature of capital gains taxation. Unrealized accrued gains at both shareholder and corporate levels must be realized and taxed to get corporate assets out of corporate solution. It could well be in the interest of a new company not to incorporate, while an existing corporation would choose to retain the corporate form.

Likewise, for an existing company, existing equity has historically been much more important than new equity as a source of additional corporate capital.[4] Regardless of how existing equity funds are distrib-

---

4. This is true even if one corrects for the large level of share repurchases of recent years. In 1986 earnings retained by U.S. nonfinancial corporations after taxes, dividends, and the capital consumption and inventory valuation adjustments were $94.9 billion. Board of Governors of the Federal Reserve System, "Flow of Funds Accounts: Third Quarter, 1988," Statistical Release Z.1 (December 8, 1988). Corporate share repurchases (most by nonfinancial corporations) were estimated to be $41.5 billion. Laurie Simon Bagwell and John B. Shoven, "Cash Distributions to Shareholders," *Journal of Economic Perspectives*, vol. 3 (Summer 1989), pp. 129–40. Thus earnings net of total distributions were $53.4

uted, shareholders must normally pay some tax to move them out of the corporate sector. If the funds are distributed as ordinary dividends, they are fully taxed. If they come out through a redemption of shares, there will be a capital gains tax liability to the extent that the current share price exceeds the redeeming shareholder's basis. This extra tax reduces the advantage of removing funds from the corporate sector. Put another way, there may be little or no disincentive to reinvest funds within the corporate sector once the cost of distributions is accounted for. Insofar as taxes on distributions are unavoidable, they do not impose a marginal burden on funds kept in the corporate sector. Taxes on future distributions simply substitute for those not paid currently by forgoing distributions. The marginal tax on retained earnings is therefore simply the corporate tax.[5]

This "new view" of the effect of double taxation has important corollaries: that the unavoidable taxes on distributions will be capitalized in the values of corporate shares and that the level of distributions tax has no effect on the decision whether to keep funds within the corporate sector;[6] the relevant comparison is between the corporate tax rate and the rate of tax on income earned outside the corporate sector. The analysis is made more complicated by the fact that there is no single tax rate on distributions. Capital gains and dividend distributions are not taxed equally, and investors are in different tax brackets. The degree to which taxes on distributions are actually capitalized remains the subject of some dispute

---

billion. In that same year, gross issues of equity were $37.8 billion. Joint Committee on Taxation, *Federal Income Tax Aspects of Corporate Financial Structures*, Joint Committee Print, Senate Committee on Finance and House Committee on Ways and Means, 101 Cong. 1 sess. (Government Printing Office, January 1989). By comparison, in 1980 repurchases were only $4.9 billion, but retained earnings were just $28.8 billion, or $23.9 billion net of repurchases. In that year, gross new issues of equity were $21.1 billion. For the entire period 1980–86, earnings net of distributions averaged $43.9 billion, while gross new issues averaged $27.5 billion.

5. For example, suppose that the individual tax rate on ordinary income and distributions is t_p, the tax rate on corporate income is t_c, the rate of return in the corporate sector is R, and that in the noncorporate sector is r. Then one dollar of funds within the firm that is distributed immediately yields the investor $(1 - t_p)$ dollars to invest, resulting in a net (after income taxes) amount of $[1 + r(1 - t_p)](1 - t_p)$ one period later. If the funds were reinvested for one year and then distributed, they would yield a distributable amount (after corporate income tax) of $1 + R(1 - t_c)$ and an amount net of taxes on the distribution of $[1 + R(1 - t_c)](1 - t_p)$. Comparing the two final amounts, one sees that they differ only with respect to the rate of return on accumulations, $r(1 - t_p)$ for distributed funds and $R(1 - t_c)$ for retained funds. For further discussion, see the paper by Myron Scholes and Mark Wolfson in this volume.

6. See Alan J. Auerbach, "Wealth Maximization and the Cost of Capital," *Quarterly Journal of Economics*, vol. 93 (August 1979), pp. 433–46.

in the literature,[7] and, as will be evident in the discussion, this uncertainty is important when one considers tax reform plans that distinguish between new and existing equity.

In summary, the effect of the extra burden of corporate tax is mitigated by three factors. First, this burden is entirely absent for debt finance. Second, it is somewhat offset for newly contributed equity by the opportunity to defer individual income taxes. Third, double taxation is to some extent unavoidable for existing equity, so that taxes on distributions should be capitalized and not affect current decisions.

The Tax Reform Act of 1986 altered the incentives both to supply new equity to the corporate sector and to take funds out of the corporate sector. For the first time the corporate rate (reduced from 46 to 34 percent) now exceeds the highest individual tax rate (reduced from 50 to 33 percent). It is no longer even theoretically possible for an investor to enjoy an absolute tax advantage by accumulating funds within the corporate sector. However, such a potential advantage had essentially already disappeared in 1981, when the Economic Recovery Tax Act cut the top individual rate from 70 to 50 percent, virtually equal to the corporate tax rate then in effect. Even an implausibly small level of individual taxes on corporate equity earnings would have made the total tax wedge on equity income exceed that on ordinary income.

While perhaps making the corporate form less attractive for high-bracket investors, the 1986 act made the corporate form *more* attractive for low-bracket investors. To see the point clearly, consider a zero-bracket investor, whose only taxes are those paid indirectly through the corporation income tax. This investor has a clear tax incentive to avoid corporate equity. However, the incentive was reduced by the 1986 act, because of the reduction in the corporate tax rate.

Were taxes the only determinant of portfolio selection and organizational form, one would never find investors with a tax advantage for debt or noncorporate equity holding corporate equity. Investors would sort out by assets, with only high-bracket investors holding those assets, such as corporate stock, for which an individual tax advantage exists, in this instance because of the preferential treatment of capital gains.[8] Hence a

7. See Alan J. Auerbach, "Taxation, Corporate Financial Policy and the Cost of Capital," *Journal of Economic Literature*, vol. 21 (September 1983), pp. 905–40; and James M. Poterba and Lawrence H. Summers, "The Economic Effects of Dividend Taxation," in Edward I. Altman and Marti G. Subrahmanyam, eds., *Recent Advances in Corporate Finance* (Homewood, Ill.: Irwin, 1985), pp. 227–89.

8. For further discussion of the effects of this process of tax arbitrage and sorting of investors by tax bracket, see David F. Bradford, "Issues in the Design of Savings and

reduction in the disincentive to hold equity for those holding none would be irrelevant. Only the tax treatment of investors at or near the margin of choice would matter for determining the effect of the tax change.

Although some theories of financial equilibrium envisage such an outcome,[9] they are clearly at variance with the empirical reality that a significant and increasing portion of U.S. corporate equity is held by investors in the zero bracket. These include not only domestic tax-exempt organizations and pension funds, but also foreign individuals and businesses,[10] which pay essentially no taxes to the United States and (depending on their home countries' treatment of repatriated income) may be liable for no taxes at home.[11] Since such investors hold corporate equity for nontax reasons despite the tax disadvantage, a reduction in the rate of corporate tax further encourages this activity. Moreover, certain other tax provisions limit the actual tax advantage that can be achieved by some low-bracket investors by avoiding the corporate form. In particular, tax-exempt organizations are subject to an income tax on unrelated business income that does not apply to passive investments, such as corporate equity, but would apply to income from some direct noncorporate investments. Thus not only did the 1986 act remove any residual possibility of using the corporate form to shelter an investor's income, but by reducing the corporate tax rate it actually encouraged the choice of a corporate solution for a significant class of investors.

Finally, the 1986 act contained several provisions that *discouraged* the transition out of corporate form, whatever the net effect of the initial incorporation decision, and may also have encouraged the retention of

---

Investment Incentives," in C. R. Hulten, ed., *Depreciation, Inflation, and the Taxation of Income from Capital* (Washington: Urban Institute, 1981), pp. 13–47; C. Eugene Steuerle, *Taxes, Loans, and Inflation: How the Nation's Wealth Becomes Misused* (Brookings, 1985); and Alan J. Auerbach, "Should Interest Deductions Be Limited?" in Henry J. Aaron, Harvey Galper, and Joseph A. Pechman, eds., *Uneasy Compromise: Problems of a Hybrid Income-Consumption Tax* (Brookings, 1988), pp. 195–221.

9. See, for example, Merton H. Miller, "Debt and Taxes," *Journal of Finance*, vol. 32 (May 1977), pp. 261–75.

10. At the end of 1987 foreign holdings of U.S. corporate equity amounted to $173.4 billion, while private pension funds and state and local government retirement funds held $633.2 billion ($460.6 billion and $172.6 billion, respectively) of equity, including foreign shares. Board of Governors of the Federal Reserve System, "Flow of Funds Accounts: Financial Assets and Liabilities, Year-End, 1964–87," Statistical Release Z.1 (September 1988). By comparison, the total value on U.S. nonfinancial corporate equity at the end of 1987 was $2,552.8 billion. Board of Governors, "Balance Sheets for the U.S. Economy, 1949–88."

11. Under the territorial system of taxation, used in France among other countries, foreign source earnings are tax exempt.

funds within existing corporations. Affecting both decisions was the increase in the individual rates of tax on capital gains. The maximum tax rate on individual gains went from 20 to 33 percent, raising the tax on shares redeemed by corporations and, potentially, lowering the effective marginal tax rate on funds and businesses kept within the corporate sector.[12] The decision to change organizational form was also discouraged by the increase in the rate of tax on corporate gains, applicable when corporate assets are sold to provide funds to distribute, from 28 to 34 percent. Further, and perhaps more important, the 1986 act repealed the general utilities doctrine, under which unrealized capital gains on the assets of liquidating corporations were not taxed. Whatever its net effect on the incentives facing new businesses and the sale of new equity by existing corporations, the 1986 act clearly reduced the tax incentives to eliminate existing corporations and, arguably, the incentives for existing corporations to engage in nondividend distributions of funds.

Dividend and Distribution Policy

Since dividends are taxed twice and retained corporate income only once, there may appear to be an incentive for corporations to retain earnings to avoid dividend taxes. But this logic is just as faulty as that leading to the opposite conclusion, that there is an incentive to remove equity funds from the corporate sector to avoid taxation.

As already discussed, taxes on distributions today offset the forgone taxes on future distributions, making the retention of funds within the corporate sector less unattractive than might be supposed. However, just as future taxes are unavoidable even if distributions are made today, today's taxes cannot be avoided simply by deferring distributions. If all distributions are taxed, the present value of distribution taxes should be capitalized and the rate of tax on distributions should not affect the distribution decision.

12. The word *potentially* is used because of the argument given earlier that an increase in the tax on distributions should have no effect on the incentive to distribute now versus in the future, in this case through share repurchases. However, insofar as shareholders expected future distributions to escape tax (for example, shares repurchased after a step-up in basis at death), the increase in the current tax rate on capital gains would raise the cost of distributing now relative to the future, thus imparting a negative contribution to the marginal tax rate on reinvested funds. Alternatively, if investors expected a portion of funds distributed in the future to be paid as dividends, the increase in the capital gains tax combined with the cut in dividend taxes would also raise the cost of *repurchasing* today versus distributing in the future.

One must distinguish here between the retention-distribution decision and the decision regarding the *form* that distributions should take. Even after 1986 share repurchases dominate dividends as a form of distribution because investors receive a deduction for their basis in the shares redeemed. The corporation certainly has an incentive to repurchase shares rather than distribute dividends.[13] But that does not explain the timing of distributions. In fact, if share repurchases are the alternative always chosen for distributions, the ability to recover basis provides an incentive to distribute funds immediately.[14]

Nevertheless, the empirical evidence suggests that dividends are sensitive to the current tax burden on dividends relative to retained earnings.[15] This sensitivity is, in part, associated with changes in tax rates over time: a *temporary* decrease in the rate of dividend taxation should cause an increase in distributions. But even when such temporary effects are controlled for, the rate of dividend tax also appears to have a permanent effect on dividend payments. In part, this estimated relationship may be due to the fact that it is empirically difficult to identify a "permanent" tax change; all tax rates are in some sense potentially temporary even if they remain in effect for more than a year.

Debt-Equity Ratios

From the tax perspective, the choice between debt and equity is closely related to the decision between corporate and noncorporate investment. Like noncorporate investment, interest payments are taxed only to the recipient. The use of debt rather than equity by corporations has been viewed as "do-it-yourself integration," since it causes corporate cash flow to be taxed as it would be in an unincorporated business. However, the parallel between the use of debt and the avoidance of the corporate sector extends to the distinction between new and existing equity. The tax con-

13. In terms of national income accounting, the use of earnings to repurchase shares rather than distribute dividends does increase retained earnings, but the repurchases then count as negative new contributions of capital to the firms. There is no net increase in accumulated funds.

14. Let R be the rate of return available to the corporation, t_c the corporate tax rate, t_p the individual tax rate, and b the basis on one dollar of funds currently held within the corporation. If the funds are distributed, the investor receives $(1 - t_p + t_p b)$ dollars. If the funds are reinvested and distributed one year later, the investor receives $[1 + R(1 - t_c)](1 - t_p) + t_p b$. The rate of return is thus $[R(1 - t_c) + bt_p/(1 - t_p)]/[1 + bt_p/(1 - t_p)] < R(1 - t_c)$. Thus the tax rate on reinvested earnings exceeds the corporate tax rate.

15. See Poterba and Summers, "Economic Effects of Dividend Taxation."

sequences of financing a new corporate project by issuing debt instead of equity differ from those of replacing existing equity with debt. As discussed, taking funds out of the corporate sector involves an additional tax cost that reduces the marginal individual tax burden on corporate equity funds retained. This makes the tax advantage of debt relative to existing equity small for high-bracket investors, because of the similarity of the corporate and top individual tax rates.

Leveraged buyouts (LBOs), a principal vehicle for increasing corporate debt-equity ratios, are typically not subject to immediate corporate tax when they occur, being treated for tax purposes like a debt-financed redemption of shares by the corporation.[16] Thus the principal changes in the tax incentives to engage in such transactions since 1986 have been the same as those affecting borrowing more generally: the reduction in ordinary corporate and individual tax rates and the increase in individual capital gains tax rates. As previously mentioned, the net effect of these changes is unclear, since for low-bracket investors the corporate rate reduction makes equity more attractive and for high-bracket investors the increase in capital gains tax rates may offset the reduction in individual relative to corporate tax rates (see note 12).

Mergers and Acquisitions

The merger wave of the mid-1980s has become the leveraged buyout wave of the late 1980s. From 1983 to 1985 the dollar value of merger activity increased by 245 percent, staying roughly constant thereafter through 1987. However, from 1985 to 1987 the dollar value of leveraged buyouts nearly doubled, representing in value nearly one quarter of all transactions in 1986 and 1987.[17] The public policy issue that began as a concern about takeovers has shifted to one more focused on borrowing and its role in takeovers. The shift in activity from takeovers to leveraged buyouts may be due in part to changes in the tax law, but the pattern of activity defies explanation by the tax code alone.

When considering the tax incentives for takeovers, one must distinguish between mergers and acquisitions that involve two public corporations and "buyouts," leveraged or otherwise, which do not entail any change in a corporation's status, just the ownership and size of its equity base.[18]

16. Joint Committee on Taxation, *Corporate Financial Structures*.
17. Joint Committee on Taxation, *Corporate Financial Structures*.
18. There may be significant changes in the firm's management incentive structure, but these are not tax related.

The tax rules that apply to the latter transactions are those that apply to any corporate equity redemptions; additional rules apply when there is a change in corporate structure through the merging of two public corporations. Thus the *tax* incentives to engage in LBOs are essentially those already reviewed to engage in debt-financed equity redemptions. As discussed, these incentives are not as large as those favoring debt over equity for the financing of new operations; they were present before the Tax Reform Act of 1986, and they were not necessarily enhanced by the 1986 act. However, other provisions of that act have discouraged mergers and acquisitions.

Traditionally (that is, before the 1986 act), the tax law provided several incentives for firms to combine through a merger or acquisition. At the corporate level, a firm with unused tax losses and tax credits being carried forward could offset these tax benefits against the taxable income and tax liability of its new partner. Alternatively, firms could choose to treat the transaction as one in which the target firm's assets were acquired by the parent firm, with an ensuing step-up in the basis of these assets and the opportunity to take larger depreciation and depletion allowances on assets normally eligible for such deductions.

Evidence for the period from the late 1960s to the beginning of the recent merger wave suggests that such tax incentives drove, at most, a small percentage of mergers and acquisitions in the United States.[19] Even so, the incentives themselves were sharply reduced by the Tax Reform Act of 1986 and subsequent acts that limited the transferability of unused tax losses and credits and, with the repeal of the general utilities doctrine, forced capital gains realized through the stepping-up of asset bases to face an immediate capital gains tax at the corporate level.

At the shareholder level, shareholders in tax-free reorganizations were and still are able to trade their shares in the target company for those in the parent company without any capital gains tax. Since parent companies are usually much larger and more diversified than target companies, shareholders gain the opportunity for increased portfolio diversification without the normal capital gains tax penalty. However, the main shareholder benefit derived from mergers and acquisitions recently is the ability to use debt, with its tax-deductible interest payments, to fund takeovers.

From a tax perspective, the use of debt in this manner and, indeed, the use of cash accumulated by one firm to purchase the shares of another

19. Alan Auerbach and David Reishus, "The Effects of Taxation on the Merger Decision," in Alan Auerbach, ed., *Corporate Takeovers: Causes and Consequences* (University of Chicago Press, 1988), pp. 157–83.

do not differ mechanically from such actions taken by a company with respect to its own shares. Since corporations can treat their own shares in this manner, it is difficult to see the incentive to use a takeover to achieve the result.[20]

Moreover, the recent provisions increasing the corporate capital gains tax and repealing the general utilities doctrine make takeovers an inferior way to distribute funds from the corporation, unless the transaction qualifies as tax-free (at the corporate level) reorganization: the immediate tax on stepped-up bases will normally exceed in present value the additional deductions received in the future. That would help explain a move away from takeovers by public corporations toward leveraged buyouts, which are not treated as realization events at the corporate level. Since LBOs are, essentially, redemptions by corporations of their own shares, the question then reverts to one previously considered: whether significant changes have occurred in recent years to encourage corporations to replace their existing equity with debt. Such changes, even if in the right direction, seem far too small to have led to the large increase in the observed level of LBO activity.

The Interaction between Tax and Nontax Incentives

It is useful to summarize the analysis to this point. The tax incentives to distribute corporate equity or to replace existing equity with debt are smaller than those favoring the issuance of debt instead of new equity, because individual taxes must be paid to get funds out of the corporate sector. Insofar as these additional taxes are unavoidable, they will be capitalized into the value of existing equity and not constitute a marginal tax on the retention of equity funds within the corporate sector. As a way of distributing funds, share repurchases dominate dividends because of the deduction of basis, but that in itself is largely separable from the question whether funds should be distributed. There are no apparent incentives to use debt to finance acquisitions. In recent years, in fact, doing

20. One possible incentive, which used the installment sale, was largely eliminated in 1987. Before then, an investor selling out and receiving cash over a period of time could report the cash as income only upon receipt, thereby avoiding tax on the interest accruing on the implicit liability of the buyer of the company. Insofar as the installment sale provisions were impractical for ordinary share repurchases from broad shareholder groups, the installment sale did represent an incentive to engage specifically in cash acquisitions. Even during this earlier period, however, there is little evidence that mergers and acquisitions led to increased debt-equity ratios. Auerbach and Reishus, "Effects of Taxation."

so has become a distinctly inferior way to redeem equity funds because of changes in the installment sale provisions and the repeal of the general utilities doctrine. That would explain the move away from public takeovers to leveraged buyouts, but not the surge in total borrowing.

Although it seems unlikely, therefore, that changes in the tax system provided the impetus for this recent surge in borrowing, it might well be that other factors encouraging the use of debt allowed firms to take greater advantage of the existing tax incentives to borrow. In this sense, the borrowing could be tax related even if it is not tax induced, and the need to reduce the remaining imbalance between debt and existing equity could have increased even if the imbalance itself had not.

This distinction requires an understanding of the nontax factors affecting borrowing. If borrowing for the purpose of distributing equity has even a small tax advantage, there must be other, nontax costs preventing equity from disappearing entirely. A reduction in any of these costs could increase borrowing, but with differing policy implications.

Reduced Perception of Risk

The last U.S. recession ended in 1983, just as the current surge in corporate borrowing began. One of the costs often associated with increased leverage is the threat of default. If the perceived (or, indeed, actual) risk of default has declined during the current sustained expansion, corporations may have become increasingly willing to borrow more in order to take advantage of the tax incentives to do so. Supposing that bankruptcy risk really has declined, this event would have lowered the corporate cost of capital even had no change in borrowing occurred. However, the ability to increase leverage in response would have benefited corporations still more.

If the risk of bankruptcy is correctly perceived to have fallen, then the social cost of borrowing is the assumption of too much risk because of the tax incentive to use debt. With a decline in the level of risk associated with any given level of borrowing but an increase in the level of borrowing, the total social cost of the excess risk-taking could rise or fall. If the risk of bankruptcy is *incorrectly* perceived to have fallen, there would certainly be an additional social cost resulting from increased borrowing.

Reduced Costs of Financial Intermediation

The ascendancy of "junk bond" financing has been a controversial part of the recent increase in borrowing. A plausible interpretation of this development is that real innovations have led to a reduction in the costs of financial intermediation. If companies that previously could not borrow at acceptable rates now have better access to capital markets, this in itself is a positive social development.

As with bankruptcy risks, a reduction in social costs is in itself a good thing. As in the previous example, the resulting increased borrowing to take advantage of tax incentives could (but need not) increase the costs of socially excessive intermediation. Similarly, if junk bonds have not reduced real costs, their increased usage is socially costly.

Improved Substitutability of Debt and Equity

Debt isn't what it used to be. As Bulow, Summers, and Summers discuss in their paper in this volume, many of the recent innovations in financial markets have worked toward reducing the distinction between debt and equity, through debt and equity strips, payment-in-kind and original discount debt obligations, and so on. The main result of these developments has been to make the debt obligation less fixed and in that sense more like equity.

Taken to the extreme, this kind of development necessarily lowers the nontax costs of borrowing to zero, because it removes any significance other than tax treatment from the designation "debt." To the extent that debt has become more of a substitute for equity but not a perfect one, the nontax costs of borrowing have declined but not been eliminated, and, as in the previous two cases, the ensuing increase in borrowing could increase or decrease the deadweight cost of excessive borrowing. The increase in tax arbitrage between debt and equity made possible through their becoming closer substitutes has an ambiguous effect on economic efficiency when the arbitrage remains incomplete.[21]

Managerial Incentives and the Market for Corporate Control

In the previous three cases, the separation of ownership and control was implicitly ignored; managers chose the best debt-equity ratio for their shareholders. Suppose, instead, that this was not true initially, that the

21. For a more complete discussion of this aspect of tax arbitrage, see Auerbach, "Should Interest Deductions Be Limited?"

social costs of borrowing at the margin were far below the tax advantages of debt, but that the marginal borrowing costs to individual managers who chose debt-equity ratios were quite large. A manager might stand to lose a much greater portion of his wealth from his company's bankruptcy than a well-diversified shareholder. Hence borrowing more could increase share prices but make a manager worse off.

Many have argued that the market for corporate control has become more competitive in recent years, that managers have increasingly faced the choice of maximizing share values or being replaced by others who would. An increase in borrowing associated with this change in environment would have reduced the noncompetitive returns to managers and made shareholders better off, but with a concomitant increase in the social costs of excess borrowing.

Summary: Why Is Reform Imperative?

Even without a change in the tax inducement to borrow, the recent increase in borrowing may have occurred to make the most of what tax advantage there is. Were there no social costs associated with borrowing, the result might be simply that corporations had lowered their costs of capital at the expense of the government. The relevant policy question would be whether this lower effective tax rate on corporate source income was appropriate.

Since borrowing does have real nontax costs, which in the aggregate may have risen with the recent increase in corporate leverage, one must consider not only the overall tax burden facing the corporate sector but also the balance between debt and equity. Even if a lower corporate cost of capital is socially desirable, the way in which it is being achieved has led to unnecessary distortions of corporate financial policy. Moreover, the shift from equity to debt may have reduced corporate tax payments without having a significant effect on the cost of capital itself.

Reforming the Taxation of Corporate Cash Flows

Proposals to reform the corporate tax vary widely in scope. At one extreme are proposals for full integration of corporate and individual income taxation, pure in concept, ambitious in scope, and unadopted in practice. At the other extreme are schemes to limit the tax benefits (or increase the tax penalties) of very specific transactions, such as proposals to limit the deduction of those interest expenses above a certain rate not actually paid in cash, or in excess of a certain fraction of corporate cash flow. Such proposals are easier to enact but are of more questionable economic pedigree. These two approaches differ in the direction from which they attack the problem of borrowing, the first reducing the tax incentives to borrow and the second making it more difficult to take advantage of these incentives. As discussed by Bulow, Summers, and Summers in this volume, the second approach requires the law to make distinctions between debt and equity that are changing and becoming more difficult over time. Because those authors discuss such issues in some detail, I focus here on broader proposals that would make the debt-equity distinction less important.

Beyond the full integration and the dividend relief schemes in use in other countries, several alternatives have been proposed in recent years. Since the ultimate objectives of each of the proposals are similar, it is not surprising that the proposals themselves have closely related characteristics. Indeed, by establishing a few criteria by which to describe the proposals, one may bring these similarities out. These criteria also help to evaluate the economic effects of the proposals on the efficiency of the tax system and on its incidence and revenue effects. Finally, they shed light on other schemes that might be constructed to achieve particular combinations of objectives.

The Overall Tax Rate on Corporate Source Income

Though all the proposals to be considered aim to tax debt and equity at more equal rates, the question remains what this rate will be. In particular, will the individual tax rate, the corporate tax rate, or some combination apply? If the corporate rate applies, then the corporate sector will still have a slight tax disadvantage relative to the noncorporate sector on its marginal investments.

The Treatment of Foreign and Tax-Exempt Investors

Under current law, foreign and tax-exempt investors have, relative to other investors, a strong incentive to hold debt for tax purposes, since the only U.S. tax they pay is at the corporate level. Changes in the treatment of such investors *relative* to the treatment of taxable investors would affect not only revenue but also the pattern of asset ownership.

The Treatment of Old and New Capital

A point emphasized earlier is the importance of distinguishing between existing equity and new equity, and between existing corporations and new ones. Schemes that are similar in their treatment of new equity capital may differ in their treatment of existing equity. Given the potential capitalization of some taxes in the value of existing equity, policies that differ in their treatment of existing equity could differ significantly in terms not only of revenue but also of short-run incidence, that is, windfalls.

Unlike the taxation of equity, the taxation of debt makes little distinction between the new and the existing. However, a proposal to change the treatment of debt could have different rules from those currently in existence. Likewise, the treatment of capital investments already in place relative to new investment is a matter for consideration. Thus there is a general question of the treatment of existing capital.

The Treatment of Economic Rents

True economic rents are fixed returns, the taxation of which is nondistortionary. The corporate tax as presently constructed automatically taxes such rents as they accrue to equity.[22] As is true of the distinction between old and new capital, proposals could differ on the treatment of rents while having similar marginal effects. Existing capital and economic rents are usually handled in a comparable manner.

Transition Problems

Any change in tax structure may have temporary problems of perverse incentives associated with it. In part, that may have to do with the treatment of existing capital; if unfavorable, investors may have incentives to attempt to "change" old capital to new. However, there are approaches with

22. Indeed, as Scholes and Wolfson point out (in this volume), once within the corporate equity base, such rents must bear some tax. If the firm attempts to offset them with interest payments by issuing debt, it must then distribute the proceeds and cause investors to incur a tax on distributions. The idea that firms might wish to maintain an equity base associated with the capitalization of rents even while financing marginal corporate projects with debt is discussed by Joseph E. Stiglitz, "Taxation, Corporate Financial Policy, and the Cost of Capital," *Journal of Public Economics*, vol. 2 (February 1973), pp. 1–34.

similarly intended treatment of old and new capital that provide different short-run incentives. In some cases these differences may depend on investor expectations about future changes in tax policy.

Alternative Proposals

I now discuss several schemes that have been proposed as a solution to the imbalance between debt and equity. Table 1 provides a summary of these proposals and some of their key characteristics, organized in terms of the criteria just set out.

Full Integration

As mentioned, full integration has been studied extensively as a potential reform of the corporate tax but has never been adopted. The incentives it would present are clear. Investors would be taxed on a partnership basis, so the corporate-noncorporate distinction would, by construction, cease to exist. Likewise, the single, individual tax on equity income would eliminate the importance of the debt-equity distinction; all corporate source income would be taxed at the individual's tax rate. For new investments or businesses, the tax system would be neutral with respect to financial policy and organizational form.

Much of the opposition to full integration has been of a technical nature,[23] but there are other difficulties as well. Because it would subject all equity income to a single tax at the individual's tax rate, an integrated tax system would relieve the double taxation of all equity earnings, thus replacing corporate and individual taxes with the individual tax alone. This situation would undoubtedly produce windfalls for the owners of existing equity because the prospective tax burden on such equity would have been reduced. More disturbing, however, is that such windfalls would bring with them little incentive to invest.

Insofar as taxes on distributions from *existing* equity are unavoidable, they should be capitalized into the value of shares and not influence the marginal cost of capital for reinvested funds. The effective tax rate on reinvested equity funds would then be 34 percent, compared with the 28 or 33 percent tax rate that most investors would face under an integrated tax system. Put simply, investors would receive a small cut in their mar-

23. See McLure, *Must Corporate Income Be Taxed Twice?*

ginal tax rates and a large windfall equal to the present value of the capitalized taxes forgiven and roughly equal to the present value of taxes or distributions from existing equity that would have been received by taxable investors.[24] These distributions would comprise all net assets, including returns to existing capital plus economic rents, net of interest payments on preexisting debt.

Because taxation would occur only at the investor level, an integrated tax system would cease to tax foreign and tax-exempt shareholders on their foreign-source income, thus treating equity income as interest income is now treated. This dispensation would increase the relative incentives for foreigners and tax-exempt institutions to hold equity.

Partial Integration through Dividend Relief

Dividend relief is much more easily implemented than full integration, for it requires measuring only dividends rather than all earnings. Given the traditional view that the serious problem of corporate double taxation applies primarily to earnings distributed as dividends, dividend relief has been seen as an acceptable solution to the distortions of the corporate tax.

The two basic approaches to dividend relief differ with respect to whether the corporation or the shareholder receives the tax rebate. Relief at the corporate level comes in the form of a full or partial deduction for dividends paid, often expressed in terms of a lower tax rate on distributed earnings, or a *split-rate system*. The equivalence between a lower tax rate and a partial deduction is straightforward. Full deductibility would be equivalent to a split-rate system with a lower tax rate of zero. More generally, the effective rate of deduction equals $(t_r - t_d)/(1 - t_d)t_r$, where t_r is the rate of tax on earnings retained and t_d is the rate of tax on earnings distributed.[25]

In practice, split-rate systems have usually allowed only partial deduction for dividends. For example, in Germany the split-rate system in

24. For further discussion, see Alan Auerbach, "Tax Integration and the 'New View' of the Corporate Tax: A 1980s' Perspective," in *Proceedings of the National Tax Association–Tax Institute of America* (1981), pp. 21–27.

25. To see this, note that one dollar of before-tax earnings distributed under the split-rate system yields a dividend of $1 - t_d$ dollars. If, instead, dividends are deductible at rate f from the corporate rate t_r, then the net dividend d per dollar is $1 - t_r + t_r fd$. Setting $d = (1 - t_d)$ yields the solution given in the text.

Table 1. A Summary of Reform Proposals

Proposals	Effects
Full integration	
Neutrality between debt and equity (overall rate of tax)	Would tax all corporate source income at the individual marginal tax rate, removing the distinction between debt and equity; no effect on debt-financed investment; reduces the effective tax rate on retained earnings from the corporate rate to the individual rate; alleviates the double taxation of earnings from new equity
Treatment of foreign and tax-exempt investors	Benefit from relief of double taxation
Windfalls to existing capital and pure rent?	Yes; all dividends would be relieved of double taxation
Significant transition problems?	No
Partial integration–dividend relief	
Neutrality between debt and equity (overall rate of tax)	Reduction in the corporate tax on distributed earnings; no change in the treatment of debt or retained earnings, so no change in the effective tax rate on reinvested funds; debt still slightly favored because of the higher corporate tax rate; reduction in the effective tax rate on new equity, depending on the extent of dividend relief
Treatment of foreign and tax-exempt investors	Benefit from dividend relief under split-rate system; do not benefit under imputation system
Windfalls to existing capital and pure rent?	Yes; all dividends would be relieved of full double taxation
Significant transition problems?	No
The ALI plan	
Neutrality between debt and equity (overall rate of tax)	Effects similar to full dividend relief under split-rate system (that is, full deduction for dividends)
Treatment of foreign and tax-exempt investors	Benefit, as under split-rate system
Windfalls to existing capital and pure rent?	No; distributions from existing assets would continue to be taxed; could be taxed more fully than at present if plan includes tax on nondividend distributions
Significant transition problems?	Yes; indefinite transition period plus disturbances if anticipated or perceived to be temporary

Table 1 (*continued*)

Proposals	Effects
Corporate cash-flow tax	
Neutrality between debt and equity (overall rate of tax)	Tax rate on debt-financed investment increases because of elimination of interest deduction; tax rate on both retained earnings and new equity reduced by immediate write-off of investment; net bias in favor of equity; comparison of overall tax burden to other systems depends on investment incentives already present under the income tax; for post-1986 U.S. tax system, cash-flow tax reduces overall burden most
Treatment of foreign and tax-exempt investors	Benefit unless separate withholding tax put in place
Windfalls to existing capital and pure rent?	No; source of reduction in tax burden, the immediate write-off of investment, provided only for new capital
Significant transition problems?	Yes; incentives to delay investment if anticipated

the 1980s had rates of 56 percent and 36 percent on retentions and distributions.[26] In Japan the rates are currently 42 percent and 32 percent.[27]

The shareholder-level alternative to the split-rate system is known as the *imputation system*, since shareholders calculate their income by adding the dividends they actually receive to imputed income equal to some or all of the taxes the corporations are assumed to have paid on the earnings distributed. The shareholders are given credit for these imputed taxes in exactly the way that taxes withheld by employers on wage and salary income are included by employees in their taxable income but are also credited against their tax liability. In the United Kingdom, for example, the imputation system permits a credit at the basic individual tax rate so that most taxable investors neither owe additional tax nor receive a refund for excess taxes withheld.[28]

As with the split-rate system, any degree of dividend relief is possible under an imputation system, depending on the fraction of corporate taxes imputed. In general, the two systems are equivalent for taxable dividend recipients, and it is perhaps easiest to see this equivalence in the case of full dividend relief. Under a system with full deduction for dividends, the

26. Mervyn A. King and Don Fullerton, eds., *The Taxation of Income from Capital: A Comparative Study in the United States, United Kingdom, Sweden, and West Germany* (University of Chicago Press, 1984).

27. Japanese Ministry of Finance, Tax Bureau, *An Outline of Japanese Taxes, 1988.*

28. King and Fullerton, *Taxation of Income from Capital.*

firm that sets aside one dollar of before-tax earnings for distribution actually distributes the full dollar to shareholders; the dollar is then taxed at the shareholders' rate. Under an imputation system with the corporate rate imputed, the firm pays its corporate tax on the dollar before distribution, but shareholders include the tax in their income, still reporting one dollar, and credit the corporate taxes fully against their own liability; there is still no *net* corporate tax on the distribution.

Aside from differing in appearance (that is, whether the tax reduction is "received" by corporations or individuals), there are real differences between the two approaches with respect to administrability.[29] In terms of the criteria laid out above, the main difference is the treatment of foreign and tax-exempt shareholders. Since the imputation system allows a credit for corporate taxes only against a shareholder's tax liability, those paying no taxes would receive no credit. Hence one may view an imputation system as being equivalent to a split-rate system plus a withholding tax at the normal corporate tax rate on dividends distributed to low- or zero-bracket shareholders.[30]

Because it provides relief at the corporate level, the split-rate system resembles full integration more closely than the imputation system does. But it differs from full integration in that, instead of taxing all income at the individual level and rate, it would tax only distributed income this way and continue to tax retained earnings at the corporate rate. For nontaxable investors, the dividends-paid deduction would then be less attractive than it would be under full integration. For taxable investors, however, the differences between the two dividend relief systems and full integration would be small under the current tax structure, because the tax rate on corporations would be similar to that on most shareholders.

A major problem with dividend relief, as with full integration, is that it is provided for all dividends paid to taxable investors, including dividends from existing equity for which there may be very little change in the incentive to reinvest funds. Since the relief would focus on dividends (and, as will be discussed, firms will have the incentive to make dividends

29. See McLure, *Must Corporate Income Be Taxed Twice?*

30. In some cases this equivalence is made even more explicit by additional provisions of the tax code. Under the imputation system in the United Kingdom, for example, there is a separate tax, referred to as the advance corporation tax (ACT), which is collected from otherwise tax-exhausted firms (those with sufficient deductions to offset taxable income) at a rate that just offsets the imputation credit these firms' shareholders receive on their dividends. For such firms a deduction for dividends paid would produce no current tax benefits. Thus the net difference between the two schemes is the ACT withheld on the dividends paid to those shareholders who cannot use the imputation credit.

the main form of distributions), either proposal can be seen as the equivalent of simply lowering the tax on distributions directly at the shareholder level. This would not change the effective tax rate on retained earnings at all; they would still be taxed at the corporate rate. Given the revenue cost of dividend relief, this lack of marginal effect is a serious drawback.[31]

Another consequence of both dividend relief and full integration is the incentive to pay dividends rather than repurchase shares. Under full integration, a dividend payment would have no tax consequences, while a share redemption could increase taxes if basis (in this event, including reinvested earnings on which individual taxes had already been paid) were less than market value. Hence there would be no incentive for share repurchases. Under a full dividend relief scheme, for a taxable investor dividends would also be preferred, even if the capital gains tax rate were zero, since they would actually reduce taxes (given the higher corporate rate). Thus the incentive to eschew repurchases is even stronger for the partial integration schemes.

Once again, it must be stressed that this incentive to pay dividends is a change in the form that distributions should take, and it is logically separable from the issue of whether firms should distribute funds or retain them. Neither full integration nor dividend relief should have much effect on this issue.

Imputation of Dividends and Interest

The difference between the two forms of dividend relief also suggests a different approach to the treatment of interest. The logic of raising revenue from tax-exempt and foreign investors by choosing to exclude them from dividend relief can be applied to other, normally deductible expenses, particularly interest. The suggestion that the debt-equity distinction should be removed by establishing an imputation system for dividends *and* interest has recently been made by Graetz.[32]

In parallel to the difference between the corporate-level and individual-level schemes of dividend relief, this shift in the treatment of interest amounts to a withholding tax on interest paid to foreign and tax-exempt

31. Up-to-date revenue estimates for full and partial integration schemes are hard to obtain. However, the 1984 Treasury proposal for a 50 percent dividends-paid deduction estimated a total (corporate and individual) revenue cost of $31 billion for fiscal year 1990 (the last year for which projections were provided).

32. Michael J. Graetz, "The Tax Aspects of Leveraged Buyouts and Other Corporate Financial Restructuring Transactions," *Tax Notes*, February 6, 1989, pp. 721–26.

holders of debt. It has the advantage, shared by a policy reform of full dividend deductibility, of entirely removing the distinction between payments to debt and to equity, although it would preserve a slight distinction, even for taxable investors, between corporate investments taxable at the corporate rate and individual investments taxable at the individual rate. Moreover, it would *introduce* a distinction between interest and other, normally deductible, expenses such as rent and lease payments. Instead of the current problem of distinguishing dividends from interest there would be a new problem of distinguishing interest from other payments that continue to receive a tax deduction, although the incentives to recharacterize interest payments would be relatively small so long as the payments were being made to taxable investors: firms would gain the expense deduction, but recipients of the payment would be taxable on it.

Since under the current U.S. system, no investor is taxable at a rate exceeding the corporate tax rate, this approach essentially represents a combination of two other policies: the allowance of a full deduction for dividends paid plus a withholding tax on corporate dividend and interest payments at the corporate tax rate, creditable up to the recipient's rate of tax. It shares with the previous integration approaches the revenue loss from providing windfalls to owners of existing equity, simply combining this policy with a withholding tax to raise revenue. That is, it does not avoid the revenue loss from these windfalls, but recoups it by imposing another tax, on entities that are not currently taxable. Its merits relative to other proposals hinge on the desirability of such an extra tax.

Avoiding the Windfalls

In 1982 the American Law Institute (ALI) published a volume about the reform of the U.S. corporate income tax that included proposals by the project's reporter, William Andrews, to provide dividend relief in a way that would avoid the windfalls common to the schemes discussed.[33] The ALI-Andrews scheme is fairly elaborate in its detail, and has gone through several draft versions,[34] with at least one more in preparation. To understand this plan and its effects, it is useful to consider first a much simpler one that shares many of its important characteristics.

33. American Law Institute, *Federal Income Tax Project, Subchapter C: Proposals on Corporate Acquisitions and Dispositions and Reporter's Study on Corporate Distributions* (Philadelphia, 1982).
34. The most recent one, as of this paper's initial draft, was American Law Institute, "Federal Income Tax Project: Tax Advisory Group Draft No. 18," Philadelphia, November 3, 1988.

The basic problem which the ALI plan addresses is that dividend relief is a windfall for equity funds already within the corporate solution. A direct attack on this problem would be to couple a dividends-paid deduction with a tax at the corporate rate on the present value of deductions received by dividends paid from existing equity. It would not be necessary to keep track of these dividends. Since dividends are normally taxable to recipients insofar as they are paid out of a firm's accumulated earnings and profits, the stock of these earnings and profits would serve as an appropriate tax base.[35] The incentive effects would be the same as under a dividends-paid deduction alone, but the revenue effects would be different. Even if the windfalls tax was made payable over several years, its revenue could well exceed that lost because of the dividends-paid deduction for many years (though not in the long run).

The idea of taxing windfalls is not new. Such a tax, associated with a reduction in the corporate tax rate, was included by President Reagan in his 1985 tax reform proposals.[36] However, plans to recoup windfalls through explicit taxes are often opposed as being retroactive and unfair, even when they may only partially offset windfall gains implicitly delivered at the same time.[37] This resistance exists despite the absence of any compelling logic or even a consistent definition of a retroactive policy. Indeed, whether such a definition is possible has been seriously questioned.[38]

The ALI Proposal

Unlike the previous strategy of providing dividend relief for all existing equity and then taxing away the windfalls, the ALI approach in effect would make the payment of the windfalls tax (the "toll charge") and qualification for dividend relief a decision of the firm, allowing it the option of not qualifying for dividend relief and not paying a windfalls tax. The distinction between old and new equity would remain for many years, until it diminished in importance as newly contributed equity overtook

35. An equivalent way to eliminate the windfalls would be to require the corporation to give the government a share of its existing equity equal to the present value of dividend taxes forgiven.

36. The tax would have recouped from corporations the tax reduction due to the corporate rate cut on that component of taxable income arising from previous accelerated depreciation deductions. That scheme would have raised considerable revenue.

37. This was the case of the 1985 scheme discussed in note 36.

38. Michael J. Graetz, "Legal Transitions: The Case of Retroactivity in Income Tax Revision," *University of Pennsylvania Law Review*, November 1977, pp. 47–87.

existing equity. This coexistence of new and old equity is one of the complicating aspects of the plan.

Despite its many incarnations and sophisticated analysis, the ALI plan has retained its basic purpose of providing dividend relief limited to newly contributed equity. It has two major components. The first would provide limited dividend relief along the lines of the dividends-paid deduction. The second would restrict the ability of firms to make tax-favored non-dividend distributions of funds not qualifying for dividend relief.

The ALI plan would distinguish between old and new equity; shares issued after its enactment would be new and would qualify for special treatment under the plan's deduction for dividends paid. The allowable deduction would be calculated by multiplying the value of funds raised from the sale of new shares by some reasonable rate of return. For example, if the plan became effective on January 1, 1991, and the allowable rate of deduction was 5 percent, a firm issuing $1 million of equity after this date would be entitled to deduct up to $50,000 of dividends annually thereafter. If the firm subsequently issued more equity, its allowable dividend deductions would increase.

As with the other forms of dividend relief discussed, this part of the ALI plan would alleviate the double taxation facing newly contributed equity capital. For such equity, the plan would be essentially identical to a standard dividends-paid deduction. Also similar is the ALI plan's encouragement of firms to make their distributions in the form of dividends, at least to the extent of the allowable deductions.

The ALI plan's provision of dividend relief for newly contributed equity is neither problematic nor controversial. It simply does for a certain class of shares what standard dividend relief would do for all. It is the second provision, which aims to curtail nondividend distributions, that has caused controversy.[39]

The tax on nondividend distributions would apply to shares repurchased by a corporation itself as well as to shares redeemed by another through a cash acquisition. It is intended to offset the current tax advantage such distributions enjoy, which is attributable to the basis that shareholders may deduct from capital gains tax liability (and, before 1987, the lower rate at which such capital gains were taxed). Under the original 1982 ALI plan, this levy would have been an excise tax on the distributions themselves, which would be added to the individual income tax burden. The

39. See, for example, Michael Jensen, "The Effects of LBOs and Corporate Debt on the Economy," remarks before the House Committee on Ways and Means, February 1, 1989.

1988 version instead includes a corporate-level minimum tax on non-dividend distributions (MTD) set at the tax rate of most high-income individual investors (28 percent) and creditable against individual tax liability on the distributions. In either case, low-bracket investors would actually face a higher tax burden on nondividend distributions than on ordinary dividends, while the burdens would be similar for high-bracket investors.

Why is the tax on alternative distributions seen as necessary by its supporters, and why is it opposed by others? As discussed, share repurchases are the tax-preferred form of distribution, since shareholders receive a deduction for their basis. If the alternative was to repurchase shares now or in the future, the capital gains tax on redemptions would play the role of the distributions tax and would largely be capitalized.[40] In that case, the increased tax on nondividend distributions would not alter incentives, but would effectively impose a capital levy, thus raising the value of taxes capitalized in corporate shares. This, in itself, partly explains the controversy. Though the tax increase may not be distortionary, it might still be viewed as unfair.

The relevant question here is what the appropriate benchmark is. The ALI plan treats dividends as the normal form of distribution and considers taxes on such distributions also normal. From this perspective, the recent reduction in taxes through increased nondividend distributions represents an unintended windfall to which shareholders are not entitled. Others, taking the current situation as the normal state of affairs, view the tightening of rules on nondividend distributions as unfair.

Because the first of the ALI provisions would reduce taxes and the second would increase them, the two parts are regarded with different degrees of enthusiasm by those who would be affected by the plan. A natural question to ask is whether the components of the plan are interdependent or whether they could be enacted separately.

An initial response might be that, if new equity is given the favorable treatment of dividends, the extra tax on nondividend distributions is important in order to prevent firms from "churning" their existing equity; that is, converting old equity into new equity and receiving the associated tax benefits. However, the analysis here suggests that the tax rate on distributions should not affect the incentive to distribute equity funds now rather than in the future. This analysis is not influenced by a reduction in

---

40. It would still have some small effect on the margin because of the declining value of the basis deduction over time. See note 14.

the tax on new equity. Enactment of the tax deduction for dividends from new equity should not, in itself, encourage distributions from existing equity.

Thus the two provisions of the ALI plan can be considered separate, each having its own purpose. The first component would provide relief from double taxation to the class of equity requiring it—newly contributed equity—without giving windfalls to existing equity. The second component would eliminate any prospective windfalls and take back those that have already occurred because of the favorable treatment of nondividend distributions. Together, the provisions would supply dividend relief for new equity while eliminating all windfalls from existing equity *relative to the full taxation of all distributions*.

All the analysis of the ALI plan to this point is based on a permanent, unannounced enactment of the plan. However, in a world of uncertain and temporary tax policy, a change in the tax on distributions could do more than change the value of taxes capitalized in equity values. Unlike the direct windfalls tax, the ALI toll charge, consisting of taxes on dividend and nondividend distributions from existing equity, would be paid only upon the distribution of these funds. Given a constant tax system, this distinction would be irrelevant; that is what makes the analogy to the windfalls tax useful. But given the option to delay distributions, there is a strong possibility of distorted behavior under the ALI plan.

If, for example, investors expected the tax on alternative distributions to be temporary, the incentive to delay share repurchases and cash-financed takeovers could be significant. In fact, if a phase-in to full dividend deductibility for old and new equity alike were anticipated, even current dividends would be discouraged.[41] Only a convincing, permanent adoption of the ALI plan would avoid these incentives, and consistency of this policy over time would require the system to maintain the distinction between old and new equity. Likewise, anticipation that the ALI plan would be enacted would increase nondividend distributions and reduce equity issues. Even if the enactment came entirely as a surprise, there would still be the inevitable question of fairness in transition; for example, how to treat the company that made a large equity issue a day before the provision of relief for new equity took effect.

41. The same incentive to delay distributions would be present under a simpler phasing in of full dividend relief with, say, the rate of deduction for dividends being increased over time.

The ALI plan attacks the important problem of windfalls but does not succeed in doing so without also introducing significant transition problems.

The Corporate Cash-Flow Tax

Direct taxes on individual consumption or cash flow have enjoyed considerable intellectual support in recent years.[42] Such a tax base would identify a household's consumption indirectly—using the identity that income is exhausted by saving, taxes, and consumption—by allowing a deduction for saving from the income tax base. Although corporations do not consume, a cash-flow tax base for the corporate tax has its attractions, too. Like the individual consumption tax, it would not alter the net return to saving. Moreover, insofar as corporate income generated by sources other than new saving is not variable, the corporate cash-flow tax is a nondistortionary tax on rent, unlike the individual consumption tax that distorts the supply of labor.

The attractiveness of a corporate cash-flow tax as part of a system of consumption taxation has been noted in the literature,[43] but more recently the corporate cash-flow tax has been proposed as a free-standing reform of the corporate tax.[44] It is possible to understand the effects of such a policy by studying its relationship to the alternatives already discussed.

There are two basic approaches to corporate cash-flow taxation, which were referred to by the Meade Committee as the R(eal) versus the R(eal) + F(inancial) bases.[45] The approaches differ with respect to their treatment of borrowing and interest payments. Whereas the R-base would eliminate interest deductions (and not tax the corporation's interest income), the R + F–base would preserve such deductions (and taxes) but add borrowing to (and deduct lending from) the tax base. Perhaps the most significant difference between the two methods would be in their treatment of financial

42. For example, William D. Andrews, "A Consumption-Type or Cash Flow Personal Income Tax," *Harvard Law Review*, vol. 87 (April 1974), pp. 1113–88; and David F. Bradford, "The Case for a Personal Consumption Tax," in Joseph A. Pechman, ed., *What Should Be Taxed: Income or Expenditure?* (Brookings, 1980), pp. 75–113.

43. Institute for Fiscal Studies, *The Structure and Reform of Direct Taxation* (London: Allen and Unwin, 1978); and Henry J. Aaron and Harvey Galper, *Assessing Tax Reform* (Brookings, 1985).

44. Martin Feldstein, "Excess Debt and Unbalanced Investment: The Case for a Cash-flow Business Tax," testimony before the House Committee on Ways and Means, January 31, 1989.

45. Institute for Fiscal Studies, *Direct Taxation*.

intermediaries, whose profits (interest receipts less interest payments) would be tax exempt under the R-base. For nonfinancial corporations, the approaches would have similar effects.

To convert the present corporate income tax to a cash-flow tax, one would replace depreciation deductions by an immediate deduction for all new investment as current expenses and, under the R + F–base, would include all net borrowing in the tax base. The resulting tax base would be the firm's receipts less expenditures; that is, its net cash flow, the sum of all the firm's current distributions to its shareholders, including dividends plus share repurchases. Given the previous discussion of the effects of taxes on distributions, it is clear that the cash-flow tax is nondistortionary: although it affects the value of the corporation, it imposes no additional tax on the return to earnings that are reinvested. Moreover, unlike other taxes on distributions (such as the dividend tax), it does not discriminate against newly contributed equity, since it is a tax on distributions *net* of new equity issues. New equity would not face a net tax, in present value, on its distributions, since it would receive an offsetting deduction upon its initial contribution. Thus a move to the R + F–base would be equivalent to replacing the current corporate tax with a tax on all distributions from existing equity. In terms of marginal incentives, this outcome would be equivalent to the abolition of the corporate tax.

A similar analysis applies to the R-base, which has been discussed more frequently as a possible tax reform. By eliminating the deduction for interest payments instead of taxing net borrowing, the R-base would add net distributions to holders of existing debt (interest payments less net borrowing) to those already taxed under the R + F–base. Again, there would be no marginal effect of the corporate tax.

A comparison of the effect of the cash-flow tax with those of the approaches previously considered reveals three significant differences:

1. unique among the proposals, the cash-flow tax would raise the corporate tax burden on debt-financed investment;

2. unique among the proposals, the cash-flow tax would reduce the tax rate on corporate equity investment *below* that on debt and noncorporate investment, reversing the direction of the present tax bias; and

3. like the ALI proposal, but unlike the other schemes, the cash-flow tax would avoid giving windfalls to existing equity.

To see these differences, it is useful to compare the corporate cash-flow tax with a tax on "real" corporate income. Such a true income tax would include economic depreciation allowances and a deduction for the real rate of interest paid to lenders (excluding the inflation premium). As is well established in the literature,[46] such a tax would provide a zero corporate-level marginal tax rate on investment financed by debt and would tax equity-financed investment at the statutory corporate tax rate. In addition, a similar deduction for the real return paid to holders of equity would provide a zero corporate-level marginal tax rate for equity.

A move to the corporate cash-flow tax from such an income tax would also lower the marginal corporate tax rate on equity to zero while maintaining the zero marginal corporate rate on debt, because the shift to immediate expensing of investment would just offset the less favorable treatment of debt (under the R + F–base) or interest (under the R-base) for debt-financed investments. Thus a corporate cash-flow tax would have marginal effects similar to the provision of a deduction for the real return to equity and debt under a true income tax.

However, this comparison only holds if the income tax system measures depreciation and accounts for inflation properly. If depreciation deductions are more generous than would be dictated by income measurement, and if interest deductions under the income tax exceed the real cost of funds, then the effective corporate tax rate on equity-financed investment is initially lower than the statutory corporate tax rate, and the effective corporate tax rate on debt-financed investment is initially negative. Hence a move to the cash-flow tax may be seen as a two-stage reform, first removing investment incentives and the deductibility of the inflation premium on debt in a shift to a true income tax, thereby increasing the effective tax rates on both debt (to zero) and equity (to the statutory rate), and then reducing the effective rate on equity to zero in a policy equivalent to providing a deduction for the real return to equity.

This combination policy lowers the effective corporate tax rate on equity-financed investment by less than the second stage alone and *raises* the effective corporate tax rate on debt-financed investment. In the extreme case that depreciation allowances and investment tax credits combined already approximated immediate expensing (a case that applied in the United States to machinery and equipment before 1986), adoption of cash-flow taxation would simply amount to a removal of the interest deduction (under the R-base) or an inclusion of borrowing in income (under an R + F–base), thus bringing the tax rate on debt-financed investments *up* to zero and not reducing the tax rate on equity-financed investments at all.

46. See, for example, Mervyn A. King, "Taxation, Corporate Financial Policy and the Cost of Capital: A Comment," *Journal of Public Economics*, vol. 4 (August 1975), pp. 271–79; and Auerbach, "Taxation, Corporate Financial Policy, and the Cost of Capital."

The foregoing analysis demonstrates the first effect of the corporate cash-flow tax in the list above. Since adoption of such a tax would not by itself alter the treatment of interest payments received from corporations by individual investors, the overall tax burden on debt-financed corporate investment would increase insofar as depreciation allowances are currently more generous than economic depreciation and corporate interest deductions include an inflation premium. Since the proposal entails no change in the treatment of investment financed by noncorporate borrowing, it would also introduce a bias in favor of that kind of borrowing over corporate borrowing.

The second effect listed also follows immediately. While the *corporate-level* marginal tax rates on debt and equity would be the same under a corporate cash-flow tax, the overall tax rates would not be. For existing equity, there would then be a *zero* marginal tax rate overall, since the zero effective tax rate at the individual level associated with the capitalization of taxes on dividends would be combined with a corporate-level tax on distributions with a zero effective tax rate. Whereas other integration proposals would continue to tax retained earnings (at either the corporate or the individual tax rate), the corporate cash-flow tax would not. As discussed, it would be equivalent to the provision of a deduction for the entire return to equity under an income tax. Thus since interest payments would continue to be taxable to individuals, existing equity would face a *lower* overall effective tax rate than debt. Indeed, even newly contributed equity would be favored over debt because of the favorable treatment of capital gains at the individual level.

Finally, the cash-flow tax differs from other forms of equity relief in avoidance of windfalls. Whereas a deduction for all dividends paid, for example, would eliminate the corporate-level tax on all distributed income, including the corporation's pure economic rents and the returns to its existing capital, the cash-flow tax would not do so. If, during the transition period, it preserved the tax treatment of preexisting assets and liabilities by maintaining depreciation allowances of existing assets, thereby allowing existing inventories to be deducted when used and (under an R-base) continuing the interest deductions of existing debt, then the cash-flow tax would not alter the tax treatment of distributions from existing equity at all. It would be equivalent at the margin to the abolition of the corporate income tax but would avoid the windfalls. Like the ALI proposal, the cash-flow tax would have an effect only at the margin. However, unlike the ALI proposal, it would raise the effective marginal tax rate on debt-financed projects and would reduce the tax burden on *all* equity-financed projects, including those financed by existing equity.

The corporate cash-flow tax would, again like the ALI plan, present serious transition problems. Even though the tax treatment of existing assets and debt was preserved, firms would have a strong incentive to wait to invest if the adoption of a cash-flow tax was anticipated, for the immediate write-off would be received only for new investment. In general, attempts at limiting windfalls by distinguishing new from old activity may be subject to similar problems.

In summary, a corporate cash-flow tax would provide more marginal equity relief than other proposals as well as raise the marginal tax rate on debt-financed investment while avoiding windfalls through the conversion of the corporate income tax to a tax on the distributions of existing corporate funds. Since the adoption of a cash-flow tax is equivalent to a two-stage policy that first removes investment incentives (including the deductibility of the inflation component of interest payments) and then introduces a deduction for returns to equity, a comparison of the cash-flow tax to other approaches that leave investment incentives untouched depends on the characteristics of the initial tax system. Because the Tax Reform Act of 1986 eliminated the investment tax credit and accelerated depreciation, this "first-stage" increase in effective tax rates would be less significant now than in the past,[47] and a move to cash-flow taxation would be relatively more generous.

Before I consider estimates of the revenue costs of the corporate cash-flow tax, a review of its effects will be useful. If the initial tax system measures income properly, providing economic depreciation allowances and a deduction of real interest payments, then adoption of a cash-flow tax that preserves these measures will neither alter the tax treatment of income from existing corporate sources nor change the tax burden on new investments financed by borrowing. The only effect will be to reduce the tax burden on marginal investments financed by new *and* existing equity. Although the policy would avoid windfalls, it would still *necessarily* lose revenue because of the reductions in marginal tax rates associated with the shift from depreciation allowances to expensing for equity-financed assets.

47. See Alan J. Auerbach, "The Tax Reform Act of 1986 and the Cost of Capital," *Journal of Economic Perspectives*, vol. 1 (Summer 1987), pp. 73–86. Some degree of acceleration of allowances remains, but this is approximately offset by the lack of indexing of allowances for deflation. The ability to deduct nominal rather than real interest payments remains.

This result is significant because recent estimates for the United States have found that a switch to corporate cash-flow taxation would broaden the corporate tax base either by raising revenue or by permitting a reduction in the corporate tax rate without a revenue loss. For 1981–83 Aaron and Galper estimated that a tax rate of only 33 percent, rather than the prevailing rate of 46 percent, would have been necessary if a cash-flow tax base had been adopted.[48] Gordon and Slemrod estimated that a switch to corporate cash-flow taxation would have increased revenues from nonfinancial corporations by $20.8 billion in 1983.[49]

There are several reasons for the discrepancy between the theoretical revenue loss and the empirically estimated revenue gains. First, both estimates are based on the pre-1986 period, when, in addition to the present deductibility of nominal interest expense, depreciation allowances were accelerated and the investment tax credit applied. Thus a shift to cash-flow taxation would have lowered the tax rate on equity-financed investment by less than what is suggested by the theoretical analysis, and it would have raised the tax rate on debt-financed investment. Moreover, both of the reported estimates are for the long run and do not properly account for transition-period revenue losses.

A careful analysis of such transition effects by Gordon and Slemrod found that roughly one-third of this long-run revenue gain would be offset by the maintenance of depreciation allowances on existing corporate assets;[50] however, they did not calculate in the additional revenue loss that would come from permitting an interest deduction for preexisting debt. When such a figure is included—based on the assumption that the existing stock of debt would be permitted the interest deduction forever—the revenue gain is reduced once more by about one-third.[51] Thus if one did

48. Aaron and Galper, *Assessing Tax Reform*.

49. Roger H. Gordon and Joel Slemrod, "Do We Collect Any Revenue from Taxing Capital Income?" in Lawrence H. Summers, ed., *Tax Policy and the Economy*, vol. 2 (MIT Press, 1988), pp. 89–130.

50. Gordon and Slemrod do not report this estimate directly, but do present various calculations that may be used to obtain it ("Revenue from Taxing Capital Income"). They estimate the present value of taxes saved from corporate deductions for depreciation, amortization, and inventory expenses associated with the initial stock of assets to be $279.0 billion. Given their estimated nominal growth rate for revenue, the 1983 revenue gain of $20.8 billion implies a present value revenue gain of $945.4 billion, of which $279.0 billion is 30 percent.

51. Gordon and Slemrod report that net (of interest received) corporate interest expense of nonfinancial corporations was $96.6 billion in 1983 ("Revenue from Taxing Capital Income"). Given their average marginal corporate tax rate of 0.318, this produces a tax saving of $30.7 billion. Discounting this figure at their assumed nominal discount rate of

not change the tax treatment of existing assets and debt of the nonfinancial corporate sector, the elimination of investment incentives from the 1983 tax system would barely pay for the reduction in marginal tax rates for equity-financed investment, raising not $20.8 billion annually but just under $7.0 billion. It would represent a shift from equity to debt in the marginal tax burden with a small increase overall. However, starting from the post-1986 tax system, with its reduced investment incentives, the same policy would probably lose revenue and reduce marginal tax rates overall. The revenue loss cannot be avoided unless less generous transition provisions are introduced.

There are ways to reduce transition relief other than limiting deductions for existing assets and debt. One approach would be to allow expensing of new investment only insofar as it exceeded some fixed base year level. The marginal effects on firm behavior would be the same but, compared with the cash-flow tax, this policy could collect a considerable lump-sum tax annually equal to the corporate tax rate multiplied by the investment floor (assuming the floor were set low enough that it fell below each firm's actual investment).[52]

The corporate cash-flow tax, like the ALI plan, provides its equity incentives through tax reductions at the corporate level. Therefore, unlike an imputation system, it would extend the benefits of equity relief to foreign equity owners. However, just as a withholding tax converts the split-rate system into an imputation system, the cash-flow tax could be coupled with a withholding tax on equity distributions to foreigners and nontaxable entities. Such a withholding tax was included in the corporate cash-flow tax considered by Aaron and Galper.[53]

Summary: Windfalls and Incentives

When designing a new tax system, one might wish to have fully integrated corporate and individual taxes. Finding that too ambitious to administer, one might choose dividend relief in the form of a split-rate system or, if relief for foreigners and tax-exempt institutions was un-

---

0.088 yields a present value revenue loss of $348.9 billion. Thus the net-present-value gain becomes only $317.5 (= 945.4 − 279.0 − 348.9) billion.

52. In 1983 gross national nonfinancial corporate investment in plant and equipment was $261.1 billion. Board of Governors, "Flow of Funds Accounts: Third Quarter 1988." Setting each succeeding year's floor equal to just over one-third of this amount would raise the same revenue as denial of any interest deductions on existing debt (see note 51).

53. Aaron and Galper, *Assessing Tax Reform.*

wanted, an imputation system. The windfalls of each of these systems make the ALI plan and the cash-flow tax attractive for the reform of the present tax system rather than the design of a new one. Whereas the ALI plan would resemble a new-equity dividend relief plan in the context of the current tax system, the cash-flow tax would combine a more significant marginal tax reduction for all equity with the repeal of base-narrowing components of the current tax system. But each system has its drawbacks. The ALI plan would require the preservation of existing equity and its distinct tax treatment; the cash-flow tax would replace the financial distortion favoring debt with one favoring equity. Although either of these complications could be avoided through direct taxation of windfalls, recent experience suggests that it would be precluded by political considerations.

Conclusions

This paper has argued that, while the tax incentives to use debt finance have not necessarily increased in recent years, an increase in the ability of firms to take advantage of existing incentives to borrow could still have increased the need to address the existing imbalance in the tax treatment of debt and equity.

The proposals analyzed vary in terms of the windfalls that they provide to owners of existing assets, their treatment of foreign and tax-exempt investors, their administrability and political acceptability, and the distortions they preserve or induce between debt and equity. Such issues may seem far removed from the current policy debate, but they are the relevant ones for evaluating changes in tax structure.

Comment by James M. Poterba

Numerous plans to alter the tax treatment of debt and equity have been proposed during the last five years. These proposals have been stimulated by the dramatic exchange of equity for debt financing by major U.S. firms, totaling over $400 billion since 1985, as well as by the growth of leveraged buyouts as devices for corporate restructuring. Although the plans vary widely in their provisions and likely economic effects, Auerbach's paper brings order to a complex and often confusing area. It isolates the central issues and explains the salient features of most of the leading reform proposals. Since I am in nearly complete agreement with the paper's analysis, my comments will underscore several points that arise in reforming the taxation of corporate earnings.

The Elusive Marginal Investor

The first and probably most important difficulty in analyzing corporate taxation is evaluating the exact nature of tax incentives under current law or various proposed reforms. This is a difficult task because of the substantial heterogeneity in the tax rates on different classes of investors. For tax-exempt investors, such as pension funds or nonprofit institutions, debt dominates equity finance for a given corporate project because it avoids corporate taxes. For individual investors, however, the corporate tax benefits of debt finance are attenuated by the personal tax benefits accorded to capital gains. Even when the statutory tax rates on dividends, interest, and capital gains are equal, the benefits of tax deferral make the effective capital gains tax rate lower than that on interest or dividends.

The net tax incentive for a firm to issue debt rather than equity depends on the identity of the "marginal investors" who determine required returns in financial markets. This can be illustrated by considering the net effect of the Tax Reform Act of 1986 on corporate borrowing incentives. For tax-exempt investors, the act's corporate tax rate reduction from 46 to 34 percent narrowed the differential between debt and equity tax burdens and made equity finance relatively more attractive. Before 1986 a project that earned $1.00 before corporate taxes could translate into a $1.00 return for a tax-exempt investor if the proceeds were paid as interest, or into $0.54 if the returns were channeled to the investor as equity. For tax-exempt investors, the 1986 act was therefore a step toward tax neutrality.

A different set of incentives apply for top-bracket individual investors, for whom the act *increased* the incentive for debt finance. The reduction in top individual marginal tax rates from 50 to 28 percent increased the after-tax income such households would receive if the corporation earned $1.00 and distributed its earnings as interest from $0.50 to $0.72. For equity, by comparison, the after–corporate tax income available for shareholders rose from $0.54 to $0.66. The average tax burden at the investor level (assuming half of earnings are distributed as dividends and that the effective capital gains tax rate is one quarter of the statutory rate) declined from 30 to 21 percent. The net after-tax income from an equity-financed project therefore changed from $0.38 to $0.52, an increase of only $0.14 versus $0.22 for debt-financed projects.

Resolving whether the Tax Reform Act of 1986 raised or lowered incentives for corporate borrowing thus depends on the relative importance of the different classes of investors. Although the rapid growth of corporate leverage points toward individuals as the "marginal investors," recent borrowing trends may simply be a delayed reaction to the Economic Recovery Tax Act of 1981, which unambiguously raised borrowing incentives since it reduced tax rates on individuals without changing the statutory corporate tax rate. The greater volume of trade, and typically lower transaction costs, faced by large institutional and normally tax-exempt investors nevertheless suggests that these investors may be important in determining market prices. There is no simple resolution to the puzzle of which investors are "marginal" in determining corporate financial policy. The uncertainty about the magnitude of current tax incentives makes it difficult to assess how various reform proposals will affect corporate financial policy.

On Capitalization and Windfalls

One of the central themes of the paper is that reforms should be structured so as to avoid generating windfalls for existing assets. This point commands nearly universal agreement among public finance economists, since windfalls have revenue costs but no desirable incentive effects. In light of this consensus, it is surprising that there is remarkably little evidence supporting the importance of these effects. Lawrence Summers and I studied the reaction of British share prices to the news in 1970 that the double taxation of dividends would be replaced with an integrated tax system.[54] We did not find large effects on stock prices, and in most cases could not reject the hypothesis that prices did not respond to these announcements.

Similarly, a recent study of the U.S. stock market's response to news about passage of the Tax Reform Act of 1986 finds little evidence of price change.[55] On the days when it became clear (in both cases somewhat unexpectedly) that the Senate Finance Committee and the House would pass tax reform bills, the stock market was no more volatile than on other days, and there was virtually no increase in the dispersion of returns across

54. Poterba and Summers, "Economic Effects of Dividend Taxation."
55. David M. Cutler, "Tax Reform and the Stock Market: An Asset Price Approach," *American Economic Review*, vol. 78 (December 1988), pp. 1107–17.

firms, even though the Tax Reform Act conveyed windfalls for some firms and raised future tax liabilities for others.

Auerbach's paper suggests a potential solution to these empirical findings: perhaps tax reforms are expected to be temporary. This view would reduce the windfall gains and losses from tax changes, thus leading to smaller asset price effects. If all tax reform is viewed as transitory, designing transition rules to avoid windfalls is a less important problem than some of the current reform discussion has suggested.

Tax Levels, Not Just Differentials, Matter

My final point concerns the objectives that should be used in evaluating different tax proposals. Recent plans have primarily focused on the relative tax burdens on debt and equity securities, largely ignoring the level of tax burdens. The overall level of taxes, and hence corporate capital costs, should be an important consideration in comparing policies. The present tax incentives for debt finance could be eliminated in either of two ways: by lowering the tax burden on equity or by increasing the tax burden on debt. Although both schemes would make firms indifferent between financing projects using debt and equity, proposals to lower tax burdens on equity, which include schemes for integrating the corporate and personal income taxes as well as dividend-deduction plans, would reduce the cost of capital. This would encourage firms to invest and ultimately enlarge the stock of productive capital. Plans to make debt more expensive by partly or completely eliminating the tax deductibility of interest payments, however, would raise the cost of capital and adversely affect investment.

The principal argument for tilting policy toward encouraging investment is that investment is a key determinant of productivity growth. During the 1980s net plant and equipment investment in the United States averaged 2.6 percent of net national product, compared with 3.7 percent during the 1960s and 1970s. In the three most recent years for which data are available, 1985–87, the investment rate was only 2.3 percent of NNP. Partly as a result, U.S. productivity growth during the 1980s (3.0 percent a year in manufacturing) lagged behind that of several of our major trading partners. Japanese manufacturing productivity grew at 4.5 percent a year, and Britain's at 4.3 percent. Tax policies that discourage investment risk exacerbating these differences and should therefore be avoided when possible. In the corporate cash-flow context, this suggests that reductions in tax rates on new investments, financed if necessary by higher tax burdens on existing projects, may be appropriate.

Comment by William D. Andrews

Auerbach's paper helps immensely to clarify the relationship between the U.S. tax treatment of corporate income and the 1980s' persistent wave of cash acquisition and LBOs. The main tax effect of these transactions is the elimination of future corporate income tax liabilities that results from any buyout or acquisition for cash or debt, or indeed any other distribution of cash or debt (or other assets, except corporate stock) out of corporate solution. That effect is not an inducement solely for acquisitions or LBOs as such, since the same tax advantage can be achieved by a simple distribution of cash or debt to a corporation's own shareholders, even as an ordinary dividend. But an ordinary dividend bears the burden of ordinary income taxes for high-bracket shareholders. The bias in favor of LBOs, cash acquisitions, and other nondividend distributions results from the elimination of future corporate income taxes without the countervailing burden of ordinary income taxation on the full amount distributed.

This bias does not provide any explanation of why corporate financial behavior changed the way it did *in the 1980s*, since the principal characteristics of the system that create the bias have been around for ages. Nevertheless, the system does create a bias in favor of nondividend distributions (and even dividends extraordinary in amount, since shareholders can avoid the full burden of tax on these by selling their shares). Before 1980 the major puzzle about corporate financial behavior was why corporations did not take greater advantage of the opportunity to make nondividend distributions. Whatever the reason was, it now seems to have been overcome to a considerable extent. In Auerbach's words, "Even without a change in the tax inducement to borrow, the recent increase in borrowing may have occurred in order to take advantage of what tax advantage there is."

As a policy matter this means that the bias in the system is more urgently in need of fixing, even if it is the same old bias that has been there all along. Auerbach's paper therefore rightly concentrates on options for alleviating that long-standing bias.

While agreeing on the major point, I would take a somewhat different view about the effects of tax rate changes enacted during the last decade. Of course, reductions in marginal tax rates reduce the effect of tax biases, other things being equal. But rate inversion—the reduction of top individual rates to below the level of the corporate tax—means that no one is left for whom the cost of capital by accumulation of equity is lower than the cost of borrowing. Auerbach points out that for tax-exempt shareholders there has been no reduction of investor taxes at all. But shareholders' influence on corporate behavior may be more a function of how many shareholders want a change than of the strength of that feeling on the part of some. In the past, tax-exempt shareholders may have been quite willing to play the role of passive investors, particularly if payment of taxable dividends caused shares to be available on the market at a discount.

In any event it is certainly the impression of many lawyers that the 1986 tax rate changes have fueled a relatively new drive to run profitable businesses in noncorporate form. The immediate tax cost of disincorporating is often still too high; in that case, serious consideration should be given to a Subchapter S election despite its restrictions on share ownership. In any new business, serious thought is given to partnership form.

Much legal activity relates to closely held corporations, but perhaps these are not quantitatively important in the greater order of things. However, closely held corporations are an important test of rational behavior when interests of shareholders and management coincide. As such, they may represent what public corporations can ultimately be driven to do.

This suggests a way of reading recent financial history: the tax law has long offered rewards for taking money out of corporate solution by nondividend routes. In a complex set of provisions for taxing redemptions as dividends under appropriate circumstances (mainly when they have a small enough effect on relative shareholdings), the tax law has also long recognized the relationship to be quite unlike ordinary sales of shares. Closely held corporations have long understood this; indeed, their financial planning has been built around it.

For reasons that are not well understood, most public corporations have not until recently aggressively exploited the opportunities to save taxes by nondividend distributions. Those reasons may have something to do with separation of management from ownership or with (mis)conceptions about market behavior and the signaling effect of dividends. But exploited or not, the opportunities have been there. The most significant development in the 1980s was the appearance of raiders willing and able to exploit the opportunity for corporations who failed to do it for themselves. Then, as the decade proceeded, corporations understood (1) the need to do the exploiting themselves as a defensive matter and (2) the opportunity for profit from doing LBOs and even extraordinary dividends, whether or not they were under threat from outsiders.

The ALI Reporter's Proposals

Auerbach describes two of the ALI reporter's proposals on corporate distributions: (1) a minimum tax on distributions (MTD), and (2) a deduction for dividends paid up to the amount of an interest-like return on equity capital paid in for shares after the effective date of the proposal.[56] He observes that these would have many of the same incentive effects as dividend integration, but that they would not create the same windfall for owners of existing equity. He then compares those proposals to adoption of a deduction of all dividends paid (dividend integration), but with a lump-sum tax imposed on future dividends from existing equity to recapture the windfall. Collecting a lump-sum tax has the advantage of avoiding distortions that could result from the hope that an ongoing tax like the MTD might be repealed or reduced.

The comparison is intriguing. My instinct tells me that collection of this lump-sum tax would be much more disruptive of business and financial operations than such a tax, in theory, is supposed to be. Measurement of a lump-sum tax liability by reference to accumulated earnings and profits is much easier to talk about than to do. Accumulated earnings and profits are the outcome of calculations going back to the beginning of a corporation's history, and prosperous corporations have often had no occasion to determine their accumulated earnings and profits. A few corporations

56. In the current version, these are proposals 1 and 3. American Law Institute, *Federal Income Tax Project—Subchapter C (Supplemental Study): Reporter's Study Draft* (Philadelphia, June 1989). (The ALI reporter is William D. Andrews.) Proposal 2 is to disallow interest deductions on debt used to finance nondividend distributions (converted equity). The combined effect is that a distribution other than an ordinary dividend is applied first in reduction of newly contributed capital, if any, and then in disqualification of debt, if any; and only the remainder, if any, is subjected to the minimum tax on distributions. For many LBO and acquisition transactions the operative effect would be to disallow interest deductions on debt, but the MTD is essential to assure a uniformity of burden on *all* distributions. The basic effect of the proposals is captured in proposals 1 and 3, or even 1 alone, with 2 serving as an alternative remedy to 1 in cases where debt is available to be treated as converted equity.

There is also a proposal 4, which deals with intercorporate equity investments: a corporate purchase of shares of another corporation would be treated as a nondividend distribution by the purchasing corporation, except in the case of mere portfolio investments, with respect to which the existing deduction for dividends received would be repealed and the investor corporation taxed in full just like any other investor.

have had to make a first relevant determinant of accumulated earnings and profits after years of existence under present law; the experience has not been encouraging.

Moreover, I do not think that the ALI reporter's proposals are quite the same as integration with a lump-sum tax to eliminate windfalls. The proposed deduction for dividends is limited to an interest-like return on the net amount *contributed* to the corporation after the effective date. *Accumulated* equity, even if accumulated out of earnings on newly contributed capital, will not qualify for the deduction. The distinction between contributed and accumulated is at least as important as that between new and old, and makes the distinction between new and old much less important than it might appear since the overwhelming preponderance of existing equity was accumulated rather than contributed and would not qualify for relief even if the proposal had always been in effect. Although many of the effects of the reporter's proposals would be considerably like integration without windfalls, their origin and overall effect is much humbler: simply to let equity contributions be treated henceforth for income tax purposes the way borrowing has been treated all along.

A Corporate Cash-Flow Income Tax

A cash-flow tax on corporate borrowing and investments has many advantages that are well described in Auerbach's paper. His conclusion that such a tax would, however, be unduly *favorable* to corporate equity unless investor taxation is also put on a cash-flow basis appears quite correct. Again, the matter turns on the fact that accumulated earnings, which are the main source of equity capital, already enjoy a substantial advantage in the form of tax deferral for investors. The corporate income tax imposes a burden on simple corporate investments, but that only serves to offset the benefit of deferral at the investor level. When corporate and investor taxes are taken into account, the effective tax rate on investment financed by not paying dividends to taxable investors is already near zero, and cash-flow treatment at the corporate level would turn it negative.

If investor taxes were also put on a cash-flow basis, then there would be no advantage to deferral and the benefits of cash-flow taxation could be enjoyed, without substantial windfalls, throughout the economy.

Distinguishing Debt from Equity in the Junk Bond Era

Jeremy I. Bulow, Lawrence H. Summers and Victoria P. Summers

BECAUSE American tax law permits corporations to deduct interest payments from profits, it creates a bias in favor of debt finance. As long as their bondholders are not heavily taxed, firms have a strong incentive to compensate the suppliers of capital with payments that are labeled as interest rather than dividends. Traditionally, distinguishing debt from equity has arisen as a problem primarily in small, closely held companies, which receive loans from their owners. Until recently the dividing line between debt and equity has seemed relatively clear in the case of large, publicly traded entities.

Recent financial innovation has raised new problems as high-yield securities, which appear to many observers to be "equity in drag," have come into vogue. As an example, consider the $8 billion pay-in-kind (PIK) securities issued in connection with the 1989 RJR Nabisco buyout, to date the largest corporate takeover transaction. These securities require no payment for a number of years, carry yields of as much as 800 basis points above Treasury bill yields, and are senior to only $2 billion of RJR's more than $25 billion capital structure. It is expected that they will wipe out RJR's taxable income for some years to come.

In this paper we consider the implications of recent financial innovations for the taxation of corporate source income. Most discussions of this issue focus on the possible costs of tax-encouraged debt finance. Such discussions presume that there are important differences between debt and equity securities. We argue that, in fact, financial innovation has reduced the difference between the investment characteristics of debt and equity. Firms are now able to issue securities that function very much like equity but are treated as debt for tax purposes. Current law and judicial precedents appear inadequate to counter this trend.

We begin by highlighting the fact that most of the recent increase in corporate indebtedness has been a consequence of restructurings that have made use of high-yield debt. We then argue that much of this debt

represents "equity in drag." Innovation has eroded each of the traditional tests for distinguishing debt and equity. Debt securities that are
effectively junior to equity, that do not require fixed payments, and
that have only a remote chance of being repaid were all issued during
the 1980s. It is only a small exaggeration to say that the principal
criterion now determining the tax status of a security is the name its
issuer gives it.

We then turn to an evaluation of the consequences of the issuance of
equity-like securities that masquerade as debt. Usually such securities are
not used to finance new investment but instead to replace outstanding
equity. Often the objective is to constrain corporate cash flow and reduce
investment. Although the use of high-yield debt to finance new investment
could be defended as leading to greater capital investment in America
through the backdoor integration of the corporate income tax, the use of
high-yield debt to replace equity is more difficult to defend. All the benefits
(except the tax benefits) said to be associated with debt-financed restructurings could be realized through the use of preferred stock. There is clear
evidence that the current American tax system subsidizes corporate restructurings and raises the premiums that acquirers can afford to pay for
corporations.

We argue that the appropriate tax treatment of corporate restructurings
depends on their external consequences. Insofar as they have benefits or
costs that are borne by the transacting parties, there is no reason for tax
subsidies or penalties. An analysis of the available evidence suggests that,
while restructurings may significantly increase economic efficiency, their
external consequences are almost certainly negative. This implies that
there is no case for subsidizing them through the tax system. If proponents'
arguments about their efficiency consequences are correct, they would
take place even without the current tax subsidy.

The paper concludes with an examination of a number of different
policy approaches to corporate restructuring transactions. We find that
corporate tax integration or dividend tax relief would be very expensive
and would confer a large windfall on current shareholders, but that it
would not fully eliminate the subsidy to restructuring transactions. General
limitations on interest deductibility would limit the subsidy to restructurings but would also raise firms' cost of capital and discourage new investment, particularly in intangibles. Our preferred approaches involve
targeted tax penalties for cases where debt is used to replace existing
equity.

Figure 1. The Corporate Debt Burden in Historical Perspective, 1952–90

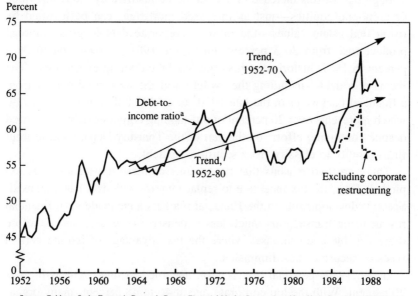

Percent

Source: Goldman Sachs Economic Research Group, *Financial Market Perspectives* (New York, December 1988–January 1989), p. 4.

a. Ratio of outstanding debt of nonfinancial corporations to gross domestic nonfinancial corporate product.

The Blurring of the Debt-Equity Distinction

Financial innovation during the 1980s has been associated with a dramatic increase in corporations' use of debt finance. During 1983–88 nonfinancial companies borrowed 60 percent more than they needed for the traditional uses of capital spending, inventory accumulation, and the acquisition of financial assets, while $420 billion of equity was eliminated through acquisitions, leveraged buyouts (LBOs), and corporate stock repurchases.[1] As figure 1 illustrates, these restructuring transactions account for all of the increase in corporate debt-equity ratios during the 1980s.

From 1984 through 1987 the nonfinancial corporate business sector increased its borrowing by an average of $153 billion a year, and a little over 70 percent of this amount was spent on repurchasing stock through either acquisitions or repurchases. Net payouts to stockholders, including dividends and repurchases but subtracting new equity issues, soared from

1. Goldman Sachs Economic Research Group, "Debt without Disaster." *Financial Market Perspectives* (New York, December 1988–January 1989).

$84 billion in 1983 to $152 billion in 1984 to over $193 billion in 1986.[2] Though part of this increase in debt could be justified by the rising value of corporate equities—just as increased mortgages can be justified by rising real estate values—the ratio of corporate debt to gross national product rose from 30.3 percent during the 1981–82 recession to 36.8 percent in 1987; historically this ratio has fallen during expansions.[3] The increase in debt—including the evolution of the junk bond market from a financial backwater in the late 1970s to a $200 billion market in 1989, which represents over 20 percent of outstanding corporate debt—occurred despite continuing efforts on the part of the Treasury Department to limit firms' ability to classify risky securities as debt.

There are two reasons that the volume of these transactions has exploded. First, the tax incentive to replace equity with debt has increased. Second, developments in the financial markets have made such financial restructuring transactions much less expensive for issuers and therefore more feasible even in cases where the tax advantage of issuing certain types of securities has diminished.

In the 1970s personal tax rates on unearned income went as high as 70 percent. With the top corporate rate at 46 to 48 percent, many organizations found the corporate form to be tax advantaged. Although money held in corporate form would be subject to a "double tax" if ever distributed to stockholders, paying a corporate tax on earnings could be preferable to issuing tax-deductible debt and having bondholders pay a higher tax on interest income.

In recent years there has been no tax incentive to leave income subject to the corporate tax. Although corporate rates did drop to 34 percent in 1986, the top personal rate fell first to 50 percent and then to 28 percent. Furthermore, the rapid growth of tax-exempt institutions such as pension funds caused the average tax rate on interest income to fall to perhaps 11 percent by 1989.[4] Any increase in stakeholders' taxable income that is offset by a dollar-for-dollar reduction in corporate income will reduce the total amount of taxes paid. These tax changes have provided an enormous

2. Joint Committee on Taxation, *Federal Income Tax Aspects of Corporate Financial Structures*, Joint Committee Print, 101 Cong. 1 sess. (Government Printing Office, January 1989).

3. Joint Committee on Taxation, *Corporate Financial Structures*.

4. See Michael J. Graetz, "Statement before the Senate Finance Committee on the Subject of Leveraged Buyouts," January 25, 1989. Only about 5 percent of corporate bonds are held by taxable households, while roughly 40 percent are held by tax-exempt institutions, and the bulk of the remainder is held by institutions such as banks and insurance companies that pay a tax rate of substantially less than the 28 percent personal rate.

incentive for firms to convert their equity into debt, or, more accurately, their taxable corporate profits into tax-deductible interest expenses.

Besides the tax incentives, the development of a large-scale, high-yield bond market has made the issuance of such securities much less expensive. New innovations enabled companies to issue original issue discount (OID) securities that gave borrowers interest deductions without requiring them to make any cash payments for several years. Put bonds, increasing rate notes, and other securities were designed to appeal to more investors. The average high-yield bond issuer was able to borrow well over a dollar for every dollar of tangible assets held.[5]

Historically most of the controversy in defining debt and equity has focused on closely held firms. The reason debt-equity distinctions previously were only a minor problem for publicly traded corporations was that financing was generally split among equity, trade credits, bank loans, and senior debt that had a first claim on some or all of the firm's assets. Some firms did perform badly, and their bonds became "fallen angels," which assumed equity-like features. However, until the late 1970s almost no original issue bonds were issued at yields that implied a high default premium. Almost invariably, all the obligations of a publicly traded corporation that were not denominated as common or preferred stock were low-risk securities that could readily be acknowledged as debt. The development of the junk bond market has made the issue one of the most important in corporate income tax policy, affecting some of the nation's largest corporations.

The Treasury's main potential defense against debt masquerading as equity has been section 385 of the Internal Revenue Code, passed as part of the 1969 Tax Act. Section 385 deferred to the Treasury's expertise, rather than legislatively spelling out the definitive rules for distinguishing debt from equity for tax purposes. But the statute did provide that the regulations were to take into account five factors "among others." Taken from earlier case law developed largely in the context of closely held corporations, these factors were (1) the ratio of debt to equity; (2) subordination to or preference over other obligations of the corporation; (3) the existence of a written unconditional promise to pay a certain sum in money on demand or in return for adequate consideration in money or money's worth, and to pay a fixed rate of interest (the most hallowed formal traits of "true debt"); (4) convertibility into the stock of the cor-

---

5. See Roger Lowenstein, "Junk Gets Junkier, and That May Explain Bond's Current Ills," *Wall Street Journal*, November 3, 1989, p. C1.

poration; and (5) the relationship between holdings of the stock in the corporation and holdings of the interest in question.

The inability of the government to find a practical way of implementing section 385, combined with new developments in "financial engineering" in the 1980s, has allowed firms to issue equity-like securities that make a mockery of the statute's list of factors. We now consider each of these criteria in turn and show why this broad-based approach for determining whether a security should be treated as debt has failed.

Debt-Equity Ratios

In their initial form the section 385 regulations used the debt-equity ratio to classify instruments constituting "straight debt" as equity if the corporation's debt-equity ratio exceeded 10:1, on the theory that a true independent "creditor" would make a loan in such circumstances only infrequently. When proposed, however, this approach led to a great outcry from the public, and the Treasury was flooded by counterexamples detailing the typical capital structures in various industries. In fact, reliance on this single factor was contrary to previous case law, where the ratio test had been used extensively but essentially always in the context of shareholder debt or "hybrid" instruments having on their face certain equity characteristics. This provision was therefore eliminated. Thus in neither case law nor regulation has mere leverage alone been sufficient to support a recharacterization of ostensible debt as equity.

Subordination

Traditionally, debt is considered senior to equity in a firm's capital structure. However, with the maze of holding companies set up in some of the fancier leveraged buyouts, this hierarchy has become less clearly defined.

That was true in the RJR Nabisco transaction in which RJR used a four-tiered capital structure. At the third level, RJR Holdings Group, Inc., the owner of the owner of the shell company (RJR Acquisition Corporation) that was formed to merge with the original RJR Nabisco, Inc., issued about $4.2 billion in "exchangeable" preferred stock. At the fourth level, RJR Holdings Corp., the owner of RJR Holdings Group, issued almost $1.8 billion in pay-in-kind senior converting debentures. Because the preferred stock is one level closer to the actual operating company, it is actually a senior security. Eventually, when RJR became capable of using even more interest deductions, the company converted the preferred stock into still more bonds and merged the top two layers of the holding company hierarchy, thus making the preferred stock pari pasu (equal priority) with the bonds.[6]

The seniority of debt over equity has been futher eroded by the lack of effective covenants in many bonds, combined with the newfound ability of companies to engage in financing schemes that hurt bondholders and that would have been impossible ten years ago. The classic examples of this sort of behavior occur when buyout specialists are able to find ways to make large payments to themselves without paying up the bondholders. Drexel Burnham Lambert, which controlled more than 50 percent of the equity in Rexene, was able to make a $7 per share payout to stockholders, returning more than their original investment to shareholders, only six months before announcing that the firm was on the ropes. Kohlberg Kravis Roberts (KKR) has managed to return to the equity investors in the Beatrice buyout all or most of their original investment, while junk bond holders now find themselves holding the paper of something called the E-II Corporation, which is controlled by Meshulem Riklis, an entrepreneur who through his Rapid American Corporation and other vehicles has been involved in financial fast dealing for over twenty years.[7]

In other examples, KKR refinanced their leveraged buyout of Storer Communications and paid the lucky equity holders $1 billion, while the unfortunate bondholders of the new SCI Communications have been left with paper selling for only a fraction of its face value. Other entrepreneurs, such as Rupert Murdoch and Carl Icahn, have been able to extract large amounts of cash from various companies while still leaving their acquisition debt outstanding. It is hard to see any meaningful way in which the bondholders in these corporations have been treated as ''senior.''

Unconditional Promise to Make Fixed Money Payments

Recent innovations in the high-yield market have circumvented the third factor listed—the promise to make regular cash payouts—the omis-

6. See Salomon Brothers, "RJR Nabisco, Inc.—Superior Returns from an Excellent Credit," New York, April 27, 1989.

7. See Connie Bruck, *The Predators' Ball: The Junk-Bond Raiders and the Man Who Staked Them* (American Lawyer, Simon and Schuster, 1988). Riklis claims to have already had over $1 billion in junk bonds outstanding in 1970, mostly in "Chinese paper" issued in acquisitions.

sion of which would trigger a default. These cash payments are often crucial in retaining a de facto seniority of debt over equity, though as we have just shown, they may not be sufficient to do so.

Pay-in-kind securities give the issuer the option of either paying interest (or dividends, in the case of high-yield preferred) in cash or in additional securities, valued at par. Since these securities almost always trade at a discount from par, particularly those securities issued as "cram down" securities given to old equity holders as part of a buyout, payments will generally be made in new securities.[8] As a result, issuers do not have to either generate the cash necessary to pay "interest" or go to the outside capital markets to provide the funds necessary to finance these payments. One of the major costs of traditional debt finance is thereby eliminated. Also, as some theorists argue, having large interest payment requirements forces managements to operate companies more efficiently, on a shorter leash, and therefore the argument does not apply to PIKs.

In the RJR case roughly $8 billion of the securities issued in the deal are of the PIK variety. Therefore noncash "payments" in 1990 should be well over one billion dollars. Although the RJR deal can in no way be called typical—since its PIK preferred stock when outstanding was larger than the rest of the market combined and its PIK debentures will exceed 70 percent of the market for all other pay-in-kind bonds[9]—this deal does illustrate the basic issues.

In addition to PIKs, companies have issued two other kinds of securities that accrue deductible noncash interest: zero coupon bonds, which pay no interest until maturity but are sold or otherwise issued at a large original issue discount (OID), and split coupon bonds, which are like PIKs in that they pay no (or low) cash interest for several years before developing into conventional junk bonds.

"Zeros" were the first of the tax-favored OID bonds to appear, making their debut in the late 1970s, when the tax law was so beneficial that issuing long-term zeros was profitable even if a company had to give the entire proceeds from its offering to its investment banker. At that time, if a company issued $50 million in zero coupon bonds, due in fifty years, and received, say, nothing in return for the bond, then the company would

8. If the company's credit rating improves, either through strong operating results or through the sale of substantial assets, the PIK securities will often be bought back early. For example, 68 percent of the PIKs issued in 1987 were already retired by April 1989. See Drexel Burnham Lambert, *1989 High Yield Market Report: Financing America's Future* (New York), p. 36.

9. See Michael Quint, "Nabisco Bonds Coming to Market," *New York Times,* May 8, 1989, p. D7.

be allowed $1 million of interest deductions for fifty years. At a 46 percent tax rate and 10 percent discount factor, the company would receive $4.56 million in tax benefits in return for committing to make a repayment with a present value of about $430,000.

Although this loophole has been eliminated and discounts must be amortized geometrically rather than linearly, zeros and other PIK securities still generate large tax advantages for the issuers. Perhaps the largest advantage relates to the tax treatment of debt forgiveness in bankruptcy. If RJR "pays" $3 billion in PIK interest over the next five years and then reorganizes, with the bondholders forgiving $3 billion of debt, then the company will have received more than $1 billion dollars in tax benefits without ever having paid a penny, and bondholders would be able to realize a loss on their securities. In the past it would have been rare for a large company to have had substantial operating profits that would be sheltered in bankruptcy because of debt forgiveness. However, as Michael Jensen has argued, a company involved in an LBO can become a candidate for reorganization even if its value falls by only 20 percent or so, when it could still be earning substantial sums from operations.

Convertibility into the Stock of the Corporation

The Treasury was concerned about convertible bonds that were certain to be exchanged for equity. Obviously, such a security would generate interest deductions while having almost all of the risk characteristics of stock. The section 385 regulations defined "equity features" of an instrument as including only (1) the right to receive at least some contingent payments, and (2) conversion features. The definitional test was whether the fair market value of these features accounted for less than 50 percent of the instrument's fair value. If so, the instrument was classified as debt. Thus the value of the "straight debt payments" would have to account for at least 50 percent of the value of the instrument in order for the instrument to constitute debt.

In response to this test, Goldman Sachs created the adjustable rate convertible note (ARCN), which was quickly adopted by other investment firms. The ARCN was designed to fit exactly within the parameters of the hybrid instrument rules of the final section 385 regulations, which were issued in early 1982. Although those rules were not yet in effect, these aspects of the regulations had not been altered from the initial regulations issued in 1980 and were arguably viewed by the "public" as being reasonably certain.

A typical ARCN was a very short-term convertible bond that would be worth converting as long as the stock did not fall by more than 40 percent over the period. The ARCN paid interest equivalent to the amount of dividends received on a similar investment in stock, with interest payments being adjustable according to changes in the dividend rate. Furthermore, the ARCN was junior to any other debt that the company might choose to issue. The ARCN was intended to meet the test of debt under the rules, but it looked remarkably like equity.

As these instruments began to hit the market, the Treasury in effect threw in the towel on the section 385 regulations. It announced its intention to study ARCNs and then issued Revenue Ruling 83-98, published by the IRS on June 24, 1983, reclassifying ARCNs as equity.[10] In analyzing the classification of the ARCNs, the IRS relied entirely on case law and never even mentioned the section 385 regulations, which were withdrawn, effective as of August 1983.

Relationship between Holdings of Stock and the Security in Question

One of the key distinctions between debt and equity is that debt holders should have interests that diverge from those of equity holders. That is, their sole concern should be that their debt, or as much of it as possible, be paid off. Similarly, if the company defaults on its debt, the bondholders should be concerned with negotiating as good a deal as possible for themselves rather than in maximizing the value of the firm.

Much of the small company litigation over the definition of debt and equity came from cases in which the owners of the firm made proportional loans to the business. Since the owners of the debt and equity were identical, there was no conflict of interest between the classes of claimants, so that de facto the firm would operate in exactly the same way (apart from tax considerations) as if the new debt were called equity. The new technique of "strip financing" has introduced this form of capital structure into some leveraged buyouts.

As described by Jensen, in strip financing risky nonequity securities (including, for example, "mezzanine financing") are held in approxi-

10. Internal Revenue Code, section 163, Rev. Rul. 83-98, 1983-2 C.B. 40, p. 40.

mately equal proportions by all outside equity holders.[11] Top managers and the sponsoring venture capitalists hold disproportionate amounts of equity. The risky securities are sold in "strips," which are "stapled" together so that an investor cannot sell his debt holdings without also selling his equity.

The substantive economic difference between this financing method and an all-equity method, wherein the managers and venture capitalists are given warrants to acquire more equity, is that management is theoretically kept on a shorter leash. That is, various slip-ups will trigger defaults in various levels of the strip financing, giving the holders new rights to intercede into the operation of the organization. However, a more important attribute of strip financing is that it allows tax deductible interest payments to be made (or "PIKed") with a minimum of conflict between debt and equity holders.

Thus the financial "debt" instruments developed in the acquisitions and restructurings of the 1980s violated almost every principle of prior law with respect to the distinction of debt and equity. The attempt to draw this distinction more finely through specific regulations proved an impossible task for the Treasury, since financial innovators found ways to structure around each such test as it was developed. This failure is perhaps unsurprising given that the task of line drawing seeks a metaphysical distinction between forms of ownership which does not actually exist.

Thinking about Debt-Equity Distortions

We have shown that in some recent transactions securities with many of the characteristics of equity were labeled as debt for tax reasons. In this section we examine the distortions in behavior that result from the deductibility of interest in general and the deductibility of interest on equity-like securities in particular. We distinguish the very different issues involved in the use of high-yield debt to finance investments in new capital and to finance corporate restructurings.

At the outset it is useful to consider as a benchmark the case in which taxpayers can freely elect whether a given security is to be treated as debt or as equity. Corporations would then choose a debt-intensive capital structure that would permit them to eliminate all their tax liabilities, and they would use equity securities only to the extent that this would benefit

11. Michael C. Jensen, "Takeovers: Their Causes and Consequences," *Journal of Economic Perspectives*, vol 2 (Winter 1988), pp. 21–48.

corporate owners who could make use of the intercorporate dividend
exclusion, or allow the company to pay dividends as untaxed "return of
capital." Firms would have no incentive to adopt inefficient contracting
structures or to incur additional "bankruptcy" costs for tax reasons. The
principal consequence would be "backdoor" integration, since the corporate tax would effectively be eliminated.

This example and the previous discussion highlight an important point
that is often overlooked. Distortions in behavior depend on the real characteristics of different securities, not on the way in which they are labeled.
It is misleading to speak of tax distortions favoring "debt" over "equity."
If securities that are treated as "debt for tax purposes" are really equity
in drag, then there are legitimate grounds for concern about the erosion
of the tax base, but concerns about bankruptcy costs and the like are
misplaced. Likewise, measures which require that "tax debt" be "real
debt" may increase bankruptcy costs by forcing firms to rearrange their
contracting structures to create conflicts between holders of different securities or to require nondiscretionary cash payments that may act to deter
investment.

The Uses of High-Yield Debt

The ability of corporations to use higher levels of leverage means lower
costs of capital for businesses contemplating new investments. If the
corporate tax is viewed as an undesirable double tax on corporate investment income, then "backdoor integration" through increased indebtedness may actually be a positive development. Indeed, higher levels
of leverage in Japan and other countries are often cited as a reason that
costs of capital are lower abroad than in the United States.[12]

The crucial issue regarding new investment is whether reductions in
effective tax rates that result from increased issuance of debt increase or
decrease the neutrality of the tax system. This question awaits further
study. Recent financial developments have in a sense "democratized"
the tax advantages of debt finance. Whereas previously only entities with
safe cash flows (for example, utilities or companies with heavy real estate

12. George N. Hatsopoulos and Stephen H. Brooks, "The Gap in the Cost of Capital:
Causes, Effects, and Remedies," in Ralph Landau and Dale W. Jorgenson, eds., *Technology and Economic Policy* (Ballinger, 1986), pp. 221–80; and B. Douglas Bernheim
and John B. Shoven, "Taxation and the Cost of Capital: An International Comparison,"
paper presented at the American Council for Capital Formation Conference on The Consumption Tax: A Better Alternative? Washington, D.C., September 1986.

holdings) could reap the tax advantages of very heavily leveraged debt finance, the increasing availability of debt has allowed other industries to obtain similar advantages. Michael Milken makes much of this argument in defending the use of high-yield debt:

> Not one investment-grade company in America is headed or controlled by a black American. . . . And only one investment-grade company, the *Washington Post*, is headed by a woman, Katherine Graham. Many states do not have even one investment-grade company. In some of the most important industries of the future—medical diagnostics, toxic waste disposal, cellular telephones—there is not one investment-grade company. . . . Further, most of these noninvestment-grade companies are not little fly-by-night operations. In 1987, the average noninvestment-grade company that borrowed money had 4,000 employees, had been in business for 36 years and had $1 billion in assets.[13]

As Milken suggests, it is difficult to see why large companies in safe industries should not be permitted to benefit from interest deductions. Limiting the deductibility of interest for all companies issuing high-yield debt would disproportionately increase the cost of capital for start-ups and for companies in risky industries. However, most high-yield bonds are issued for purposes other than financing new investments. According to Drexel Burnham Lambert, in 1988 only 2 percent of new high-yield bonds were issued for internal growth, whereas more than 40 percent of high-yield debt was associated with LBOs; of the remainder, 31 percent was associated with acquisitions, 12 percent with recapitalization, and 15 percent with general refinancing. It appears that an even higher fraction of PIK and increasing rate note (IRN) securities are associated with restructurings rather than with internal growth.[14]

Debt-financed restructuring clearly involves different issues from debt-financed new capital investments. Arguments that lower costs of capital caused by the use of debt will spur investment cannot be used to defend any tax revenue losses associated with restructuring transactions. Indeed, proponents of these transactions normally cite investment cutbacks as one of their important virtues. Thus Michael Jensen writes: ''Debt creation *without retention of the proceeds of the issue* helps limit the waste of free

13. "History Is Bunk, The Future Is Junk," Interview with Michael Milken, *New Perspectives Quarterly*, vol. 6 (Fall 1989), p. 14.

14. See Drexel Burnham Lambert, *1989 High Yield Market Report*, p. 20, fig. 2.4, and appendixes F and G.

cash flow by compelling managers to pay out funds they would otherwise retain. Debt is . . . a mechanism to force managers to disgorge cash rather than spend it on empire-building projects with low or negative returns.''[15]

The Use of Debt in
Corporate Restructurings

Traditionally, economists have argued that debt finance is tax favored because corporate interest payments are tax deductible whereas dividend payments are not deductible. It is more accurate to say that firms have an incentive to attribute a large fraction of their taxable income to the holders of debt securities. This incentive is especially strong for debt owners in the zero tax bracket. Because taxable and economic income may differ in the case of risky bonds, these securities may be particularly attractive as tax-reduction vehicles. This situation creates an extra bias in favor of issuing high-yield securities whose stated interest rate is such that they are expected to suffer capital losses to balance their extra yield.[16]

The view that debt in general and high-yield debt in particular is tax favored has led most experts to conclude that the tax system subsidizes leveraged buyouts. The subsidy may be quite substantial as is illustrated by the case of the recent RJR-Nabisco deal.

In that record buyout, shareholders, managers, and investment bankers were paid roughly $19.3 billion in cash and were given $1.8 billion in converting debentures (as well as $4 billion in PIK preferred stock). In addition, Kohlberg Kravis Roberts injected $1.5 billion of equity into the deal. Total indebtedness of the firm thus increased by roughly $20 billion. At an average interest rate of 13 percent, this amount of new debt should be sufficient to entirely eliminate RJR's tax bill for the next several years.

The financial projections made by KKR and Drexel Burnham confirm the expectation of low future income taxes, even if the buyout is as profitable as the principals hope.[17] Projections indicate expected earnings before interest and taxes of $3.4 billion in both 1989 and 1990, and $3.7 billion in 1991. However, current income taxes (that is, income taxes net

15. Michael C. Jensen, "Eclipse of the Public Corporation," *Harvard Business Review*, vol. 67 (September–October 1989), p. 67.

16. The argument here parallels discussions of discount securities.

17. Drexel Burnham Lambert, "Private Placement Memorandum" for $3,000,000,000 of First and Second Subordinated Increasing Rate Notes, December 1988, and Supplement, January 1989.

of "deferred taxes") were projected to be *negative* $48 million in 1989 and (positive) $73 million in 1990. However, the early conversion of RJR's PIK preferred into bonds has generated additional tax deductions, so taxes may be negative in 1990 as well.

Note that the sale of some of RJR's assets to other firms, combined with the retirement of bank debt, does not alter the economics of the transaction. Unless the acquirer issued new equity to finance its acquisition of KKR assets, the purchase would not alter the net financial liabilities of the corporate sector or the aggregate corporate tax burden. In fact, one can argue that because the cash and noncash interest payments of the "new" RJR will drain much more equity from the company than the dividend payments made in the past, the equity base of the assets represented by RJR will continue to fall, and debt will continue to rise, unless either RJR or the acquirers of its assets issue enough equity annually to finance the increase in the company's cash payout burden plus the increase in debt incurred through "paying" PIK interest.

Hayne Leland has estimated that 80 percent of the premium paid in the RJR deal can be explained by interest deductions and that other tax savings and transfers from bondholders bring the total fraction of the premium explainable without any efficiency gains to almost 90 percent.[18]

True, KKR has made some real changes at RJR. Their projections include a reduction in corporate overhead from $153 million per year to $75 million. They have eliminated the much-maligned Premier smokeless cigarette, taking a large write-down, and have stopped overstocking cigarette retailers (which incidentally will also save the company some taxes). But these savings are small when compared with the eleven-figure premium that was paid for the company.

This argument that the tax system subsidizes LBO transactions has recently been challenged by opponents of tax reforms to limit interest deductions. In a widely cited study, Michael Jensen, Steven Kaplan, and Laura Stiglin argue that LBOs actually benefit the Treasury.[19] They cite five sources of revenue gains to the Treasury from LBOs: capital gains taxes paid by bought-out shareholders, corporate taxes paid on increases in operating income, taxes on LBO creditors, taxes paid because of the more efficient use of capital, and capital gains taxes on the sale of LBO assets.

18. Hayne E. Leland, "LBOs and Taxes: No One to Blame but Ourselves?" Finance Working Paper 185 (University of California, Berkeley, School of Business, May 1989).

19. Michael C. Jensen, Steven Kaplan, and Laura Stiglin, "Effects of LBO's on Tax Revenues of the U.S. Treasury," *Tax Notes*, February 6, 1989, pp. 727–33.

Table 1. The Revenue Implications of Marginal and Average Leveraged Buyouts
Dollars unless otherwise specified

Item	Average LBO	Marginal LBO
Critical values		
Prebuyout market value of equity	360	360
Buyout purchase price	500	360
Tax basis of prebuyout shareholders	290	290
Postbuyout value of equity	750	360
Percent increase in operation profits	25	0
Percent reduction in capital investment	20	0
Postbuyout debt fraction (percent)	86	86
Present values of Treasury revenues		
Revenue gains		
Capital gains taxes	54.2	13.7
Taxes on increased operating income	85.0	0.0
Taxes on LBO creditors' income	40.8	31.6
Taxes on increased capital efficiency	29.9	0.0
Taxes on sales of assets	17.0	0.0
Total incremental revenues	226.9	45.3
Revenue losses		
Tax deductibility of interest payments	−81.6	−63.2
Taxes on forgone dividend payments	−35.3	−35.3
Total incremental losses	−116.9	−98.5
Net incremental revenues to Treasury	110.0	−53.2
Ratio of gains to losses	1.9	n.m.

Source: Calculations for the average LBO are taken from Michael C. Jensen, Steven N. Kaplan, and Laura Stiglin, "Effects of LBOs on Tax Revenues of the U.S. Treasury," *Tax Notes*, February 6, 1989. Marginal LBO calculations follow those of this study, adjusted for the different transaction.
   n.m. Not measured.

The first column of table 1 presents their analysis of the tax consequences of an average LBO. Following Kaplan's work, they assume that the standard LBO occurs at a substantial premium and produces substantial increases in operating income. Given these suppositions, they predict increases in government tax collections. Making similarly optimistic assumptions about LBO effects on operating income, they also conclude that the RJR-Nabisco deal was a boon to the Treasury.

As we will discuss, their premise that operating income increases following LBOs are entirely attributable to efficiency gains is questionable. There is, however, a more fundamental difficulty with their analysis. Jensen, Kaplan, and Stiglin's conclusions are relevant to the question of what the revenue effect of a law that abolished LBOs would be. But they are not germane to the question whether the tax system subsidizes LBOs as that question is usually understood. It would not be appropriate to conclude that real estate was not tax subsidized just because positive taxes are collected on profitable real estate investments. Likewise, the right question about tax subsidies to LBOs is whether the tax system tips the balance in favor of an LBO that would otherwise be marginally profitable.

This question is examined in the right-hand column of table 1, which assesses the tax consequences of an LBO that had no effects on operating income or capital investment decisions. Such a marginal LBO would in fact reduce the Treasury's tax collections. The value of increased interest deductions exceeds the capital gains taxes paid by bought-out shareholders. It follows that LBOs are tax subsidized—LBO transactions that would otherwise not be profitable become profitable because of tax considerations. This conclusion is entirely consistent with Jensen, Kaplan, and Stiglin's claim that total tax collections on profitable LBOs are positive.

So far we have focused on LBO transactions as a whole. Regardless of whether the tax system encourages more LBO transactions to take place, there would seem to be little doubt that they encourage the use of more debt in the transactions that do take place. This reduces corporate tax collections, and unless marginal debt produces marginal increases in operating efficiency, it reduces total tax collections as well.

In conclusion, it seems clear that current tax rules permitting the deduction of corporate interest and prohibiting a deduction for dividends can be said to subsidize LBOs in three senses. First, tax payments by restructured companies are lower than they would be without interest deductibility. There is no evidence that the government recoups these losses in the form of extra capital gains collections. Second, leveraged transactions that would break even in the absence of tax considerations become profitable when taxes are taken into account. Third, the incentive to use debt in structuring a given transaction is increased.

The Role of Debt in
Corporate Restructurings

Proponents of LBOs, notably Michael Jensen, cite four primary benefits of the LBO form of organization over the traditional corporate form.[20] Similar benefits are said to come from restructurings in which firms' leverage is increased but no buyout takes place. First, LBOs typically limit free cash flow by requiring that cash payments of interest be made. Second, LBOs force midcourse corrections more quickly than traditional forms of organization because as soon as trouble arises, companies can

20. Jensen, "Eclipse of the Public Corporation," pp. 61–74.

no longer meet their interest obligations and are forced to negotiate with their creditors. Third, LBO managers usually have a significant equity stake in the companies they manage, thus increasing their incentive to manage effectively. Fourth, LBOs facilitate close monitoring of managers by concentrating equity ownership.

Do these efficiency improvements require the use of debt in general and exotic financial instruments like those described above in particular? It is difficult to see why. Preferred stock that includes in its terms provisions requiring voting control to shift to the preferred stockholders if a dividend is missed would limit managers' access to free cash flow to the same extent that debt obligations do, with respect to corporate control issues. Indeed, preferred stock would bring more near-term financial pressure to bear on management than would PIK bonds or other debt securities which have streams of payments that increase over time but require little or no current and near-term cash payments. Examples of firms that have used preferred stock in this way are Rupert Murdoch's News Corp. and Ted Turner's TBS (in its acquisition of the MGM film library). The principal difference between the use of preferred stock and bonds is that interest payments reduce corporate tax liabilities, whereas preferred stock dividends do not. Note, however, that from the point of view of economic efficiency, if free cash flow is typically wasted, then a tax on it is not likely to be distortionary and may even increase economic efficiency.

Nor would the compensation of top management on a performance-based contract seem to require the use of high levels of leverage. In the instances cited by Jensen, top management typically does not hold more than a small fraction of the company's equity. In unleveraged companies there would be no difficulty in writing a contract making executive compensation a function of stock price in a manner that would have the same incentive effects as the contracts used following restructuring transactions. Indeed, in a number of cases (for example, Disney and United Airlines) executives in companies with relatively low levels of debt have profited handsomely when their companies have succeeded. Stephen Ross of Warner negotiated a contract that earned him more than $100 million in the Time-Warner merger.

The final argument for the use of large amounts of leverage is that by concentrating ownership, it facilitates the monitoring of managers. Again, it would seem that the same objective could be achieved by using preferred stock. Holding companies could also be used to pressure managers. British-based Hanson Trust has attained LBO-like returns for its shareholders by buying and selling firms and maintaining a lean corporate staff without accumulating colossal leverage. Indeed, the original rationale offered for conglomerates in the 1960s was that an active corporate staff would ensure that free cash flow was not wasted. In 1969 Harold Geneen, then chief executive officer of International Telephone and Telegraph, offered many of the same defenses for conglomerates that are offered for LBOs today:

> [Our] management group makes [it] possible [for us] to contribute innovation and new levels of competition to the companies that have joined us. . . . *The conglomerate is one of the most efficient and effective forms we have developed.* . . . The sales per employee of these companies that have joined us have increased 10–15 percent a year . . . about three times as fast as the national average. . . . Diversified companies such as ITT, by continually meeting the changing markets' needs as the primary basis of selecting their areas of business activity, maximize the efficient use of scarce resources of the economy.[21]

The point here is not to defend conglomerates but only to observe that keeping a close eye on operating managers does not require the use of large amounts of debt. To the extent that efficiency gains are achievable through restructuring, they can be achieved without increased reliance on debt finance.

The Private and Social Consequences of Debt-Based Corporate Restructurings

Thus far we have argued that corporate restructurings are subsidized by current tax rules favoring debt over equity finance, and that debt finance is in no way necessary to realize the real economic benefits of corporate restructurings. Here we examine whether there is a rationale for tax subsidies for restructuring, or whether an ideal tax system would penalize them. This calculation does not depend on their overall efficiency consequences. Rather, it depends on their external consequences for those who are not parties to LBO transactions. Insofar as there are private benefits to restructurings, these benefits will not be realized without government intervention. It is only the consequences of LBOs for third parties that warrant any public action.

21. Harold S. Geneen, "Diversification: The Road to World Competition," *Vital Speeches*, vol. 36 (December 15, 1969), pp. 148, 149.

Without a doubt LBO transactions have historically been beneficial for those who have engaged in them on both the buying and the selling sides. Perhaps the most thorough study of management buyouts (a subset of LBOs) concludes that the seventy-six MBOs of greater than $50 million in equity value that took place between 1980 and 1986 increased the initial value of the company by about 37 percent.[22] The forty-eight MBOs that subsequently went public again produced a total return to investors of 50 percent relative to a market portfolio with equal risk, and produced a 25 percent increase in operating profits and an 80 percent increase in cash flow, when adjusted for industry and business cycle trends.

Even aside from any bias created by looking only at the ex post returns on firms that did well enough to return to the public markets, we are somewhat skeptical about the relevance of these statistics to recent transactions. First, the number of transactions for which there are any long-term data is quite small. The mean company in Kaplan's data set was bought out for $524 million in equity, implying a total value for the forty-eight firms that returned to the public market of about one RJR. The 50 percent premium earned on these investments must be contrasted, for example, with the $32 billion loss that junk bond holders suffered relative to Treasury bond holders during the first eleven months of 1989.[23]

Second, the Tax Reform Act of 1986 repealed the general utilities doctrine, substantially reducing the tax advantage available in mergers. Firms were no longer able to reap huge increases in depreciation allowances without having sellers incur sizable capital gains taxes. The implication is that transactions completed before 1987 were sufficiently tax favored to look profitable even without any real efficiencies or increased leverage.

Third, the reason for the profitability of LBO investments in the middle to late 1980s may have as much to do with securities mispricing as with improved management. Although Kohlberg Kravis Roberts and other top LBO investors have done well, they have not significantly outperformed the top "value investors" who play no role in management but invest according to similar criteria as the buyout specialists. The portfolios of

22. Steven N. Kaplan, "Sources of Value in Management Buyouts," Ph.D. dissertation, Harvard University, 1988.

23. Drexel Burnham Lambert estimated the size of the junk bond market as of the beginning of 1989 to be $183 billion (*1989 High Yield Market Report*). *Business Week* reported that the total returns on junk bonds for the first eleven months of the year came to 1.1 percent (interest received less capital losses) against 19 percent for Shearson's Treasury bond index. Leah J. Nathans, "Junk Bonds Are Climbing Out of the Grave," *Business Week*, December 25, 1989, p. 134.

stocks managed by top "value investors" such as Warren Buffet, Mario Gabelli, and Michael Price have yielded excess returns comparable to those produced by the top buyout specialists. As for MBOs, it is also possible that managements may have had inside information that their firms were good values. In addition, the decline of the junk bond market in 1989 indicates that those securities may have been overpriced during the period of Jensen, Kaplan, and Stiglin's study, thus inflating returns.

Junk bonds have historically outperformed securities of equivalent risk, yet the original issue high-yield debt of the late 1980s may be much riskier than the "fallen angels" of old. Whereas the old high-yield bonds that were originally issued as senior obligations had a good chance of being substantially repaid even if the firm's value fell by half, today's junk debt is often junior to bank debt and senior bonds representing 60 or 70 percent of the firm's capitalization, as in the case of RJR. As bondholders in Integrated Resources, Resorts International, SCI, Seaman Furniture, Southmark, and Western Union have discovered, owners of original-issue junk can end up with very little in a corporate reorganization.

The yield premiums that original-issue junk requires are influenced not just by the probability of default (which is a function of the firm's total debt load, though not of the seniority structure of that debt), but also by the amount of debt that is senior to it and its PIK characteristics. Holders of junior debt that receives current interest will at least have received something if a firm defaults several years after the securities are issued. PIK debt holders may end up with nothing. A recent study by Barrie Wigmore, a limited partner in Goldman Sachs, indicated that for the average junk bond issuer in 1980 total debt amounted to 60 percent of tangible assets, but by 1988 this figure had grown to 202 percent, and that earnings before interest and taxes had fallen from 1.99 times interest expense (despite the 1980s' record high interest rates) to 71 percent of interest, including PIK interest.[24] It may be that the market has finally begun to recognize the reduced quality of junk in the high-yield market collapse of 1989.

But this point is subsidiary. The crucial issue is whether there are external consequences to third parties that are not captured by the parties to LBO transactions. This in turn depends critically on the source of the dramatic increase in value created during LBO transactions. There are three possibilities. The first, stressed by Michael Jensen and other proponents of restructurings, is that these transactions increase efficiency and

24. See Lowenstein, "Junk Gets Junkier."

that the increases in asset values that accompany them simply capitalize the value of these increases. Consider the case in which a competitive firm discovers a way of reducing its costs. Assuming it remains small relative to the entire market, it captures the full value of its innovation as its costs decline and the market price remains constant. If a firm with market power reduces its costs, it may reduce its prices as well, creating a benefit for consumers. Thus there is some possible external benefit to increased efficiency. However, this gain is of the second order. Evidence that efficiency increases may play some role in restructurings comes from reports that restructurings usually involve reductions in the size of firms' headquarters staff and the curtailment of some wasteful investment projects.

A second possibility, stressed by Shleifer and Summers as well as by many opponents of corporate takeover activity, is that increases in shareholder value may come at the expense of corporate stakeholders. If, for example, increases in leverage lead firms to lay off employees who go on to suffer wage losses, or to reduce the wages of persons who remain employed, or to drive a harder bargain with suppliers, or to charge higher prices to consumers, they will create value by forcing transfers. In that case, third parties will be made worse off by takeovers. Is this hypothesis consistent with the evidence? Shleifer and Summers offer several examples in which wages were reduced after takeovers. Bronars and Deere find empirical evidence that increases in debt levels are helpful in forestalling union wage increases. It has also been reported that restructurings have sometimes been followed by dramatic increases in prices that burden consumers.[25]

A third possibility is that the apparent value created in hostile takeovers reflects market misvaluations. This kind of value creation may take several forms. For instance, companies may be restructured because they are undervalued. A natural example here is closed-end mutual funds, organizations whose only asset is a portfolio of readily marketable stocks. Such companies would be expected to consistently sell for the value of their assets. Yet closed-end funds normally sell at a fluctuating discount of up to 25 percent of their value. Purchasing and liquidating undervalued assets is obviously profitable. But it has only second-order effects on

25. See Andrei Shleifer and Lawrence Summers, "Breach of Trust in Hostile Takeovers," in Alan J. Auerbach, ed., *Corporate Takeovers* (University of Chicago Press, 1988), pp. 157–83; Stuart Flack, "Who's Really Picking Up the Tab?" *Forbes*, October 30, 1989, pp. 38–39; and Stephen G. Bronars and Donald R. Deere, "The Threat of Unionization, the Use of Debt, and the Preservation of Shareholder Wealth," Texas A&M University, Department of Economics, January 1990.

social welfare, the sign of which is not obvious. Suppose all the closed-end funds were liquidated tomorrow. The result would probably be an increase in the perceived wealth of consumers, which would lead to increased consumption and reduced saving. The same is true of increases in asset values from restructuring transactions. A related possibility is that some of the value in restructuring transactions reflects the ability to market debt at excessively high prices. Selling overvalued debt increases equity values. As Michael Milken put it: "In the early 1980s, when stock valuations were low, it was better to put debt in one's capital structure. In 1989, equity is a better deal."[26] This suggests an important role for market misvaluations in determining capital structure.

Another example of value creation through misvaluation effects concerns subsequent acquisitions. In advocating restructuring transactions, Jensen stresses the danger that firms with excess cash flow will overpay for acquisition targets and harm the acquirer's shareholders. If correct, this argument does not imply a first-order social gain from curbs on restructurings. Rather, restructuring may prevent an excessively large transfer to the owners of acquired companies. Unless it changes acquisition patterns, it will have no effect at all on economic efficiency. Even if it does change acquisition patterns, the social gain will be overstated by the total volume of excessive payments prevented, since much of the overpayment represents a transfer.

A final example comes in the case of "breakup" restructurings in which companies spin off a number of different divisions to willing buyers at premium prices. In buying a company "wholesale" and selling it "retail," LBO firms are providing the same sort of benefit to the economy, though on a grander scale, as the real estate investors of ten years ago who bought up rental buildings and converted the apartments into condominiums for resale. Insofar as companies overpay for individual divisions because of a misplaced faith in synergy arguments, breakup transactions will create value for shareholders at the expense of those who subsequently overpay. It is ironic that proponents of LBO transactions often decry the waste of free cash flow on poor acquisitions and then cite the marketing of divisions to acquiring companies as a major efficiency advantage. A good example is Ford's $2.5 billion acquisition of Jaguar. Jensen specifies Ford as an example of a firm that was dissipating its free cash flow by wasting it on acquisitions and other projects instead of turning it over to shareholders.[27]

26. "History Is Bunk," Interview with Milken, p. 17.
27. Jensen, "Eclipse of the Public Corporation," p. 66.

Table 2. RJR's Declining Net Investment
Millions of dollars

Year	Sales	Gross investment	Depreciation	Net investment
1984	8,200	642	191	451
1985	11,622	946	354	592
1986	15,102	1,022	605	417
1987	15,766	936	652	284
1988	16,635	1,176	708	468
1989	18,136	1,179	644	535
1990	13,309	561	510	51
1991	14,359	486	528	− 42
1992	15,382	447	531	− 84
1993	16,484	445	527	− 82

Source: For 1984–88, Drexel Burnham Lambert, "Private Placement Memorandum" for $3,000,000,000 of First and Second Subordinated Increasing Rate Notes, December 1988, p. 10; for 1989–93, Drexel Burnham Lambert, "Private Placement Memorandum," Supplement, January 1989, pp. 5–6.

Yet if an LBO firm had bought Jaguar and then resold it to Ford at the current high price, the gain would be considered an example of the efficiency gains possible from buyouts.

There are several additional channels through which LBOs may have negative external consequences. First, they reduce at least some forms of investment activity. Kaplan reports that the typical firm in his sample of LBOs reduced its gross investment by 20 percent following the buyout.[28] Although he does not present figures, this means a reduction of more than 50 percent in net investment. Even if these reductions in investment raise shareholder value, they are probably socially inefficient given the wedge taxes drive between the social and private returns to capital. In the presence of substantial capital income taxes, private "mistakes" that lead to excessive investment are likely to be welfare enhancing rather than welfare reducing.

Again it is instructive to consider the projections of RJR Nabisco. As table 2 shows, net investment is projected to fall from an average of $458 million in 1984–89 to an average of negative $39 million in 1990–93. As regards the cigarette business, society probably gains from these cuts in investment. But, more generally, investment usually generates positive external consequences.

Second, there is some evidence that LBOs reduce spending on research and development. Although the finding is challenged by many LBO proponents, a recent National Science Foundation study concluded, "Of the 200 companies that together account for almost 90 percent of total industrial R&D funds, 16 large R&D performers were identified as recent mergers and an additional eight firms were involved in LBOs or other

28. Kaplan, "Sources of Value in Management Buyouts."

restructurings. The 24 companies had a combined 5.3 percent reduction in R&D spending in current dollars between 1986 and 1987. In contrast, all other R&D–performing companies reported a 5.4 percent increase in their R&D expenditures during that period."[29] Insofar as R&D generates external benefits, these reductions have private benefits that exceed their social benefits.

Third, as Shleifer and Summers argue, there are "reputational externalities" associated with the breaches of implicit contracts that go on in many restructuring transactions. If, because of the possibility of restructuring, it becomes more difficult for firms to enter into long-term implicit contracts with workers or suppliers, efficiency will be reduced. For example, it may be difficult to get suppliers to make relationship-specific investments if restructuring is an ever-present possibility.

Fourth, there are the risks stressed by Henry Kaufman, Benjamin Friedman, and others who maintain that increases in corporate indebtedness reduce financial stability and run the risk of either exacerbating the next recession or forcing monetary policy to be excessively expansionary. If valid, these concerns would represent an external cost of the use of leverage. Because leverage levels are much higher in foreign countries than in the United States, and because financial innovation has probably reduced the costs of the renegotiations associated with bankruptcy, we are somewhat skeptical of the importance of these costs.

Against these considerations, one must weigh the positive external consequences of the use of high levels of leverage to restructure companies. These seem more difficult to identify, but they might include the long-term benefits to workers and consumers of better management if increases in efficiency are not captured by shareholders. Insofar as financial innovators are not able to capture the full benefit of their innovation because of emulation, there might be some positive external consequences associated with financial innovation.

It seems very unlikely that the external benefits of LBOs are nearly as large as their external costs. Regardless of whether they are desirable on the whole, this imbalance suggests that the laissez-faire outcome will involve more use of leverage to control free cash flow than is socially desirable. Put differently, there are marginal transactions that are privately profitable but socially undesirable. Current tax provisions that encourage the use of debt only serve to exacerbate this distortion.

---

29. National Science Foundation, "Corporate Mergers Implicated in Slowed Industrial R&D Spending," Washington, March 1989.

What Should Be Done?

The analysis so far has established four propositions. First, the rise of the junk bond market and associated financial innovations largely accounts for increases in corporate debt-equity ratios during the 1980s. Second, the tax law as it is currently enforced makes it relatively easy for firms to issue debt securities that function as "equity in drag." Large-scale replacement of equity by securities labeled as debt during the 1980s reflects not only an increase in the tax incentives for the use of debt but also the institutional innovations that make it possible for corporations to capture the tax benefits associated with using debt without accepting the costs traditionally associated with excessive indebtedness. Third, recently junk bonds have largely been used to replace corporate equity rather than to finance new investment. Fourth, although the government heavily subsidizes restructuring transactions because of current tax laws, these transactions would take place even in the absence of tax subsidies if the arguments of their proponents are correct. The external consequences of restructuring transactions are almost certainly negative, so there is no case for subsidizing them through the tax system.

These conclusions suggest that a strong case exists for policy measures that would eliminate the current tax subsidy to the use of high-yield debt in corporate restructuring activity if this could be accomplished without excessive collateral costs. Tax reform strategies directed at this objective can generally be divided according to two criteria. First, some approaches rely on the carrot of dividend deductibility to reduce the tax bias in favor of debt finance,while others rely on the stick of interest nondeductibility in some situations. Second, some approaches involve radical reform of the corporate tax system; others involve much more limited changes in current tax rules. We begin this section by describing our reasons for preferring an approach that narrowly limits interest deductibility. Then we describe and evaluate the reforms enacted in 1989 that move in this direction. Finally, we suggest some directions for future policy changes.

Carrots versus Sticks

It is often suggested that some form of dividend tax relief or corporate tax integration is the appropriate way to reduce or eliminate the current tax bias in favor of debt finance. West Germany, France, Japan, and the United Kingdom all provide some form of relief from the double taxation of dividends, either through a shareholder tax credit for corporate taxes paid on dividend income (France and the United Kingdom) or through partial deductibility of dividends (Japan and West Germany). The argument is made that relief from the double taxation of dividends would cause firms to substitute equity for debt finance and would also encourage investment by reducing firms' cost of capital.

Although corporate tax integration may have some advantages, we have suggested that it is not an appropriate response to the problem posed by corporate restructuring transactions. First, large-scale dividend relief would permit on a large scale what restructurings have already permitted on a small scale—the tax-favored distribution of profits on past investments. The case for conferring such a windfall on corporate shareholders at the present time is especially weak. Most of the corporate capital now in place was encouraged by highly accelerated corporate tax deductions taken at the 46 percent, not the current 34 percent, corporate tax rate. To allow full dividend deductibility would be exactly equivalent to permitting firms to replace all their current stock with discretionary, income-related, coupon bonds.

Second, integration would do very little to encourage new investment. Just as high-yield debt often serves to discourage investment by limiting the cash flows that managers can use at their discretion, integration would put more pressure on managers to pay out profits as cash dividends. As with high-yield debt, the windfall gains conferred by integration would serve to increase the demand for consumption goods and push up real interest rates and costs of capital. Since start-up, high-technology, and other fast-growing companies rarely pay out a large fraction of their profits in dividends, integration most benefits the least dynamic parts of the economy.

Third, it is questionable whether dividend deductibility would have as large an effect on corporate debt equity ratios as is often supposed. Only through the use of zero coupon or PIK bonds is it possible for firms to receive tax benefits without disbursing cash. In addition, unless dividend relief was given on dividends paid to tax-exempt shareholders, firms would still have a tax reason for preferring debt to equity. And most important, dividend deductibility is far more likely to affect the choice between share repurchases and dividends than the choice between debt and equity. If the presence of a share repurchase option means that firms can now return existing equity to shareholders in the future on favorable tax terms, their incentive to prepay the shareholder tax by replacing existing equity with debt is limited.[30] Despite the absence of dividend tax relief, and the full (if deferred) taxation of capital gains, American firms rely less on debt finance than do those in most other countries.

Depending on just what option was selected, corporate tax integration could cost the Treasury as much as $40 billion. Since this figure dwarfs any estimate of the Treasury's loss from current financial manipulations, and since it is far from clear that integration would have a significant positive effect on investment or a negative effect on indebtedness, integration does not seem to be a cost-effective solution to the problems posed by recent financial innovation.

Some have suggested that the tax system be integrated prospectively by permitting dividend deductibility only for new equity issues. Over the short run this proposal would be quite inexpensive for the Treasury. In the relatively rare cases in which high-yield bonds are now issued to finance new investments, this reform might encourage the use of equity rather than debt finance. But it is not clear in these instances whether there is much cost associated with the use of high-yield debt. In the more common restructuring case, where high-yield debt is used to finance equity repurchases, it is unlikely that more favorable treatment of new equity issues would have any effect at all.

On balance, apparently the only tax carrots that would reduce debt-financed restructuring activity would be extremely expensive and might well fail to limit the adverse consequences now associated with restructuring activities. We turn therefore to the possible use of "tax sticks," which limit in some way the deductibility of interest.

How Should Interest Deductions Be Limited?

Given budgetary realities, tax measures that simultaneously correct distortions and raise revenue are attractive policy options. Many proposals have been put forward to limit the deductibility of corporate interest. They range from disallowing a constant fraction of interest deductions, to limiting the share of operating profits that could be paid out as interest, to limiting the yield securities could carry and still be treated as debt, to enacting measures that would look to the purpose for which debt was incurred in determining whether the resulting interest was deductible.

30. This point is developed in Alan J. Auerbach, "Tax Policy and Corporate Borrowing," forthcoming in Federal Reserve Bank of Boston conference volume, *Are the Distinctions between Corporate Debt and Equity Disappearing?*

Any limit on interest deductibility would serve to discourage the restructuring transactions that have accounted for most of the increases in corporate debt ratios during the 1980s. A crucial question then becomes whether some general reform is desirable, or whether it would be better to focus on reforms directed at the financial innovations associated with restructuring transactions. General restrictions are difficult to defend on any principle as long as some kind of debt-equity distinction is maintained. Furthermore, as we discussed earlier, most of the increase in corporate debt-equity ratios during the 1980s resulted from restructuring transactions; and so general restrictions on interest deductibility may not be necessary to address recent financial innovations. Finally, such general restrictions have the defect of raising the cost of funds and therefore the cost of capital for firms undertaking new investments. The widespread concerns about the myopia of American business and about relatively high American costs of capital make this a serious problem.

Many have suggested that reductions in the corporate tax rate could offset any adverse effect that limits on interest deductibility might have on investment- or business-planning horizons more generally. This suggestion is not correct for two reasons. First, reductions in the corporate rate would do nothing to encourage intangible investments in R&D, worker training, or marketing because these investments are currently written off in the year in which they are made. With the tax authority sharing equally in their costs and their fruits, changes in the tax rate do not affect the incentive to undertake them. In fact, because these investments carry a negative effective tax rate to the extent that they are debt financed, reductions in the corporate rate would actually reduce the incentive to undertake them. Second, reductions in the corporate rate would primarily benefit old capital rather than encourage new investment. Therefore reductions in the corporate tax rate that offset the revenue gains associated with limits on interest deductibility would be associated with increases in capital costs.

The 1989 Act and Beyond

These concerns and the current political reality call for considerations of specific reforms targeted at restructuring transactions. Such an approach was taken by Congress in the Revenue Reconciliation Act of 1989. Rather than seek to resolve the metaphysical question of what constitutes debt, the act tries to eliminate some of the subsidy element in restructuring transactions. It also breaks new ground by permitting individual securities to be treated partly as debt and partly as equity.

The most important provision of the act was a change in the tax treatment of "high-yield original issue discount obligations" with an initial maturity of five years or more. Almost without exception, these obligations are issued in connection with restructuring transactions. The approach taken in the act bifurcates such instruments; it treats a part of what is labeled "interest" as interest and the rest, the yield in excess of the applicable federal rate of interest plus six points, as distributions with respect to preferred stock. No deductions are permitted from the "interest" portion of the yield until cash interest payments are actually made. This eliminates the advantage of PIK and other OID instruments, where under current law interest is deductible even when it is not currently payable.

In addition, the act precludes deductions from "corporate equity reduction transactions" from being carried back as net operating losses and offset against previous years' income. It also limits the ability of firms to deduct "interest" paid to nontaxable foreign-related parties, thereby curbing U.S. tax avoidance by foreign-owned firms. Finally, the act instructs the Treasury to attempt yet again to write regulations providing tax definitions for debt and equity. This time the Treasury is explicitly authorized to treat single instruments as part debt and part equity, the approach taken by the act in an effort to curb the use of high-yield original-issue discount obligations.

These steps will certainly reduce the tax subsidy to corporate restructuring transactions. However, a considerable subsidy element remains. PIK securities that have maturities of less than five years are not covered by the act, and very high yield securities that do not have original issue discount elements are also neglected. Although restructuring activity has subsided for the moment because of adverse developments in the junk bond market, there is still an argument for further restrictions on restructuring transactions.

At least two strategies appear viable. The first would disallow interest deductions for debt incurred or continued for the purpose of repurchasing equity. This would involve difficult tracing problems. Firms that purchased either their own equity or equity in other firms would lose the deductibility of interest on a corresponding amount of debt. Special provisions would be needed to handle cases in which firms first repurchased shares and then took on debt. A reform of this kind would eliminate firms' tax incentive to replace equity with debt. At the same time, it would not have any effect at all on firms' incentive to invest in new capital.

A second strategy, suggested by William Andrews and an American Law Institute working group, would tax all corporate "nondividend" distributions to shareholders as if they were dividends.[31] Thus transactions removing assets from corporate solution, which are currently treated at least in part as a return of capital, would be subject to tax on the full amount. That could be accomplished by a tax on shareholders or, more plausibly, by a corporate tax at the 28 percent rate that was creditable to taxpaying shareholders. In either case, a repurchase of shares either by a single corporation or in conjunction with a takeover would be taxed more heavily than a dividend, since the tax treatment would be equivalent for top-bracket taxpayers and more onerous for low-bracket taxpayers and tax-exempt entities. Presumably firms would then substitute dividends for share repurchases. The incentive for restructuring transactions that replaced equity would then be eliminated. This proposal goes beyond the first one in that it would apply to share repurchases that were not debt financed. As with the limitation on interest deductions proposal, there would be no increase in the cost of capital for firms considering new investments. In fact, the second part of the ALI proposal would institute dividend deductibility for *new* equity issues.

Proponents of restructuring transactions argue that the interest limitation and the ALI proposal would each discourage corporate restructurings and therefore reduce economic efficiency. Although these proposals would make restructurings less attractive than they are now, it is desirable to do so. As we have discussed, current tax rules make acquisitions that reduce real economic efficiency profitable. Either of the plans advocated here would be approximately neutral. Under the interest limitation plan, firms would not be able to take advantage of interest deductions unless they undertook new investments. The ALI proposal would require firms to pay a penalty tax on their repurchases that would approximately equal in present value their subsequent interest savings. Under either plan corporate restructuring would still trigger capital gains tax liabilities for shareholders, but these would largely be a prepayment of taxes that would in any event be paid in the future. Moreover, even this small disincentive to restructurings could be mitigated by permitting investors to trade their common stock for preferred stock in the restructured corporation.

These reforms would eliminate the current subsidy to restructurings without affecting in any way firms' ability to finance new investment.

31. See American Law Institute, *Federal Income Tax Project—Subchapter C (Supplemental Study): Reporter's Study Draft* (Philadelphia, June 1989). (Hereafter ALI, *Reporter's Study Draft*.)

They would provide a natural experiment for testing the claims of proponents of corporate restructurings that they greatly increase real economic efficiency. If the proponents are correct, the transactions would continue, albeit with buyers paying smaller premiums. If not, the elimination of the tax benefit would greatly reduce the number of restructurings. In either case, it is difficult to see what would be lost.

Comment by David F. Bradford

The lack of an equilibrium model of corporate financial behavior consistent with observations continues to plague the analysis of income tax policy. As much as I found the Bulow, Summers, and Summers paper full of information and insights, and as much as I enjoyed reading it, I was struck by an inconsistency at its heart. The first part of the paper documents the inability of the tax authorities to produce an operational definition of debt. Without offering an operational definition of their own, the authors proceed in the second part of the paper to describe the uses of debt, especially high-yield debt, in corporate restructuring transactions and to argue that defective tax rules are inducing an excessive or inappropriate use of debt.

I do not think a coherent definition of debt can be inferred from the second half of the paper. But I do think something can be learned about the important economic phenomena at issue. And a depressing amount can be learned about the shortcomings of an income tax system that makes large tax distinctions among transactions without economic differences.

In the old-fashioned conception of a corporation, there were two kinds of securities, debt and equity. With debt, the amount the creditor was due was independent of the success or failure of the corporation, so long as bankruptcy was avoided. The equity holder got the residual. In the old-fashioned conception, the main function of debt was to permit a reallocation of risk; those who didn't like risk held bonds. The only tricky part was bankruptcy. A lot of attention was paid to its costs, since the efficiency consequence of any tax bias in favor of a high-debt equilibrium was excessive bankruptcy costs.

It has long been recognized that the costs of bankruptcy include not just the lawyers' fees but also the skewed incentives of managers associated with attempting to avoid bankruptcy. Such incentive effects are central to the new-fashioned conception of corporate finance. Recent thinking has shifted away from the idea of corporate capital as an asset that generates a return according to some exogenously given random draw, with the proceeds arbitrarily divided between riskless interest and a residual return to equity, toward an emphasis on the corporation as a web of contracts designed to cope with costly information. In a word: how do you keep the employees hard at work in pursuit of the employer's interests?

At one point in their discussion, the authors note that "one of the key distinctions between debt and equity is that debt holders should have interests that diverge from those of equity holders." This captures the essence of the incentive function of what might be an economic definition of debt. The owner of a highly leveraged firm (in this sense) has a strong incentive to pay attention to the productivity of the organization, and the incentive is all the stronger, the more compelling is the actual obligation to deliver the contractual payments to debt holders. Note that this has nothing to do with whether the payments are in cash now, rather than in the future (as with a PIK security). Nor does it have anything to do with the riskiness of the security per se: a promise to duplicate the performance of General Motors stock would obviously have the risk characteristics of equity in one sense, but it would serve as "debt" in the economic sense just described if issued by, say, IBM.

Bulow, Summers, and Summers correctly emphasize that if what is favored by the tax system is debt in some purely nominal sense, and not debt in the economic sense, then the associated costs are not the efficiency losses that customarily attract the attention of economic analysis. If the tax-favored item is purely a label, then there is no waste directly involved. Having at least established a presumption that the current tax rules are indeed of this character, the authors do not clearly justify their later views that the tax system results in an inefficiently large amount of "leverage" (undefined) and that policy measures are called for to eliminate the use of high-yield debt in corporate restructuring activity. The policy measures to which they are inclined involve one form or another of limiting interest (undefined) deductibility.

I would draw somewhat different lessons. First, and this is implicit in the authors' discussion, their analysis suggests the major tax benefits from the financial gymnastics of recent years have been in the nature of rewards for discovery of tax loopholes. That is, the innovating financial schemes probably have little effect on the margin of significance for the incentive effects of contractual arrangements, for the reasons so well laid out in the first part of the paper. Instead, they have the effect of transferring wealth from the government to the innovators. They undoubtedly do impose significant costs in the form of the legal talent required to put the deals together, and they may have even more significant costs in weakening the confidence of the general public in the integrity of the financial system, but they may well have no consequences for the efficacy of forward-looking contractual arrangements. But even if the rules have no efficiency effects when viewed in isolation, it would be incorrect to conclude that recent events do not have efficiency consequences. Somehow the revenue has to be raised, and most ways of obtaining it have efficiency costs. A lump-sum giveaway of a dollar implies an efficiency cost of the excess burden of raising that dollar back by the usual methods. Nor should one neglect the distributional aspects of the situation. I am not happy when the present value of my future taxes goes up by a dollar by virtue of a lump-sum grant by the government to someone else. (Compare the S&L crisis.)

The second lesson I draw is a reinforcement of the general point that a tax system which treats very differently transactions with equivalent economic effects is a recipe for major problems. Most of the games described by Bulow, Summers, and Summers are not profitable when both sides of the transactions are taxed with the same timing and the same tax rates. Take their example of $50 million of fifty-year OID bonds under the now-outdated rules of "ratable" (linear) deduction by the borrower and inclusion by the lender. These rules clearly mismeasured income in an economic sense (something like the present geometrical amortization is certainly closer, when inflation is ignored), but the mismeasurement would have been of no significance if both borrower and lender had the same tax rate. The mischief results from differences in rates, which require accurate accrual income measurement (the economic substance of the transaction).

A similar remark applies to the tax treatment of forgiveness of debt in bankruptcy described in the authors' hypothetical future of the RJR PIK interest on $3 billion. Debt forgiveness is supposed to result in taxable income to the forgiven and a tax deduction for the forgiver. If the PIK interest is deducted and included at the same tax rates, and the same holds true for the forgiveness in bankruptcy, then there is no tax gain to be had on the PIK-plus-bankruptcy scheme.

The evolution of the tax law in regard to corporations, and to capital income more broadly, has in many respects been driven by the effort to keep ahead of the ingenuity of financial technicians. To avoid losing tax revenue without addressing the fundamental source of the problems, the rule writers have had to resort to ever more complex provisions. It is certain that complying with these provisions has its own significant costs (has anyone tried to deal with the limits on deductibility of home mortgage interest lately?). If the government cannot formulate a workable measure of accrual income, I see no prospect for an end to this process except by a move toward uniformity of the tax treatment of both sides of transactions, including the applicable tax rate. To do this systematically raises profound issues (for example, the treatment of pension plans), but in my view this is the general direction in which policy should go in the interest of equity, efficiency, and simplicity.

Comment by Martin D. Ginsburg

In this very good paper the authors state, with what they term "only a small exaggeration," that "the principal criterion now determining the tax status of a security"—as debt or as equity—"is the name its issuer gives it." I agree without reservation. Indeed I think it no exaggeration at all, and whereas the authors spotlight recent financial innovation as the miscreant, I would argue that the instruments and the tactics of the 1980s have merely served to highlight and exploit a formalism in the tax law that has been with us from the beginning.

Visiting at Stanford Law School a dozen years ago, I asked a corporate tax student, one who in previous exchanges had convincingly demonstrated a wholesome lack of financial background, to catalogue the tax law's means of distinguishing corporate debt and corporate equity. The conventional response, of course, would have proffered that unconvincing litany of five factors or thirteen factors—unconditional promise to pay, fixed maturity, fair rate of interest, divergent ownership of debt instruments and stock, nonsubordination, and on and on—that has played so large a part in the judiciary's debt-equity devotions.

Unable or unwilling to mouth cant, my student responded thus: "If the yield is deductible, it's debt; if not, it's equity."

Struck nearly dumb by this blazing insight, I foolishly inquired, "But how can you tell?"

"Well," responded the student with some patience, "if it's a public company, you look to see if the certificate says 'debenture' or says 'preferred stock.' "

Recent financial innovations did not create the reality my student so well perceived a dozen years ago. There is in federal tax law an important difference between debt and equity, but it is precisely that the yield on debt is deductible and the yield on equity is not. Of other cataloguing distinctions, in public company instruments the "debenture" or "preferred stock" label has always mattered enormously, but except in the most marginal circumstances the rest is façade. Appearance carries the day because, other than in terms of outcome, in the tax law there is not and never was "reality" to a debt-equity distinction.

Converts to that conclusion are likely to focus, as did my student, on outcome—yield on debt is deductible, yield on equity is not—and to urge some form of about-face: (1) perhaps partial integration, what the authors nicely refer to as "the carrot of dividend deductibility"; (2) alternatively, "the stick of interest nondeductibility" or at least a limitation on interest deductibility in identified circumstances; (3) alternatively still, the carrot and the stick in a grand package. The authors argue that corporate tax integration, whatever its other merits, is potent with concerns of windfall benefit and provides to the debt-equity problem a response that is inappropriate, inadequate, or extremely expensive. As for interest deduction limitations, the "stick" of the package, the authors applaud a focus on debt issued in restructuring transactions, leveraged buyouts, and the like, as they find merit in the Revenue Reconciliation Act of 1989,[32] but they doubt the feasibility ("difficult tracing problems") of a fully fleshed, targeted solution that would "disallow interest deductions for debt incurred or continued for the purpose of repurchasing equity."[33]

32. In particular, the authors refer (although not by number) to new section 163(e)(5) of the Internal Revenue Code of 1986, which disallows part and defers the balance of a corporate issuer's interest deduction on certain high-yield OID debentures and PIK debentures. The new provision is extraordinarily complex, even for the Internal Revenue Code, and one's enthusiasm for it is likely to be inversely proportionate to the likelihood that one will be required to work with it hereafter. As economists rather than tax practitioners (or tax teachers), two of the authors need never again look at section 163(e)(5). For a detailed analysis of the provision identifying a number of uncertain or discordant applications, see Martin D. Ginsburg and Jack S. Levin, *Mergers, Acquisitions, and Leveraged Buyouts* (Chicago: Commerce Clearing House, Tax Transaction Library, 1989), para. 1303A.

33. The authors' point seems to me a strong one, although I do not know that we would define "tracing problems" the same way. Assume, for example, that P corporation using borrowed money purchases a large operating division from T corporation. At a later time T sells to others the balance of its operating assets and liquidates. In the liquidation the

Having scattered straw men, the authors identify as their solution of choice the minimum tax on distributions (MTD) proposal recently developed by William D. Andrews of Harvard Law School and a group of consultants in the American Law Institute's ongoing Federal Income Tax Project.[34] As the authors, somewhat pinched for space, sum it up, "Transactions removing assets from corporate solution, which are currently treated at least in part as a return of capital, would be subject to . . . a corporate tax [at the shareholder rate, currently 28 percent] creditable to *taxpaying shareholders*" (emphasis added). Thus the incentive in current tax law for restructuring transactions—a corporation's repurchase of its own shares or its purchase of the controlling shares of another corporation—would be eliminated or greatly restricted, and, under the ALI reporter's study, that would be true whether the restructuring is financed by the issuance of debt or the application of accumulated earnings.

Before joining the MTD crusade, however, it would be well to read and comprehend the whole text of the recruitment poster. "The aim of the MTD is to limit what shareholders can get by way of distribution from their corporation to what they could have got in a rational market contemplating continued corporate operations without distributions other than ordinary dividends."[35]

If T corporation distributes a dividend that is not "ordinary,"[36] the 28 percent MTD special corporate tax applies. If T corporation winds up its affairs and liquidates, obviously that distribution is no ordinary dividend and, subject to a couple of partial relief rules that need not detain us, the entire distribution is subject to 28 percent MTD withholding.

The MTD proposal reduces the premiums in corporate takeovers, not by foolishly trying to identify and condemn this or that deplorable transaction, but rather by heavily taxing any and every corporation that pays out to its public shareholders (or indeed to the shareholders of any non-

---

outstanding T shares are retired and exchanged for cash distributed by T. Much of that cash can be "traced" to the money P borrowed and used, some time earlier, to purchase T's large operating division. Would we, at the time T liquidates—which, after all, is the event that reduces outstanding corporate equity—inform P that it suddenly has lost its interest deduction? But if we do not take that step, the targeted solution of a disallowed interest deduction is doomed to impotence.

34. The current incarnation of this work is ALI, *Reporter's Study Draft*.

35. ALI, *Reporter's Study Draft*, p. 72.

36. Under ALI, *Reporter's Study Draft*, proposal 1, ordinary dividend is defined as not exceeding the greater of 133 percent of the prior four years' average ordinary dividends, average earnings over that period, and (if T corporation is public) 8 percent of average share market value during the distribution year.

subsidiary corporation) more than a modest part of its net worth. This poison pill is endemic, not selective.

What of the credit to "taxpaying shareholders" to which the authors refer? If "the aim of the MTD" is as quoted above, it is not easy to justify any shareholder credit. The ALI reporter's study nonetheless proposes one, but in reality not much of one: the credit is available only to "taxpayers"—pension plans and charities need not apply—and the credit is not cashable. Thus, while shareholder Jones, who has long owned T shares at a low-cost basis, will benefit from the credit if T liquidates (in effect he will pay no tax on the distribution he actually receives), Mr. Smith, who bought his shares yesterday at full price from Ms. Brown, will obtain no benefit from the credit because he has no gain. Ms. Brown, more's the pity, must pay full tax on yesterday's sale gain and enjoys no credit; had she not sold to Smith and instead participated in the liquidation, she, like Jones, would have benefited from the credit and would have paid no tax on her liquidation gain.

Is there in our system an implied covenant that a corporation, once embarked on an enterprise, will forever continue to operate, reinvest profits, and earn more profits on which regular corporate tax will forever be paid? Is there a quiet agreement that the corporation will not seek to reduce its stream of corporate earnings and corporate tax payments by distributions that will significantly reduce or, in the case of a complete liquidation, eliminate the corporate tax base? If you think yes, you will have no trouble with the ALI reporter's study proposals. But if you are less sure, you may wish to think long before embracing a program that makes the corporation, for breach of an implied promise to pay corporate tax forever, pay to the fisc up-front damages equal to 28 percent of its net worth.

Converting Corporations to Partnerships through Leverage

Myron S. Scholes and Mark A. Wolfson

IN THIS PAPER we explore the degree to which debt financing can reduce the corporate-level tax on income in the United States. Although we show that debt is capable of shielding the competitive rate of return on projects from the corporate-level tax, debt financing cannot shield the positive net-present-value portion of project returns. Because nontax factors preclude corporate activities from being 100 percent debt financed, part of the competitive return to corporate activity is also subject to double taxation.

We also consider alternative mechanisms that would convert the corporate tax to a personal tax (or a partnership tax). These include other claims that give rise to tax deductible payments to the corporation, such as obligations to employees, lessors, and suppliers. As we show, all these alternatives are limited in their ability to eliminate the corporate-level tax.

The Evolution of the Tax Treatment of Debt and Equity

Whether debt financing is tax favored relative to equity financing depends on the magnitude of shareholder-level, corporate-level, and personal taxes. The tax laws in the United States have always treated debt differently from corporate equities. Whereas interest paid on debt is tax deductible to corporate borrowers, dividends paid on common and preferred stock is not. And whereas gains and losses on the repurchase of corporate bonds are taxable events to corporate issuers, that is not true of share repurchases. On the investor side, interest from bonds is taxable as ordinary income whether paid out currently or not, while dividends and changes in the value of stocks are taxable only when realized. Moreover, dividends re-

We have benefited from conversations with Alan J. Auerbach, Laurie Simon Bagwell, Jeremy Bulow, John B. Shoven, and the participants of the conference on Taxes and Corporate Restructuring.

ceive tax-favored treatment for corporate shareholders, and capital gains, besides being granted favorable tax-deferral treatment, have also been taxed at rates well below that of ordinary income for many shareholders.

Since the returns to corporate stock are tax favored relative to bonds, investors are willing to accept lower pretax equity returns, on a risk-adjusted basis, to invest in them. That is similar to what occurs in the market for tax-exempt bonds, where the pretax yields are substantially below those of fully taxable bonds. The same can readily be observed in the market for adjustable-rate preferred stocks in the United States, held almost exclusively by corporations for whom the dividend income is largely tax exempt.

The pretax return differential on corporate common stocks is more difficult to document than it is for preferred stocks and tax-exempt bonds. The variability of stock returns is very large relative to the size of the possible tax effects. Moreover, a consensus is lacking on the appropriate risk adjustment to make to stock returns (for example, single-factor pricing models such as the capital asset pricing model versus multifactor pricing models) so that they can be compared with the returns of equally risky corporate bonds. But the tax-favored treatment of corporate stock in the hands of investors should result in lower risk-adjusted pretax returns. This reduction in rates exacts an implicit tax from investors. Symmetrically, the rate reduction represents an implicit tax subsidy to issuers of corporate stocks that compensates, at least in part, for the nondeductibility of dividends.[1]

Holding everything else constant, increasing the tax rate to investors on income from share ownership reduces the pretax wedge between shares and bonds (and therefore reduces the implicit tax subsidy to issuing shares). That makes stock more expensive for corporations to issue than bonds. Similarly, increasing corporate tax rates relative to personal tax rates favors corporate debt financing insofar as such financing moves taxable income from the corporate to the noncorporate sector.

---

1. See Joseph E. Stiglitz, "Taxation, Corporate Financial Policy, and the Cost of Capital," *Journal of Public Economics*, vol. 2 (February 1973), pp. 1–34; Merton H. Miller, "Debt and Taxes," *Journal of Finance*, vol. 32 (May 1977), pp. 261–65; Alan J. Auerbach, "Taxation, Corporate Financial Policy and the Cost of Capital," *Journal of Economic Literature*, vol. 21 (September 1983), pp. 905–40; Myron S. Scholes and Mark A. Wolfson, "The Cost of Capital and Changes in Tax Regimes," in Henry J. Aaron, Harvey Galper, and Joseph A. Pechman, eds., *Uneasy Compromise: Problems of a Hybrid Income-Consumption Tax* (Brookings, 1988), pp. 157–94; and Scholes and Wolfson, *Taxes and Business Strategy: A Global Planning Approach* (Prentice Hall, forthcoming).

Before 1981 top marginal tax rates in the corporate sector were well below top marginal personal tax rates. Top personal rates were 70 percent from 1965 to 1981, whereas top corporate rates were in the 50 percent range. In the two decades before 1965, top personal rates were in the 90 percent range. During that time top long-term capital gains rates to individuals ranged from 25 to 35 percent. Such a configuration of tax rates should have caused common stocks to bear substantial implicit taxes, and corporate debt financing might not have been at all tax favored for many corporations in those years.

With the passage of the Economic Recovery Tax Act of 1981, personal tax rates were reduced dramatically, whereas corporate rates were not. But at the same time capital gains rates were also slashed. Furthermore, with interest rates then at record levels, the tax advantage of capital gains deferral was particularly high. Because top personal tax rates were set at a level just above top corporate tax rates, the 1981 tax act began to move incentives toward increased corporate borrowing, although this effect was mitigated by the reduction in capital gains tax rates and high interest rates. By 1984 interest rates had decreased dramatically, reducing the tax-sheltered nature of common stocks, which further promoted corporate debt financing over equity financing.

As always, important nontax factors were also influencing corporate financing decisions during the early 1980s. In particular, mature corporations were discovering that it was efficient, from the standpoint of corporate control, to restructure by buying back equity with the proceeds of debt issues, thereby committing themselves to distribute "free cash flows" to investors through bond interest and principal repayments.[2] Moreover, increased reliance on strip financing (in which institutional investors acquire combinations of junior debt and equity or senior debt, to reduce conflicts of interest among classes of investors) and the rise of active bondholders enabled more debt to be issued without the fear of incurring excessive dead weight restructuring and bankruptcy costs if the corporation defaulted on its commitments to creditors.[3] But it does not seem right to view these developments as being entirely independent of the evolution of the tax law. The tax law may well have provided important incentives for the proliferation of these institutional arrangements.

2. Michael C. Jensen, "Agency Costs of Free Cash Flow: Corporate Finance and Takeovers," *American Economic Review*, vol. 76 (May 1986, *Papers and Proceedings, 1985*), pp. 323–30.

3. Michael C. Jensen, "Capital Markets, Organizational Innovation, and Restructuring," working paper, Harvard Business School, Division of Research, 1989.

Corporate restructuring took a decided turn in 1984. Net new borrowing by corporations exploded to nearly $160 billion a year during 1984–86 from $66 billion a year during 1978–83. At the same time there was a quantum leap in the magnitude of both share repurchases ($37 billion a year in 1984–86 versus $5 billion a year in 1978–83) and other equity retirements through corporate acquisitions ($75 billion a year in 1984–86 versus $15 billion a year in 1980–83).[4]

The 1986 Tax Reform Act had an even more dramatic effect on the tilt toward corporate debt financing. Personal tax rates were reduced to a level well below that of corporations (28 percent for wealthy individuals versus 34 percent for corporations by 1988), and capital gains tax rates were greatly increased. That, in conjunction with relatively low interest rates, greatly reduces the implicit tax on shares and makes equity financing a particularly expensive way to finance corporate investment.

That debt financing has become more tax favored with the 1981 and 1986 tax acts is closely related to the fact that noncorporate forms of organization have become more tax favored relative to the corporate form. If all corporate earnings before interest and taxes could be distributed to investors as interest, the corporation would essentially be converted to a partnership for tax purposes. No entity-level tax would be imposed on the corporation,[5] and all owners would pay tax at the personal level on interest income. It would be as if the shareholders owned income bonds.

There are many ways in which the firm can "lever up." One method that has received considerable attention is leveraged buyouts, or LBOs. Others include debt-for-equity swaps, dividend-for-debt exchanges, cash redemption of stock financed with debt, deferred compensation plans, partnership arrangements involving deferred payments, and leveraged employee stock ownership plans (ESOPs). An important tax issue that arises in leveraged buyouts and other debt-increasing recapitalizations is whether the Internal Revenue Service (IRS) will claim that the debt issue is really

4. Joint Committee on Taxation, *Federal Income Tax Aspects of Corporate Financial Structures*, Joint Committee Print, 101 Cong. 1 sess. (Government Printing Office, January 1989), tables I-A, I-B, pp. 8–9. The 1984 Deficit Reduction Act also eliminated withholding taxes on newly issued bonds and other evidences of indebtedness that generate portfolio interest income to foreign investors. Bonds purchased by foreigners skyrocketed from less than half a billion dollars per quarter over the preceding decade to more than 10 billion dollars per quarter over the next three years. Board of Governors of the Federal Reserve System, "Flow of Funds Accounts: Fourth Quarter, 1988," Statistical Release Z.1 (March 1989).

5. This ignores any corporate "alternative minimum tax" that may be assessed.

equity in disguise.[6] As we show, all these alternatives are limited in their ability to eliminate the corporate-level tax.

A Simple Model of the Tax Advantages of Debt

Assume that the corporation has an investment project that will return Y dollars of taxable income and cash before interest and taxes. The required investment in the project is $1. For an all-equity-financed firm, the after-tax return on the investment would be

$$Y(1 - t_c)(1 - t_s),$$

where t_c is the corporate marginal tax rate, and t_s is the annualized share-holder-level tax rate. If shareholders sell shares, they pay tax at rate gt_p, where g is the fraction of realized income from shares that is taxable, and t_p is their marginal tax rate at the time the sale occurs. Shareholders, however, can defer the realization of capital gains and in some cases avoid paying capital gains taxes entirely by donating stock to charity or by realizing a stepped-up basis on death. Moreover, capital gains tax rates

6. Other problems arise if the debt is issued with original issue discount (that is, when a debt or preferred stock issue has a redemption price that exceeds its respective issue price or when a debt issue pays interest at a below-market rate). Tax issues arise over how these discounts are to be amortized over the life of the instruments. Nontax costs arise for taxpayers who accrue taxable income without receiving cash payments. Some taxpayers might need to borrow to make their tax payments. As a result of deadweight financing costs, certain taxpayers might be the wrong clientele for these original-issue bond or preferred stock issues.

In an LBO effected by management, the target's management usually borrows to buy shares in the new firm (Newco). Individuals, who are partners or S corporation shareholders, also borrow to acquire the target's stock. These taxpayers, however, might not be able to take tax deductions for all the interest on their debt. Under section 163(d) of the tax code, individual taxpayers can deduct "investment interest" only to the extent of their "net investment income," which includes interest, dividends, and net capital gains realized on the sale of assets. The excess is carried forward to future tax years. Because of this restriction, management may face high after-tax costs to finance its part of the acquisition. As an alternative, Newco management could argue that it had to borrow to buy its shares as part of its trade or business. The investment interest limitation under section 163(d) would thereby be avoided by treating interest as an employee business expense. After the 1986 Tax Reform Act, however, that would be a losing strategy. Interest payments on this type of debt are now considered interest on personal debt and are no longer tax deductible. To some extent managers could use first and second home mortgages to buy the stock of Newco and still deduct the interest payments.

are not necessarily constant over time (both g and t_p can change), and shareholders have an option to time their realizations strategically to coincide with periods of relatively low tax rates. As a result, the marginal tax rate on the returns to shares on an annualized basis, t_s, is lower than the current values of gt_p.

To ease notation, we define t_d by the following identity:

$$(1 - t_d) = (1 - t_c)(1 - t_s).$$

From this identity, t_d can be interpreted as the total tax rate that shareholders pay on income earned by their all-equity-financed corporations. The subscript d is chosen to denote a "double" tax, once at the corporate level (t_c) and then again at the shareholder level $[t_s(1 - t_c)]$. With this notation, the after-tax return to shareholders from investing in an all-equity-financed corporate project that yields Y dollars of corporate taxable income is

$$Y(1 - t_d).$$

If the firm financed the project with debt instead of equity, which reduces taxable income by the interest payments at rate R_b, the after-tax return to stockholders would be

$$(Y - R_b)(1 - t_d),$$

and the after-tax return to the firm's bondholders would be

$$R_b(1 - t_p).$$

If the interest on the debt, R_b, was equal to Y, then corporate taxable income would be zero. The corporate-level tax would disappear, and the firm's debt holders would realize a return of

$$R_b(1 - t_p) = Y(1 - t_p).$$

That could happen if the firm's only shareholders were its bondholders and all the firm's income was paid out as interest. In effect, the firm's owners (the bondholders) would be taxed as if they were partners in a partnership, and the income earned by the corporation would escape an entity-level tax.[7]

In general, this strategy will not work. A corporation must have shareholders. In principle, the firm's capital structure could consist of some form of strip financing in which each investor acquires both debt and equity in constant proportions and the firm "overpays" on the debt component of the package. In the extreme, if interest rates are set high enough, the stock portion of the strip would receive no return and have a market value of zero. Were it not for tax rule restrictions, this ruse would avoid the double taxation of corporate income. All the payments on the debt would be tax deductible, even though they included equity returns (in the form of interest) to shareholders. The IRS, however, would consider this arrangement to be a sham. For debt to be distinguished from equity under section 385 of the tax code, there must be a disproportionate interest in the profits of the firm: the debt holders and equity holders cannot be one and the same investor, directly or indirectly through related party ownership of securities. A significant proportion of the shares must be held by shareholders who are not also bondholders. This necessity defeats the ability of strip financing to eliminate the corporate tax completely, and partnerships remain tax advantageous relative to corporations.

Corporate Taxation of Economic Rents versus Competitive Returns

Surprisingly, if the corporation earns a noncompetitive rate of return on its investments (that is, a return above its cost of capital), its shareholders must pay a full corporate and personal tax on these excess profits even if the firm finances the investments with debt. To illustrate this, assume that the corporation finds an investment project that will return Y percent before interest and taxes (for example, 20 percent a year on a risk-adjusted basis, when the risk-adjusted borrowing rate is 8 percent before tax). If the project is financed with equity, shareholders pay a full double tax on the corporate income, and they are left with $Y(1 - t_d)$ after corporate-level and shareholder-level taxes.

Suppose that shareholders finance their equity investment in the corporation by borrowing on personal account at rate R_b. If so, their after-tax annualized net return, assuming the interest is tax deductible at rate

7. The corporation could still face corporate-level capital gains taxes on its liquidation. A partnership does not pay partnership-level taxes on any gains realized on the sale of its assets.

Table 1. The Degree to Which Debt Financing Avoids Double Taxation

Form of debt-financed investment	Net after-tax return to investor	Double tax avoided?
Case I. Equity-financed corporation	$Y(1 - t_d) - R_b(1 - t_p)$	Not at all
Case II. Debt-financed partnership	$(Y - R_b)(1 - t_p)$	Completely
Case III. Debt-financed corporation	$(Y - R_b)(1 - t_d)$	On R_b only
Advantage of II over I	$Y(t_d - t_p)$	
Advantage of II over III	$(Y - R_b)(t_d - t_p)$	
Advantage of III over I	$R_b(t_d - t_p)$	

Y = taxable project return before taxes;

R_b = pretax interest rate on debt;

   t_d = total tax rate to shareholders on income earned at the corporate level. The rate equals t_c, the corporate tax rate, plus $t_s(1 - t_c)$, where t_s is the annualized shareholder-level tax rate paid on gains from holding corporate stock: $(1 - t_d) = (1 - t_c)(1 - t_s)$;

   t_p = tax rate paid on ordinary income earned at the personal level, including income earned by partnerships (passed through to its partners) and interest income or expense.

t_p, would be $Y(1 - t_d) - R_b(1 - t_p)$—see case I in table 1. But to use these interest deductions fully, shareholders must have investment income from other sources. That is, because of the restrictions imposed by section 163(d), interest deductions in any tax year cannot exceed realized investment income.[8]

If the same investment undertaken by the corporation was instead undertaken through a partnership, the after-tax return to investors would be $Y(1 - t_p)$. If the partners borrowed on personal account to finance this project, their net return would be $Y(1 - t_p) - R_b(1 - t_p)$ or $(Y - R_b)(1 - t_p)$—case II in the table. This case serves as a useful benchmark against which to evaluate the taxation of corporate investment returns, since there is no double taxation of partnership investment income. Note also that the net return to partnership investors would be the same whether the borrowing is undertaken on personal account or through the partnership. As will be seen, that is not true for corporate investors.

A comparison of cases I and II shows that personal leverage does nothing to eliminate the double tax on the all-equity corporate investment. If, instead, the corporation borrows to finance this project at the corporate level, it returns to shareholders $(Y - R_b)(1 - t_d)$—case III. Here the advantage of the partnership form over the corporate form, even for 100 percent debt-financed investments, is

$$(Y - R_b)(t_d - t_p).$$

8. One way to generate investment income is to realize capital gains on shares. But if shares are sold early to enable the deduction of interest expense, shareholders lose some of the advantage of the deferral of the shareholder-level tax. In other words, t_s increases, and this increases t_d as well.

Corporate-level financing succeeds in eliminating double taxation on R_b of income (the competitive return), but not on the excess.

To illustrate, if $Y = 20\%$, $R_b = 8\%$, $t_c = 34\%$, $t_p = 28\%$, and $t_s = 20\%$, then a corporate debt-financed investment (case III) yields a profit to shareholders after interest and taxes of $(20\% - 8\%)(1 - 34\%)(1 - 20\%)$, or 6.34% of the amount invested in the project, versus 8.64% [or $(20\% - 8\%)(1 - 28\%)$] to partnership owners. The excess return to the partners is 36 percent higher than to corporate shareholders.

Because of nontax factors, however, the pretax return on projects might differ between corporations and partnerships. To generate the same after-tax return as partners, the pretax return on the corporate project would have to increase from 20 to 24.36 percent. Moreover, because of such nontax factors as restructuring costs, it might be undesirable to finance projects with 100 percent debt even if the taxing authority would allow it.[9] That would further favor partnerships. For example, if projects were 50 percent debt financed, the project would have to earn 25.82 percent in corporate form to provide the same after-tax return as the 20 percent partnership project.[10] In other words, corporate profitability before interest and taxes would have to be 5 percent higher for the 50 percent debt-financed corporation than for the 100 percent debt-financed corporation to provide identical net returns to shareholders.

The Effect of Borrowing for Multiple Periods

Some firms borrow a sufficient amount to wipe out their current taxable income. Does this strategy convert the tax rate on the total return (the required plus the excess return) to the personal tax rate as in a partnership? The answer is no. To illustrate this point, assume that the firm earns Y percent a year in perpetuity on a project and borrows at rate R_b to finance it. Its before-tax excess return is $Y - R_b$ each year. To eliminate its entire before-tax income, the firm could borrow an additional $(Y - R_b)/R_b$ dollars. The interest payments on this loan would be supported by the annual

9. However, in the event of bankruptcy, there may also be benefits from transferring control of the firm to a management team that can do a better job than the incumbents would. See, for example, Phillippe Aghion and Patrick Bolton, "An 'Incomplete Contract' Approach to Bankruptcy and the Financial Structure of the Firm," Working Paper 484 (MIT, Department of Economics, and Harvard Institute of Economic Research, 1988).

10. Remember that risk is held constant across these financing alternatives, because any equity investment in the corporation is financed by borrowing on personal account. This avoids a comparability problem.

project cash flows of $Y - R_b$. But what would the firm do with the loan proceeds? If it cannot pay out the loan proceeds to its stockholders (perhaps because of loan covenant restrictions) and it invests in competitive projects, it would earn at rate R_b per dollar invested in the additional projects. That generates taxable income of $(Y - R_b)$, or $[(Y - R_b)/R_b] \times R_b$. This strategy leaves the firm exactly where it started before undertaking additional borrowing.

Alternatively, the firm might try to engage in some form of clientele-based arbitrage. That is, it might take a long position in tax-favored assets financed with debt that give rise to fully deductible interest payments. For example, suppose the firm purchased tax-exempt assets, such as municipal bonds, with the loan proceeds. Even if the tax rules allowed the firm to deduct interest after the purchase of such assets, the firm could convert only the corporate-level tax rate to the marginal tax rate that sets prices in the tax-favored asset market. That is, though explicit taxes would be reduced, so would pretax returns on the investment, an implicit tax.

If the corporation borrows $(Y - R_b)/R_b$ to eliminate corporate taxable income and is permitted to pay out the entire loan amount to its stockholders, either as a dividend or a repurchase of shares, that would not eliminate the double taxation either. Shareholders would realize current taxable income on the distribution.[11] The amount of taxable income normally depends on whether the distribution is a dividend or a share repurchase, as well as on the magnitude of "earnings and profits" in the corporation and the shareholders' basis in shares. If the shareholders have a zero cost basis in their shares (after all, the projects are all debt financed), then any distribution will be fully taxable as a dividend or a capital gain. In this case, after paying the shareholder-level tax, the firm's shareholders retain

$$\frac{(Y - R_b)}{R_b} (1 - gt_p),$$

where, as before, g denotes the fraction of the income that is fully taxed at rate t_p.

Note that if shareholders can reinvest this after-tax amount at rate R_b, before tax, they generate an annual after-tax cash flow stream of

$$(Y - R_b)(1 - gt_p)(1 - t_p).$$

11. If the firm had no accumulated earnings and profits, many state laws would prevent the firm from distributing the loan proceeds to shareholders.

Compare this to the annual cash flow to partners in a partnership if they finance a project at rate R_b that returns Y percent a period in perpetuity:

$$(Y - R_b)(1 - t_p).$$

So the corporation cannot avoid a second level of tax on the excess return on corporate projects through additional corporate borrowing even if the proceeds are distributed to shareholders. That is true even if the distribution takes the form of a share repurchase and shareholders have some cost basis in their shares. In such a case, g would be less than one, but it would still be positive, resulting in one round of taxes more than in a partnership.

To illustrate this point, assume that the firm can generate 20 percent on its $1.00 debt-financed investment each year forever. The required annual return on projects of this risk is 8 percent. On the strength of these cash flows, the firm borrows an additional $1.50, or $(0.2 - 0.08)/0.08$, for a total loan of $2.50 per $1.00 of investment and pays no taxes each year. The firm requires $1.00 for investment in the project, which generates $0.20 of taxable cash income a year forever. After it pays $0.08 in interest to bondholders for the $1.00 borrowed, the corporation is left with $0.12 of before-tax income. By borrowing $1.50 more, it pays an additional $0.12 in interest each year at 8 percent. As a result, its net income is $0 (or $0.2 - 0.08 - 0.12$), assuming that no additional corporate taxable income is generated with the excess $1.50 loan.

But the firm must do something with the $1.50 debt proceeds. If it could pay out the $1.50 to its shareholders, the payment would be at least partly taxable as a dividend or capital gain. If the entire distribution is taxable at t_p of 28 percent, shareholders would net only $1.08, or $1.50 \times (1 - 0.28)$. The present value of the same opportunity in partnership form is $1.50, a perpetuity of $(Y - R_b)(1 - t_p)$, discounted at $R_b(1 - t_p)$, or $[(0.2 - 0.08)(1 - 0.28)]/0.08(1 - 0.28)$.

The Effect of Recapitalizing and Distributing the Loan Proceeds

If the firm has undertaken a project that returns Y percent a year forever and has issued debt at an interest rate of R_b to finance the entire project, then it would realize $(Y - R_b)(1 - t_c)$ a year after corporate-level tax. Since shareholders can defer paying the tax on this excess return until they realize a gain, their annualized effective shareholder-level tax rate,

t_s, is usually less than t_p. For example, because of deferral opportunities, t_s might be only 20 percent when t_p is 28 percent. For the firm's shareholders, the present value of this investment opportunity is

$$\frac{(Y - R_b)(1 - t_d)}{R_b(1 - t_p)}.$$

Substituting the parameter values from the illustration yields

$$\frac{(0.2 - 0.08)(1 - 0.34)(1 - 0.2)}{0.08(1 - 0.28)} = 1.10.$$

With full borrowing and immediate taxation of the gain at the shareholder level, the present value of the investment opportunity is $1.08. Without borrowing, and deferral of the shareholder-level tax, the present value of the opportunity is $1.10. More generally, the firm must trade off realizing shareholder-level taxes earlier than necessary against the advantage of converting the corporate-level tax rate to the shareholder-level tax rate (for example, 34 percent to 28 percent) on corporate taxable income. Recapitalization may not be a tax-advantaged strategy for fully taxable shareholders. Note, however, that with heterogeneous shareholders a partial recapitalization allows those for whom deferral is unimportant (such as pension funds) to step forward to liquidate their interests in a share repurchase.

Let us define gt_p as the shareholder-level tax today, and t_{sn} as the annualized shareholder-level tax rate if the capital gain is realized in n years. Then in the presence of a perpetual investment opportunity yielding Y a year, the advantage of undertaking a 100 percent leveraged recapitalization of the firm with a complete payout to shareholders today over borrowing an amount only up to the required investment level is

(1) $$\frac{(Y - R_b)}{R_b}\left[(1 - gt_p) - \frac{(1 - t_c)(1 - t_{sn})}{(1 - t_p)}\right].$$

As seen in the equation, if gt_p, t_{sn}, and t_p are equal to one another (which requires, among other things, that $g = 1$, that is, no capital gains exclusion), then the advantage of leverage is to allow corporate income to be taxed at the personal rate (for example, 28 percent) rather than at the corporate rate (for example, 34 percent). If deferral of the capital gain is tax advantageous (that is, gt_p exceeds t_s), then some of the advantage is offset because shareholders are forced to pay taxes early. In fact, in our example it was tax disadvantageous to increase leverage because the firm's shareholders paid tax early on their gains.

Gains to Tax-Exempt Holders of Common Shares

As seen from equation 1, tax-exempt holders gain by levering up to eliminate corporate taxes and distributing the proceeds to shareholders. They gain $t_c(Y - R_b)/R_b$ by escaping the corporate-level tax on their investment. Using our illustration, tax-exempt holders realize $1.50 after tax. If the corporation payed corporate tax, the present value of the firm would be only $0.99 (or $0.66 \times \$1.50$) to these tax-exempt entities. So if tax-exempt institutions succeed in pressuring corporations to restructure (that is, add leverage and use the loan proceeds to pay out dividends to shareholders), they gain, though perhaps at the expense of individual shareholders. On net, therefore, it might not be tax advantageous to restructure.[12] But if the distribution is made by way of a share repurchase rather than a dividend, the conflict may be mitigated, since tax-exempt holders can step forward to sell their shares.

Foreign investors may also benefit from a strategy of corporate leverage and share repurchase. Such investors are exempt from U.S. capital gains taxation, but they face withholding taxes on dividends that range from a rate of 5 to 30 percent, depending on the treaty the foreign investors' home countries have with the United States. The degree to which the foreign investor benefits also depends on how the home country taxes U.S. dividends and capital gains, as well as whether the home country allows a foreign tax credit for U.S. taxes paid on dividends.

Finite Duration Debt

If the firm's cash flows will generate abnormal profits forever, there is some advantage, at least for tax-exempt entities and certain foreign investors, for the firm to increase its leverage and make payments of the

---

12. Increasing the firm's leverage increases the likelihood of bankruptcy. In the event of bankruptcy, shareholders can deduct the capital loss only against other realized capital gains (plus $3,000 each year). All realized capital gains, however, are fully taxable in the year incurred. This asymmetric treatment might increase the tax on shares. However, shareholders can time their sales to realize losses earlier than they realize gains.

loan proceeds to stockholders. When the firm faces the prospect of earning abnormal profits for only a limited time, however, the advantage of corporate leverage is lessened, and the partnership form becomes even more tax advantageous relative to the corporate form.

To eliminate corporate taxable income, the firm must borrow $(Y - R_b)/R_b$ to generate $Y - R_b$ of interest payments each year. If the firm's projects will generate abnormal returns for only n years, the firm cannot afford to pay out the entire loan proceeds to its stockholders. To ensure repayment of the loan, it must retain an amount sufficient to repay the loan principal at its maturity in n years. Because interest on the loan will be exactly offset by cash flows from the project, no residual cash flows will be available to repay loan principal unless some loan proceeds are retained within the firm. Assuming that the corporation can invest at the annual rate of R_b, before tax, on marginal investments, netting $R_b(1 - t_c)$ after tax per dollar invested, it must retain an amount ρ such that

$$\rho[1 + R_b(1 - t_c)]^n = \frac{(Y - R_b)}{R_b}.$$

This ensures that the loan can be repaid. So the amount that must be retained is equal to

(2) $$\frac{(Y - R_b)}{R_b} \bigg/ [1 + R_b(1 - t_c)]^n.$$

Note that this retention precludes the corporate-level tax from being eliminated entirely, let alone the shareholder-level tax.

If the firm borrows $(Y - R_b)/R_b$ dollars and retains the amount specified in equation 2, it can distribute

$$\frac{(Y - R_b)}{R_b} \left(1 - \frac{1}{[(1 + R_b(1 - t_c)]^n} \right)$$

to its stockholders. After paying the shareholder-level tax, shareholders retain

$$\frac{(Y - R_b)}{R_b} \left(1 - \frac{1}{[1 + R_b(1 - t_c)]^n} \right) (1 - g t_p).$$

Compare this to a strategy of *no* additional corporate borrowing beyond that required to finance the project. If the corporation retains the excess profits of $Y - R_b$ each period for n periods and reinvests them at rate $R_b(1 - t_c)$, the present value of this annuity, after corporate tax but before shareholder-level tax, would be

$$(Y - R_b)(1 - t_c) \left(\frac{1 - [1 + R_b(1 - t_c)]^{-n}}{R_b(1 - t_c)} \right),$$

which simplifies to

$$\frac{(Y - R_b)}{R_b} \left(1 - \frac{1}{[1 + R_b(1 - t_c)]^n} \right).$$

If this amount is then distributed to shareholders, the net amount available is exactly the same as when the corporation undertook additional borrowing. As a result, there is *no advantage whatsoever* for the corporation to undertake additional borrowing beyond its project financing requirements to eliminate its current taxable income. By contrast, if the project was undertaken through a partnership, the shareholder-level tax would be avoided, and the excess returns would compound net of the partnership tax rate, t_p, rather than the higher corporate tax rate, t_c.

Restructured Firms and the Corporate Tax

It is commonly believed that corporate restructurings involving large amounts of newly created debt enable the corporate tax to be eliminated.[13] But we have demonstrated that this is not really so. Why, then, do so many restructured firms seem to pay no corporate tax? Several factors may be at work here.

First, insofar as debt is issued in sufficient quantity to eliminate corporate taxable income, significant amounts must be distributed to shareholders, thereby triggering immediate realization of taxable gain at the individual level. A 1989 study illustrates this phenomenon in the context of the recent leveraged buyout of RJR Nabisco by Kohlberg Kravis Roberts.[14] Second, insofar as taxable income in the post-restructuring period

13. For example, see Laura Saunders, "How the Government Subsidizes Leveraged Takovers," *Forbes*, November 28, 1988, pp. 192–96.

14. Michael C. Jensen, Steven N. Kaplan, and Laura Stiglin, "Effects of LBOs on Tax Revenues of the U.S. Treasury," *Tax Notes*, February 6, 1989, pp. 727–33.

is temporarily low because of nonrecurring expenses associated with the restructuring, future taxable income at the corporate level can be significant. Examples of such nonrecurring expenses are costs associated with plant closings, the sale of other assets that have declined in value, severance pay for employees, and consulting, legal, and certain investment banking fees associated with the restructuring that are currently tax deductible. Third, restructuring may occur during periods of transitory operating losses. And fourth, the restructured firm may invest in tax-sheltered assets that avoid explicit taxes but at the expense of paying implicit taxes through reduced pretax returns on investment.

Whatever the reason, if corporate restructuring does not eliminate all positive net-present-value projects to the corporation, a second level of tax on the excess return generated by the corporation will not be avoided. Moreover, a second level of tax on projects undertaken in the past, whether positive net present value or not, cannot be avoided because of the shareholder-level tax that results from replacing equity with debt. This misunderstanding may have contributed to the recent interest expressed by many congressmen in removing the interest deductibility for some or all of the debt issued by corporations. We now turn briefly to this subject.

Deductibility of Interest
on High-Yield Debt

Recent proposals to eliminate the deductibility of interest on high-yield debt would place considerable strain on the corporate form of organization. Partnerships would look much more attractive if this vehicle for mitigating double taxation of corporate income were eliminated. Although one might argue that few would abandon the corporate form, because it achieves risk-sharing and liquidity efficiencies among investors, that argument has not been fully tested.

Some might contend that the Tax Reform Act of 1986 provided an opportunity to test the elasticity of demand for the corporate form with respect to changes in the tax cost of using that form. For example, although at the end of 1986 there was an explosion of conversions of regular corporations to so-called S corporations (corporations with thirty-five or fewer shareholders electing to be taxed at the personal level each year, as in partnerships, rather than at the corporate level), there were relatively few large corporations that converted to partnership form.[15] While there

15. See Myron S. Scholes and Mark A. Wolfson, "The Effects of Changes in Tax Laws on Corporate Reorganization Activity," *Journal of Business*, vol. 63 (January 1990), pp. S141–64.

was a substantial burst of activity undertaken through master limited part-nerships (partnerships whose interests trade on organized exchanges), tax law changes passed in 1987 quickly halted this trend. Indeed, the uncer-tainty over the form such legislation might take was probably sufficient to choke off a good deal of this activity. The 1986 tax act did prompt substantially increased interest in pass-through corporate tax entities, such as real estate investment trusts and real estate mortgage investment con-duits.

Over the last decade a trend toward active investors and concentrated ownership has developed.[16] This trend reflects in part a recognition that in most relevant settings effective monitoring and managerial performance in organizations requires leading investors to have a large stake in orga-nizational performance. Apparently, the favorable incentive effects of concentrated ownership have become increasingly important relative to the risk-sharing benefits that dispersed ownership confers. So partnerships may well become viable as alternatives to even large-scale corporate ac-tivity, particularly if there is a great difference in the tax cost of the two organizational forms. And unless tax planners could conceive of alter-natives to high-yield debt as a way of distributing corporate profits in a tax-deductible manner, corporations would surely begin to lose their dom-inant position.

Of course, alternatives to high-yield debt would be devised if Congress enacted legislation precluding the tax deductibility of interest on such debt. For example, trade credit at low interest rates with corresponding increases in the price of goods and services exchanged would be one obvious response. Closely related would be the use of bank credit at below-market rates, tied to a requirement to maintain interest-free compensating balances.[17] Operating leases would increase as well, with rental expense substituting for interest. Alternatively, key lenders might demand more managerial input in exchange for tax-deductible compensation and reduced interest rates. Still another response would be to reverse the trend toward deconglomeration of corporate America so as to increase the low-risk debt capacity of the firm. Unfortunately, all these responses would exact ef-ficiency costs on the economy.

16. Jensen, "Capital Markets."
17. Such a strategy was widely used in Japan in the face of interest rate ceilings before deregulation in the 1980s, and in the United States under interest-rate ceilings specified in Regulation Q before deregulation. See Takeo Hoshi, Anil Kashyap, and David Scharfstein, "Bank Monitoring and Investment: Evidence from the Changing Structure of Japanese Corporate Banking Relationships," Working Paper 3079 (Cambridge, Mass.: National Bureau of Economic Research, August 1989).

Finally, eliminating interest deductibility on high-yield debt would accelerate the recent trend of foreign acquisitions of U.S. corporations, particularly by investors who reside in tax jurisdictions that do not tax foreign-source income (so-called territorial tax systems). For such investors the U.S. tax exemption on capital gains means that the shareholder-level tax on U.S. corporate income can be avoided.

Alternatives to Debt to Reduce
the Corporate-Level Tax

ESOPs. Employee stock ownership plans (ESOPs) offer three ways to distribute corporate profits to investors in a tax-deductible way: interest on ESOP loans (at specially subsidized rates), employee compensation, and dividends on employee-owned shares. Theoretically, a 100 percent ESOP-owned firm provides a way to eliminate the corporate tax even if substantial physical capital is invested in the firm. The firm can distribute all the firm's before-tax income to its employee-owners in the form of either compensation or dividends that are paid on ESOP-held shares. Compensation is tax deductible, and the dividends paid on the shares held in the ESOP are tax deductible if the dividends are paid to employees (or used to pay down an ESOP loan that was used to acquire the shares held in the ESOP). Such strategies are not possible in 100 percent employee-owned corporations that are not organized as ESOPs, because attempts to distribute, as compensation, 100 percent of precompensation taxable income from a business that requires nontrivial amounts of physical capital will be met with IRS claims of excessive compensation and disguised dividends.

ESOPs have exploded in popularity since 1986, and they provide an opportunity to test the importance of tax and nontax factors in explaining their proliferation. For example, to secure ESOP tax benefits, employee ownership must be allocated in ways that may provide poor performance incentives compared with alternative incentive compensation arrangements. As regards special tax treatment, ESOPs can be viewed as being highly tax subsidized or not subsidized at all, depending on the benchmark against which they are compared. To the extent ESOP plans replace existing stock bonus plans or the investment in employer stock held through a firm's other pension plans, ESOPs offer distinct tax advantages. But to the extent ESOP plans replace debt-financed pension contributions into a plan that holds no employer securities, ESOPs may actually be tax disfavored. If the latter was the relevant case, then the recent popularity of

ESOPs would probably be attributable largely to the voting control they help incumbent managements secure.[18]

Elimination of interest deductibility on high-yield debt would greatly increase the attractiveness of ESOPs. First, employee ownership becomes desirable, since both compensation and ESOP dividends are ways to distribute profits out of the corporation in a tax-deductible way. And second, with 50 percent of interest income on qualified ESOP loans tax exempt to qualified lenders, competition results in interest rates on ESOP loans being reduced. This means that high-risk ESOP loans may bear interest rates comparable to those of low-risk fully taxable loans. Unless a different standard for interest deductibility applied to ESOP loans, the formation of ESOPs would clearly expand tax-deductible debt capacity.[19]

Partnerships and other organizational arrangements. The firm could also form a partnership with its shareholders. That is, if the firm undertakes new investments in a partnership with its shareholders, the new investment escapes corporate-level and shareholder-level taxes if all the income can be passed through directly to the shareholders, who pay tax on this income at their own personal tax rates. But even here, restrictions under section 704(b) of the tax code prevent certain disproportionate allocations of income to specific partners unless such allocations have "substantial economic effect." Also, supplier or customer transfer pricing opportunities can move income from corporate to partnership form. Franchise arrangements could be used. The supplier or customer entity might be set up with current shareholders as owners. The corporation could then set prices strategically to shift corporate-level income to the shareholder partnership. Section 482 of the code restricts these types of transfer pricing opportunities.

Shareholder-Level Taxes and Pension Funds

At the end of 1987, more than 30 percent of all corporate equity was held by pension funds, self-administered pension plans, and insurance

18. For further discussion of these issues, see Myron S. Scholes and Mark A. Wolfson, "Employee Stock Ownership Plans and Corporate Restructuring: Myths and Realities," Working Paper 3094 (Cambridge, Mass.: National Bureau of Economic Research, September 1989).

19. The supposed tax advantages of ESOPs have not escaped the notice of members of the congressional tax committees. As a result, the 1989 tax act curtailed some of their tax advantages.

companies.[20] A common misconception is that the shareholder-level tax for ownership interests held by these entities is zero.[21] But in fact pension funds merely enable their beneficiaries to postpone the tax on investment income until it is distributed.[22] That is true of the income earned through both the corporate and partnership forms. Moreover, if a pension fund invested in the equity, as opposed to the debt, of a partnership, it would normally face a tax liability on "unrelated business income." This tax would be assessed at the corporate rate, t_c. For these reasons, pension fund investors find the corporate form to be less tax disfavored (relative to partnerships) than other investors do, but *not* because such investors avoid shareholder-level taxes.

Retained Earnings and Dividend Policy

An interesting question that has arisen since the passage of the 1981 and 1986 tax acts, which favor partnerships over corporations, is whether existing corporations should liquidate or whether they should continue to reinvest their retained earnings at the corporate level. To answer this question, we begin by ignoring information costs.[23] Suppose a corporation issued equity at its inception and used the proceeds to invest in research and development projects. After deducting the cost of the investment as an expense, it has received a cash return from the project equal to the initial cost of the investment. So the firm has no taxable income or retained earnings, but it has generated cash equal to the original equity issue. It also expects additional cash income in the future from the R&D effort.

Assume that the firm distributes these cash returns to investors. In the absence of any "earnings and profits" in the corporation, any cash dis-

20. Board of Governors of the Federal Reserve System, "Flow of Funds Accounts: Financial Assets and Liabilities, Year-End, 1964–87," September 1988.

21. Conversations with Richard Leftwich have clarified our thinking on this point. Studies that estimate the revenue consequences to the U.S. Treasury of leveraged buyouts and other forms of corporate acquisitions routinely err in assuming that merger premiums received by pension funds that hold shares in target companies generate no tax revenues. (See, for example, Jensen, Kaplan, and Stiglin, "Effects of LBOs on Tax Revenues.") But, in fact, the return premium generates both (deferred) income tax as well as (deferred) estate tax to be paid by beneficiaries.

22. Although a tax deduction for pension contributions followed by full taxation of pension benefits is well known to be equivalent to tax exemption of pension investment income when the pension fund invests exclusively in zero net-present-value projects, this result is not robust to investment in positive net-present-value projects.

23. As discussed earlier, much of corporate activity might not be displaced, because operating in corporate form might dominate partnerships for nontax reasons. These benefits, however, may be overstated.

tributions made to shareholders represent a return of capital that is untaxed but that reduces the tax basis of shares until it falls to zero. As a result, the shareholders have a tax basis of zero on their shares. This basis reduction means that when the shares are sold in the future, taxable capital gains will be increased by the same amount. Moreover, any future after-tax distributions made by the corporation will generate fully taxable income to the stockholders (that is, the shareholder basis cannot be reduced below zero).

When the firm earns another $1 of after-tax corporate income, should the firm retain it or pay out the $1 as a dividend? The answer depends on several factors, but we wish to emphasize that it especially depends on whether there are projects that generate returns above the competitive rate.

When only competitive projects are available, undertaking them through the corporation is approximately equivalent to having investors undertake them on private account after a dividend distribution. If the firm pays out the $1 as a dividend today, shareholders pay taxes at their own personal tax rates, t_{po}, and reinvest the after-tax income on their own account for n periods at an after-tax rate of $R_b(1 - t_{pn})$, or r_{pn} per period.[24] If the firm retains the $1 of after-tax corporate income, in contrast, and invests it on corporate account, it returns $R_b(1 - t_{cn})$, or r_{cn} per period after tax, until it finally distributes the accumulated amount of retained earnings. At that time, shareholders pay tax on the distribution at tax rate t_{pn}. The after-tax accumulations in n periods for the two alternatives are as follows:

Liquidate and invest on personal
    account for n periods: $\$1(1 - t_{po})(1 + r_{pn})^n$

Retain and invest on corporate
    account for n periods before
    liquidating: $\$1(1 + r_{cn})^n(1 - t_{pn})$,

where r_{pn} and r_{cn} should be interpreted as annualized rates of return available over the n-period horizon.

The best strategy depends on two factors. One is the investor's marginal tax rate today, t_{po}, versus the investor's marginal tax rate in the future,

---

24. Note that dividend income is investment income against which investment interest can be deducted. Hence, if t_{po} exceeds the implicit tax on tax-favored investments, borrowing to purchase such assets could reduce the taxpayer's tax burden to a lower level that includes implicit taxes. For elaboration, see Scholes and Wolfson, *Taxes and Business Strategy*.

t_{pn}. A decreasing tax rate, or an ability to convert dividend income into a capital gain taxed at a reduced rate, favors dividend deferral. The other factor is the corporate versus investor after-tax rate of return on investment. A higher corporate rate favors current payout.

If tax rates are constant over time and if corporate and personal after-tax rates of return coincide, it is a matter of indifference whether the competitive projects are undertaken in corporate or partnership form when the corporation is an all-retained earnings firm and shareholders have a zero tax basis in their shares. This is the now-traditional trapped-equity argument from the public finance literature.[25] At first blush, this may seem to be a counterintuitive result. After all, corporate income generates both an entity-level and a shareholder-level tax. The explanation lies in the fact that, marginally, investments financed by retained earnings do not generate a shareholder-level tax.

Notice that investors have an important *timing option* in that they may be able to sell their shares when their tax rates are lower than current rates. For example, if investors find themselves at times in an alternative minimum tax (AMT) position (a 21 percent marginal tax rate) and at other times in a 28 percent or even 33 percent marginal tax rate, they could find that the timing option is quite valuable. By waiting to sell shares (and pay full tax at personal rates on the sale proceeds because their basis in the stock is zero) until they face the potential of paying the AMT, investors would be better off by 10 percent, or $(1 - 0.21)/[(1 - 0.28) - 1]$.[26]

Retained Earnings and Positive Net-Present-Value Projects

The analysis changes when positive net-present-value projects are available. In particular, a marginal round of shareholder-level tax cannot be avoided on the return above the competitive rate. To see this, suppose a

25. See, for example, Mervyn A. King, *Public Policy and the Corporation* (London: Chapman and Hall, 1977); and Alan J. Auerbach, "Wealth Maximization and the Cost of Capital," *Quarterly Journal of Economics*, vol. 93 (August 1979), pp. 433–46.

26. Taxpayers who make large charitable contributions of property that has appreciated in value or hold investments in municipal bonds might find themselves subject to the AMT and not eligible for AMT credit in the future. The same is true for taxpayers who have substantial sums of state income and property taxes and miscellaneous itemized deductions, none of which are tax deductible in calculating the AMT. These taxpayers might want to accelerate the recognition of taxable income to the point where the next dollar of income is taxed at a 28 percent marginal rate currently and the next dollar of expense reduces taxes at the AMT rate of 21 percent.

project is available that yields a return of Y per dollar invested, where Y exceeds the competitive rate R_b. If the project is financed through retained earnings, and the after-tax profit is distributed to shareholders a year later, the net return to the shareholder per dollar invested is

$$[1 + Y(1 - t_c)] (1 - t_p).$$

If, however, a dividend is declared now, and the project is undertaken outside the corporation (say, through a shareholder-owned partnership or proprietorship), an immediate tax of t_p is levied per dollar of dividend. So t_p will have to be borrowed by the individual at rate R_b to finance the entire project. The net to the shareholders becomes

$$(1 - t_p)[1 + Y(1 - t_p)] + t_p[Y(1 - t_p) - R_b(1 - t_p)].$$

This result simplifies to $(1 + Y - t_pR_b)(1 - t_p)$. Comparing the after-tax accumulations in the two strategies reveals that an immediate dividend beats a reinvestment in the corporation by

$$(t_cY - t_pR_b)(1 - t_p).$$

Even if t_c was no larger than t_p, reinvestment of retained earnings in the corporation would subject the excess return on the project to one additional round of tax. With $t_c > t_p$, the advantage of a current dividend is increased.

The intuition behind this result is as follows. When shareholders in an all-retained-earnings firm have a zero tax basis in their shares, they face a tax liability equal to t_p on every dollar of net asset value in the firm. Shareholders have an option of paying off the liability now by distributing corporate property to the owners, or they can pay the tax later, *with interest*, by reinvesting the corporate income. In the second case, the interest rate that shareholders pay on this liability if corporate distributions are postponed is equal to the rate of return the corporation earns on its investments after paying corporate tax. If the corporation invests exclusively in zero net-present-value projects, it earns a competitive rate of return, and shareholders are indifferent about whether they pay their liability now or later. If the investments generate *excess* returns, however, shareholders will prefer to pay the tax liability now rather than pay interest at the high rate earned on the positive net-present-value projects.

The foregoing analysis assumes that the positive net-present-value project can be managed no more effectively in the corporation than in a partnership that might be formed by shareholders to invest corporate distributions in favorable projects. If the positive net-present-value project is available only if undertaken with the corporation, then reinvesting retained earnings in the corporation could prove to be the most efficient strategy.

Concluding Remarks

U.S. tax reforms in the 1980s introduced significant tax disincentives to operate in the corporate form rather than in organizational forms that impose no entity-level tax. There have been two kinds of responses to this shifting of tax costs across organizational forms: (1) direct conversion of regular corporations to organizational forms that avoid entity-level tax; and (2) changes in capital structures of corporations that allow them to avoid some of the entity-level tax by distributing corporate profits to capital suppliers in forms that are tax deductible.

In this paper, we examined the degree to which corporate restructuring can result in the same tax treatment for income earned by corporations, as for that achieved in partnerships. We found that the presence of the tax rule restrictions alone allows corporate projects to avoid double taxation on, at most, the competitive portion of their pretax return streams. Any economic rents earned by corporations face double taxation. That is true of returns to both human capital and physical capital, even when the latter is 100 percent debt financed. Moreover, the presence of market frictions, which leads firms to moderate their propensity to issue debt, causes part of even the competitive return to corporate activity to be taxed twice.

Comment by Laurie Simon Bagwell

The 1980s have been marked by a dramatic realignment in the choice of securities for financing corporate investments. Negative net equity issuance and increases in the use of debt have coincided with substantive tax reform. Interest in and concern about these trends have focused attention on the differential taxation of debt and equity in the United States, especially the controversial "double taxation" of corporations. Corporate income is taxed twice, at both the corporate and personal levels. Unlike equity income, however, interest income paid to bondholders is deductible on the corporate level. A partnership is taxed at the personal level but not as a separate entity. Hence, relative to unlevered corporations, the government subsidizes the use of debt and partnerships.

Scholes and Wolfson give an excellent summary of the arguments explaining the extent to which debt financing can reduce the corporate-level tax. Their most important contribution, however, is an innovative analysis of why corporations are unable to escape the double levels of taxation on economic rents even if they are debt financed. This analysis raises new concerns about the incentives created by current tax treatment.

Despite the double taxation of equity, debt has not always been the more lightly taxed method of financing. Before the Tax Reform Act of 1986, the top corporate tax rate was dominated by the top personal rates. For some investors the combined corporate and personal taxes borne on equity income were outweighed by the massive marginal rate paid on interest income. After the Economic Recovery Tax Act of 1981, reductions in personal rates encouraged an increase in the use of corporate borrowing. Following the 1986 tax act, the favorable tax treatment afforded debt (the corporate rate of 34 percent being greater than the top personal bracket), combined with a decline in interest rates, has further enhanced the relative attractiveness of debt. This effect is consistent with the vast buyback of more than $435 billion of equity between 1984 and 1987, through repurchases and cash acquisitions, which John Shoven and I have documented elsewhere.[27]

The authors first review the possibilities for a corporation to avoid corporate-level taxes on its competitive return, and therefore be taxed as a partnership. They consider an all debt firm in which the interest payments on debt equal the taxable return on the investment project being financed. All income earned by the corporation escapes the corporate-level tax by interest deductibility, and the corporation is taxed identically to a partnership. Bondholders realize the after-personal-tax rate of return on the income.

There are many limits to the implementation of such a strategy. Tax rule restrictions preclude this tax avoidance strategy by requiring the existence of a significant proportion of shares held independently of bonds whenever one security is taxed as debt. Because total tax avoidance requires the entire competitive return to be paid out to bondholders, these

27. Laurie Simon Bagwell and John B. Shoven, "Cash Distributions to Shareholders," *Journal of Economic Perspectives*, vol. 3 (Summer 1989), pp. 129–40.

restrictions limit the ability of corporations to recreate the partnership tax treatment.

The costs of restructuring also limit avoidance of corporate taxation. There may be nontax costs and benefits associated with the different securities used to finance investments. For example, debt may act to monitor management, or to signal an optimistic future for the firm. Increased debt, however, may cause conflicts over risk sharing and wealth expropriation between debt and equity claimants, and may increase the probability of financial distress and bankruptcy. These nontax factors may limit the use of debt in tax avoidance.

The most important contribution of this paper is demonstrating that double taxation is unavoidable on any return the firm earns above the competitive rate, even in a completely levered corporation where the limitations discussed above do not exist. Full corporate taxes will be owed on any excessive return the firm is able to generate, thus implying a true tax advantage to partnerships. Additional corporate borrowing, when the proceeds are distributed to shareholders, fails to convert the tax rate on the excess return to the personal tax treatment granted partnerships. When the firm earns only abnormal returns for a limited time, moreover, the partnership form is even more tax advantaged relative to the all debt corporation.

This paper, therefore, increases the concern about the incentives created by the current tax system. First, the differential tax treatment of debt and equity causes an obvious distortion in the choice of capital structure. Firms have a greater incentive to look to debt alternatives for reducing the corporate-level tax. The prevalence of employee stock ownership plans (ESOPs) may in part be motivated by their tax advantages, so that their use in the presence of important nontax considerations may be distorted. By augmenting the stake in ownership, ESOPs may increase employee motivation and productivity, as well as deter takeovers. In an era of meteoric increases in the cost of health benefits, ESOPs often alter employee compensation in favor of lower fixed-benefit costs. But they also alter employee retirement benefits toward a portfolio highly concentrated in the firm's own equity. When firms choose whether to implement such a strategy, these alternative considerations are weighed against the favorable tax treatment.

Second, since partnerships avoid double taxation, the choice of corporate form is also distorted. Recent proposals to eliminate the deductibility of interest would imply that even less of the competitive return could escape corporate-level taxation. This would make partnerships even more attractive. A recent explosion has occurred in the conversion of regular corporations to S corporations, which are taxed only at the personal level. This conversion is not yet the case for large corporations, perhaps because of the benefits of risk sharing and liquidity that partnerships fail to provide. Since the incentive and informational issues differentiate the organizational forms, we all must be concerned about the efficiency implications of government-induced distortions in the choice of organizational form.

Most important, this paper allows us to consider whether excess returns are encouraged or penalized by taxation. Since corporations cannot escape the corporate tax on the positive net-present-value portion of a project's return, the asymmetric taxation of competitive and abnormal returns may cause investment distortions. A firm with constrained liquidity that must choose among positive net-present-value projects will choose to maximize after-tax return. The projects chosen may not be those with the highest pretax net present value.

Assume that there are two positive net-present-value projects, each of which requires a dollar investment. Because the corporation has only one dollar to invest, this liquidity constraint implies that the firm will have to choose only one project. Taxation exists at both the personal and corporate levels. Following the paper, let the corporate marginal tax rate (t_c) be 0.34, the shareholder-level tax rate (t_s) be 0.20, and the marginal tax rate on income (t_p) be 0.28. This example shows how double taxation on excess returns may induce the firm to distort its investment choices toward lower net-present-value investments.

Assume that the risk-free rate (R_f) is 8 percent. The first project requires zero risk premium $(\pi = 0)$; thus its competitive rate of return (R_b) is 8 percent. However, it has economic rents such that it earns a return (Y) of 20 percent. This project has a pretax net present value of 11 percent, as found by this equation:

(1) $$pretax\ NPV = (1 + Y - \pi)/(1 + R_f) - 1.$$

Its total after-tax return, to both bondholders and shareholders, is found by the following equation to be 12.1 percent:

(2) $$after\text{-}tax\ return = (Y - R_b)(1 - t_c)(1 - t_s) + R_b(1 - t_p).$$

The second project demands a risk premium of 12 percent $(\pi = 0.12)$; thus its competitive rate of return (R_b) is 20 percent. However, it also has economic rents such that it earns a return (Y) of 30 percent. This project has a pretax net present value of 9.3 percent, as found by equation 1. With a lower net present value than the first project, the second project is not expected to be chosen. The differential taxation of competitive and excess returns, however, will result in a distortion whereby the second project, which has a higher after-tax return, will be chosen. Its after-tax return is found by equation 2 to be 19.7 percent.

This example raises an important concern: is the current tax policy subsidizing lower net-present-value projects? An optimal tax policy would avoid such investment distortion. Current policy, however, may be inducing the implementation of lower net-present-value projects owing to the nondeductibility of excess returns.

With so much attention being paid to the revenues raised by, and incentives created by, taxation, debate about the tax treatment of securities for financing corporate investments will certainly continue. By revealing the extent to which double taxation is unavoidable on excess returns, Scholes and Wolfson focus on a new facet of the incentives implicit in current tax treatment. This will add to the controversy.

Comment by Jeremy I. Bulow

Myron Scholes and Mark Wolfson have as sophisticated a knowledge of the U.S. tax code as any two academic economists. In their paper they show how difficult it is to escape at least some "double taxation" when assets are held in corporate form. In their analysis they stress the importance of looking at the tax system as a whole, noting that though some firms may reduce their corporate tax burden, they will at the same time trigger the payment of other taxes.

While I do not disagree with the authors' results, I would have expressed them differently. For example, they argue that the corporate tax particularly hits positive net-present-value projects. That is, they contend that corporations can escape corporate-level tax on zero net-present-value projects by using debt finance, but cannot do the same with the excess return portion of positive net-present-value projects. This description is somewhat misleading. If a corporation purchased a positive net-present-value project at market value, then according to the authors' model it *would* be able to avoid corporate tax by using debt finance. Similarly, as stated in the paper, a firm cannot avoid the corporate double tax by selling a positive net-present-value project to a noncorporate entity.

Moreover, if a corporation's positive net-present-value investments are in tax-sheltered areas, very little, if any, tax may be paid by a corporation. For example, if a corporation invests in an asset that grows in value at the inflation rate but only generates taxable income at the real interest rate, then the tax payable on a positive net-present-value investment will be much less. If for some reason part of the realized income is excludable from tax, then a positive net-present-value project might not yield any explicit tax even when held in corporate form.

More generally, the authors' results about the difficulty of escaping corporate tax apply not to positive net-present-value projects but to assets for which the market value exceeds the tax basis. Furthermore, I question whether they apply to all assets or exclude certain assets such as real estate. Real estate is the asset most likely to have a market value far above its tax basis. The restructuring of Hospital Corporation of America and some of the large hotel chains indicates that by spinning off real estate assets, a corporation can avoid corporate-level tax on these assets.

Scholes and Wolfson's argument that corporate pension assets are taxed also bears some clarification. As a benchmark case, consider a defined-contribution pension in which workers own all the assets in the fund. Those assets should obviously be managed to maximize pretax return. The government shares in the pension fund's profits only in that the pension beneficiary will owe more personal tax if the fund earns a higher return. This suggests that to the extent that pensions will invest in high-yielding, tax-disfavored investments such as junk bonds to capitalize on their ability to accumulate money tax free, the government can expect to recapture some of these excess returns through the personal tax.

As for well-funded defined-benefit plans, where the corporation may bear the risk of any changes in the value of fund assets, the logic is about the same. If a fund earns an extra dollar in returns, then the government will recapture some extra tax revenue whenever that extra dollar is removed from the pension fund, either through direct withdrawal or through lower future contributions. If the fund earns an extra dollar and the firm immediately has to reduce its pension contributions by a dollar, then the tax revenue is the same as if the firm earned an extra fully taxable dollar on corporate account. It still seems appropriate to think of the pension fund as a tax-free corporate savings account, simply with the recognition that limitations on future contributions may be reduced by superior investment performance.

The authors are also correct in noting that any attempts to curtail the interest deduction on debt will lead to the increased use of various techniques ranging from financial leases to higher prices and lower interest rates charged by suppliers. However, I am unconvinced that no changes should be made in this area. For example, an indexed tax system should sharply reduce the tax advantage of debt financing and create the same incentives to increase leasing and other debt-like activities. But that does not seem to be a compelling argument against indexation.

In summary, Scholes and Wolfson have written a thought-provoking paper about how to view the corporate income tax, especially when personal and other taxes are taken into account. However, I would have expressed some of their results somewhat differently.

Contributors

ALAN J. AUERBACH
Department of Economics
University of Pennsylvania

WILLIAM D. ANDREWS
School of Law
Harvard University

LAURIE SIMON BAGWELL
Kellogg Graduate School of Management
Northwestern University

MARGARET M. BLAIR
Brookings Institution

DAVID F. BRADFORD
Woodrow Wilson School
Princeton University

JEREMY I. BULOW
Graduate School of Business
Stanford University

MARTIN D. GINSBURG
Georgetown University Law Center

JANE G. GRAVELLE
Congressional Research Service
Library of Congress

ROBERT E. LITAN
Brookings Institution

JAMES M. POTERBA
Department of Economics
Massachusetts Institute of Technology

MYRON S. SCHOLES
Graduate School of Business
Stanford University

JOHN B. SHOVEN
Department of Economics
Stanford University

SCOTT SMART
Department of Economics
Stanford University

C. EUGENE STEUERLE
Urban Institute

LAWRENCE H. SUMMERS
Department of Economics
Harvard University

VICTORIA P. SUMMERS
School of Law
Harvard University

ROBERT A. TAGGART, JR.
Wallace E. Carroll School of Management
Boston College

JOEL WALDFOGEL
Department of Economics
Yale University

MARK A. WOLFSON
Graduate School of Business
Stanford University

Index

Aaron, Henry J., 97n, 119n, 124, 125, 174n
Adjustable rate convertible bond (ARCN), 143–44
Advance corporation tax, United Kingdom, 112n
Agency costs, for monitoring corporate managers: under free cash flow theory, 56; LBOs reduction of, 44, 55
Aghion, Phillippe, 181n
ALI. *See* American Law Institute
Alternative minimum tax, 194
Altman, Edward I., 96n
American Law Institute (ALI) corporate tax reform proposal, 10, 11, 18–19; cash flow tax compared with, 125, 126; drawbacks, 118–19; evaluation of, 132–33; by minimum tax on nondividend distributions, 15–16, 116–17; to remove windfall from dividend relief, 10, 114, 115–18, 126; for tax deductibility of new equity dividends, 15, 115–16, 117–18
Andrews, William D., 114, 119n, 171
ARCN. *See* Adjustable rate convertible bond
Auerbach, Alan J., 1n, 5n, 10, 11, 18, 33n, 95n, 96n, 97n, 101n, 102n, 104n, 109n, 121n, 156n, 162n, 174n, 194n

Bagwell, Laurie Simon, 94n, 197n
Bankruptcy: costs, 5; indicators of risk of, 8; and investment spending, 50; social costs of risk-taking associated with, 103, 105; tax treatment of debt forgiveness in, 143, 168
Berle, Adolf A., 55n
Bernanke, Ben S., 9n, 46n, 65n, 85
Bernheim, B. Douglas, 146n
Blair, Margaret M., 5, 8, 13–14, 18, 55n

Bolton, Patrick, 181n
Bonds: adjustable rate convertible, 143–44; original issue discount, 50, 51, 139, 142; zero coupon, 142–43
Bosworth, Barry P., 79n
Bower, Dorothy H., 84n
Bower, Richard S., 84n
Bracket creep: effect on individual debt, 12, 27; inflation-induced, 39
Bradford, David F., 33n, 96n, 119n
Brealy, Richard, 58n
Bronars, Stephen G., 156
Brooks, Stephen H., 146n
Browne, Lynn E., 82n
Bruck, Connie, 141n
Buffet, Warren, 155
Bulow, Jeremy I., 10, 17–18, 104, 106

Campbell, John Y., 9n, 46n, 65n, 85
Capital: existing versus new equity as source of, 94–96; free cash flow theory of, 56, 82, 84; increase in debt-financing, 61; LBO activity and returns to, 67, 73, 87; manufacturing industries ranked by cost of, and returns to, 14, 57–59; measures of cost of, 57–59, 83, 86; opportunity cost, 57, 58; pecking order theory of, 82, 85; pretax return on, 57, 59; return to, by industry, 59, 67, 71; static trade-off theory of, 81–82, 83, 84; tax treatment of existing versus new, 107–08
Capital gains tax, 3; and debt-to-asset ratios, 41–42; Economic Recovery Act of *1981* and, 175; Tax Reform Act of *1986* elimination of preferential treatment for, 3, 41, 43, 93, 98, 101–02
Cash flow: defined, 56n; ratio of interest payments to, 14, 50–52, 65, 73; stability

205

of, by industry, 78, 88. *See also* Cash flow tax; Free cash flow theory

Cash flow tax: to avoid windfalls, 122, 126; described, 11, 16–17; disallowance of interest deduction under, 119–20, 121; effects, 122–23; evaluation of, 123–26, 133; as part of consumption taxation, 119; problems relating to, 123; treatment of existing equity, 16–17, 122

Chandler, Alfred D., Jr., 55n

Corporate business: agency costs for managing, 44, 55; conflict of interest between shareholders and management, 55–56; elasticity of demand for, 188–89; new equity issues by, 6, 53; taxation of investments financed by retained earnings, 192–94; taxation of unincorporated business versus, 93–98; tax on positive net-present-value projects, 194–96. *See also* Corporate debt; Corporate income tax

Corporate debt: changes in management style related to, 61, 135; expected increases in share of total debt, 22, 35–36, 37; functions, 61; increase in, 35–36, 137–38; Internal Revenue Code rules for distinguishing equity from, 17, 139–45; model of tax advantge of, 177–79; nontax factors influencing, 103–05, 175; ratio to GNP, 9, 25, 138; risk associated with, 36, 103; social costs, 103, 105; substitutability of equity and, 1, 5, 6, 61, 91, 104; tax reform to reduce bias in favor of, 106–08, 160; tax system bias in favor of, 3–4, 19, 27, 31–32, 40–41, 83, 91–92, 135, 138–39, 173–74, 176. *See also* Debt-equity ratio; Debt-to-asset ratio

Corporate income tax: bias toward LBOs and other corporate restructuring, 100, 130–31, 148–49, 151; borrowing strategies to eliminate, 181–83; characteristics of provisions applied to, 92–93; corporate restructuring to eliminate, 187–88; and dividend distribution versus earnings retention, 98–99; employee stock ownership plans to avoid, 19, 190–91; and equity-to-debt ratios, 32–33, 99–100; on excess returns, 195, 199–200, 201–02; on existing versus new coporations, 94; leverage increase to eliminate, 184–86; noncorporate income tax versus, 93–98; problem of analyzing, 127–28; proposed full integration of individual income tax and, 92, 105, 108–09;

proposed reduction in, 163; on reinvestment of retained earnings, 192–95; Tax Reform Act of *1986* and, 35, 43, 96, 97

Corporate restructuring, 1–2, 6–7; consequences to third parties from, 155–56; debt incurred in connection with, 54; efficiency gains from, 152–53; to eliminate corporate tax, 187–88; and increase in debt-equity ratio, 137–40; interest rate movements and 78–79, 89; investment opportunities associated with, 73, 81, 84, 89; predictions of, 88; proposed tax reform for, 160–66; securities market reaction to, 81; tax system effect on, 5–6, 153, 161; timing of, 5–6, 81, 89. *See also* Leverage; Leveraged buyouts; Mergers and acquisitions

Cutler, David M., 128n

Debt, total: deregulation and, 12, 31, 34; fiscal policy and, 30–31; foreign investment preference and, 38; problem in predicting future of, 41–42; ratio to GNP, 12, 29–30; role of pension and insurance reserves in increasing, 38, 39; sectoral allocations, 21, 24–25; sectoral differences in growth, 9, 12, 25–26; stability in postwar, 23–24. *See also* Corporate debt; Debt-equity ratio; Debt-to-asset ratio; Farm sector debt; Federal government debt; Household sector debt; Individual debt; Noncorporate debt; Private sector debt

Debt-equity ratio: book-value versus market-value calculation of, 46; corporate income tax and, 32–33, 99–100; as indicator of leverage, 50; Internal Revenue Code regulations on, 140; LBOs and, 100

Debt-to-asset ratio: to measure LBO activity, 66; to measure leverage activity, 65; predictions of, by industry, 76–77; risk associated with, 33; sectoral differences in, 21–22, 31, 33–34, 35; tax system effect on, 40–41, 42

Deere, Donald R., 156

Deficit Reduction Act, *1984*, 176n

Deregulation, financial, and debt increase, 12, 31, 34

Dividend relief: ALI proposal for, 10, 15–16, 18–19, 114–19; avoiding windfalls from, 114–15; comparison of plans for, 125–26; drawbacks, 112–13, 161; to eliminate tax bias in favor of debt, 10, 160;

foreign countries use of, 160–61; imputation system for, 111, 112; by minimum
tax on nondividend distributions, 117,
132; partial integration through, 15, 92,
109, 160; split-rate system for, 109, 111–
12
Dividends: corporate retention of earnings
versus, 98–99; "new theory" of, 33, 36;
percent of total cash distributions, 6; taxation of equity from share repurchases versus, 15, 95, 99, 102, 117. *See also*
Dividend relief; Double taxation
Double taxation: ALI plan to alleviate, 10,
116–18; burden on equity, 10, 92, 94–95,
179–81; corporate inability to avoid, 182,
197–98; of corporations versus partnerships, 180–81, 182. *See also* Dividend relief
Drexel Burnham Lambert, 141, 147
Dworin, Lowell, 30n

Economic Recovery Tax Act of *1981*, 96,
175, 197
Economic rents, taxation, 107, 179–81, 197
Employee stock ownership plans (ESOPs):
avoidance of corporate tax with, 19, 190–
91; employee compensation and benefits
under, 198
Equity: accelerated versus contributed, 133;
capital from existing versus new, 94–96;
double taxation of, 10, 92, 94–95, 179–
81; "in drag," 17, 135, 136, 160; Internal Revenue Code rules for distinguishing
debt from, 17, 139–45; methods for retiring 6–7, 91, 137; revenue from selective
share repurchases of, 36n; substitutability
of debt and, 1, 5, 6, 61, 91, 104; Tax Reform Act of *1986* and, 4, 97–98
ESOPs. *See* Employee stock ownership plans

Farm sector debt: increase in, 12, 22, 24; inflation effect on, 24–25; ratio to assets,
31, 33
Fazzari, Steven M., 73n
Federal government debt: fiscal policy and,
11–12; postwar reduction of, 24; private
sector absorption of funds from declining,
29; ratio to GNP, 9, 12, 30; results of, 23
Feldstein, Martin, 119n
Fiscal policy: and changes in federal indebtedness, 11–12, 30; and interest rates, 30–
31; and total debt increase, 11, 12

Flack, Stuart, 156n
Ford Motor Company, acquisition of Jaguar,
157–58
France, dividend relief from double taxation,
160–61
Free cash flow theory: agency costs of monitoring management, 56; described, 13,
56n; on disciplinary investment management, 82; evaluation of, 89; to explain leverage and LBO activity, *1980*s, 44, 54–
56, 59, 61, 67; regression technique to
test, 45, 75–77, 87
Friedman, Benjamin M., 23n, 29n, 43, 50n
Fullerton, Don, 111n

Gabelli, Mario, 155
Galper, Harvey, 97n, 119n, 124, 125, 174n
Gay, Robert S., 36n
Geneen, Harold S., 153
General utilities doctrine, repeal, 98, 101–
02, 154
Ginsburg, Martin D., 170n
GNP: corporate debt ratio to, 9, 25, 138; to-
tal debt ratio to, 12
Goldman Sachs: creation of adjustable rate
convertible note, 143; estimates of restruc-
turing-related debt, 54, 61
Gordon, Rogert H., 124
Graetz, Michael J., 113, 115n, 138n
Gravelle, Jane G., 44n

Hatsopoulos, George N., 146n
High-yield securities: change in tax treatment
of, *1989*, 164; as "equity in drag," 17,
135, 160; to finance new capital investment, 146–47; indebtedness from restru-
curings use of, 135–36, 147–48; proposed
elimination of interest deductibility on,
188–90; tax incentives for, 139, 143, 148
Hoshi, Takeo, 189n
Household sector debt: increase in, 11, 12,
22, 24; interest rate decline and, 24; ratio
to GNP, 9, 12
Hubbard, R. Glenn, 73n
Hulten, C. R., 97n

Individual debt, 12; bracket creep and, 27;
factors influencing, 21; future share of total debt, 35; tax system encouragement of,
27, 29
Individual income tax: progressivity, 94; proposed full integration of corporate income

tax and, 92, 105, 108–09; rate, 35, 91, 138, 175; Tax Reform Act of *1986* and, 176

Individual retirement accounts (IRAs), tax arbitrage gain from, 32, 39

Inflationary economy: benefits of debt finance in, 39–40; effect on noncorporate debt, 24–25; marginal tax rate increase in, 39; taxation of interest-bearing assets in, 25

Insurance funds: corporate equity held by, 191–92; debt relative to GNP, 39

Interest–cash flow ratio: increase in, 50–52; measure of leverage, 14, 65; predictions of, by industry, 74–77; relationship of debt-asset ratio and, 73

Interest payments: proposed tax disallowance for, 113–14, 162–63, 167; ratio to cash flow, 14, 50–52, 65, 73; stock prices and, 52–53

Interest rates: corporate restructuring in response to, 78–79, 86, 88; fiscal policy and, 30–31; investment response to, 74, 79; removal of ceilings on, 12, 31, 34; and use of debt, 13

Internal Revenue Code, section 385; rules for distinguishing debt from equity, 17, 139–40; violations of, 140–45

Investment, corporate: cash flow retained for, 56; correlation between returns on capital, leverage activity, and, 72–73, 81; high-yield securities to finance, 145, 146–47; indicators of opportunities in, 73; leverage associated with opportunities in, 73, 81, 84; measures to evaluate, 57–59; opportunity cost of capital and, 57; response to interest rates, 74, 79; tax policy to encourage productivity growth through, 129

IRAs. *See* Individual retirement accounts

Japan: interest rate for bank trade credit, 189n; relief from double taxation of dividends, 160–61

Jensen, Michael C., 13, 18n, 36n, 44, 54–56, 82n, 83n, 88, 89, 116n, 143, 144, 145n, 147, 148n, 149, 150, 151, 155, 157, 175n, 187n, 192n

Jorgenson, Dale W., 146n

Junk bonds, 5; "backdoor integration" with, 17, 19; leverage and LBO response to market for, 45; performance, 155; role in

corporate income tax policy, 139; social costs, 104

Kaplan, Steven N., 18n, 36n, 89, 149, 150, 151, 154, 155, 187n, 192n

Kashyap, Anil, 189n

King, Mervyn A., 111n, 121n, 194n

Kohlberg Kravis Roberts, 80n, 141; profitability of investment, 154; and RJR Nabisco buyout, 148–49

Landau, Ralph, 146n

Lawrence, Robert Z., 50n

LBOs. *See* Leveraged buyouts

Leftwich, Richard, 192n

Leland, Hayne E., 149

Leverage: benefit to foreign investors, 185; correlation between investment returns on capital and, 72–73; debt-asset ratio to measure, 7–8, 46, 50, 65; equity retirements and, 6–7; free cash flow and, 44, 54–56, 59, 61, 67; hybrid measures of, 9; increase in, by industry, 63, 65–66, 67; interest payments–cash flow ratio to measure, 8–9, 50–52, 65; relationship with LBOs, 6, 13, 44, 85; secular trend in use of, 74–75; sources of increase in, 43–45, 176

Leveraged buyouts (LBOs), 14, 16; benefits from, 151–53, 154, 159; consequences for third parties, 156–59; and debt-equity ratios, 100, 140–41; and economic efficiency, 151–53, 155–56, 165; increase in, by industry, 63, 65, 66–67; measures of, 63–66; misvaluation of value created in, 156–57; as percent of all takeover activity, 46, 55; profitability of investments, 154; R&D expenditures by firms in, 80, 89, 158–59; relationship with leverage, 6, 13, 44, 85; reorganization of companies involved in, 143; revenue results from, 36n, 149–51; sources of increasing activity in, 43–45, 55–56; tax subsidy for, 18, 100, 130–31, 148–49, 151; and total growth in corporate debt, 54

Levin, Jack S., 170n

Lichtenberg, Frank R., 80n, 89

Litan, Robert E., 5, 8, 13–14, 18, 50n

Logue, Dennis E., 84n

Long, William F., 80n

Lowenstein, Roger, 139n, 155n

McLure, Charles E., Jr., 92n, 108n, 112n
Management buyouts (MBOs), 154–55
Manufacturing sector: cost of, and net return
    on capital in, 14, 57–59; mergers and ac-
    quisitions in, *1986*, 46; pretax return to
    capital in, 59
Means, Gardiner C., 55n
Mergers and acquisitions: shift to LBOs
    from, 100; tax laws effect on, 100–02; up-
    ward trend in number of, *1978–88*, 46
Milken, Michael, 147, 157
Miller, Merton H., 4n, 83n, 97n, 174n
Minimum tax on distributions (MTD), pro-
    posed: benefits, 132, 171–72; on equity
    from share repurchases, 15–16, 117, 132,
    171
Modigliani, Franco, 83n
Moody's AAA corporate bond rate, 58, 83,
    86
Morgan Stanley: LBO data base, 54; "origi-
    nal issue discount" bonds data, 51
MTD. *See* Minimum tax on distributions
Myers, Stewart C., 58n, 81n, 83

Nathans, Leah J., 154n
National Income and Product Accounts
    (NIPA), interest data, 50, 51, 65n
National Science Foundation, study on R&D
    expenditures, 158–59
Nelson, Susan, 30n
NIPA. *See* National Income and Product Ac-
    counts
Noncorporate business, taxation of corporate
    business versus, 93–98, 106
Noncorporate debt: factors influencing, 38;
    future, 22; increase in, 12, 22, 24–25; ra-
    tio to assets, 33–34, 35, 38; risk in, 34,
    36; tax system effect on, 40

Original issue discount bonds (OIDs), 50; In-
    ternal Revenue Code of *1986* on, 170n;
    percent of corporate debt obligations, 51;
    tax advantages, 139, 143; zero coupon
    bonds as, 142

Partnerships: avoidance of double taxation,
    180–81; elimination of interest deductibil-
    ity effect on, 198–99; pretax return on
    projects, 181; tax advantage for corpora-
    tions versus, 188–90, 192–96; tax on
    high-yield debt of, 188–90; tax on positive

net-present-value projects of, 194–96; tax
    on retained earnings of, 192–94
Paulus, John D., 36n
Pay-in-kind securities: interest payment op-
    tion on, 142; Internal Revenue Code of
    1986 on, 170n; issued in RJR Nabisco
    buyout, 135, 140–41, 142, 143, 148–49,
    168; performance, 155; tax advantages,
    143
Pechman, Joseph A., 97n, 174n
Pension funds: corporate equity held by,
    191; debt relative to GNP, 39; investment
    in corporations versus partnerships by,
    192; taxation of assets, 201
Petersen, Bruce C., 73n
Petroleum refining industry, leverage activ-
    ity, 71–72
Positive net-present-value projects: double
    taxation of, 200; net return from rein-
    vested retained earnings versus dividends,
    195; tax liability of corporation versus
    partnership, 195–96, 197; tax on excess
    returns portion of, 199–200
Poterba, James M., 96n, 99n, 126, 128n
Price, Michael, 155
Price-earnings ratios, 9; free cash flow
    theory and, 73–74, 87
Primary metals industry, leverage activity,
    71
Private sector debt: factors influencing allo-
    cation, 21; postwar increase in, 24, 29; ra-
    tio to assets, 21–22

Quint, Michael, 142n

Rasche, Robert H., 29n
Ravenscraft, David J., 80n
Reishus, David, 1n, 101n, 102n
Research and development, LBO firms and,
    80, 89, 158–59
Revenue Reconciliation Act of *1989*, 163–
    64, 170
Riklis, Meshulem, 141
RJR Nabisco buyout, 168, 187; pay-in-kind
    securities issued in, 135, 140–41, 142,
    148–49; projected net investment, 158; tax
    subsidy in, 148–49
Roach, Stephen S., 54
Rosengren, Eric S., 82n
Rubber and plastics industry, leverage activ-
    ity, 71

Saunders, Laura, 187n
Scharfstein, David, 189n
Scholes, Myron S., 19, 83, 95n, 174n, 191n
Scholz, John Karl, 4n
Schultze, Charles L., 50n
Share repurchases: benefit to foreign inves-
    tors, 185; under full versus partial integra-
    tion, 113; proposed minimum tax on
    distributions from, 16, 117, 132, 171; rev-
    enue from selective, 36n; taxation of divi-
    dends versus equity from, 15, 95, 99,
    102, 117; Tax Reform Act of 1986 and,
    97–98
Shay, Robert P., 24n
Shleifer, Andrei, 156, 159
Shoven, John B., 33n, 94n, 146n, 197
Siegel, Donald, 80n, 89
Slemrod, Joel, 124
Steuerle, C. Eugene, 9, 11–13, 27n, 97n
Stiglin, Laura, 18n, 36n, 149, 150, 151,
    155, 187n, 192n
Stiglitz, Joseph E., 107n, 174n
Stone, clay, and glass industry, leverage ac-
    tivity, 71
Stocks: corporate interest burden and prices
    of, 52–53; preferred, 152, 174; pre-tax re-
    turn differential on returns from, 174; tax
    structure effect on dividend versus nondi-
    vidend distributions from, 98–99. See also
    Equity; Share repurchases
Strip financing, 144–45, 175
Subrahmanyam, Marti G., 96n
Summers, Lawrence H., 10, 17–18, 33n,
    50n, 96n, 99n, 104, 106, 124n, 128, 156,
    159
Summers, Victoria, 10, 17–18, 104, 106

Taggart, Robert A., Jr., 5n, 82n
Tax arbitrage: and debt increase, 12, 32, 34,
    38; debt-equity, 32, 104; noncorporate sec-
    tor, 40; real estate opportunities for, 27, 29;
    tax advantage from pure, 32; tax rates on
    interest income under normal, 27, 32
Tax integration: adoption of partial, 92; and
    corporate restructuring, 161; failure to
    adopt, 92, 105; junk bond finance and
    "backdoor," 17, 19; and new investment,
    161; share repurchases under partial versus
    full, 113; windfalls from, 10, 15, 18,
    108–09

Tax rates: corporate, 35, 43, 96, 97, 138,
    175; effect on debt holdings, 12, 13, 138;
    individual 35, 91, 138, 175; reform pro-
    posals for, 106, 108
Tax Reform Act of 1986: and capital gains
    taxation, 3, 43, 98, 154; and corporate
    debt finance, 41, 83, 127–28, 176; corpo-
    rate income tax rate, 35, 43, 96, 97, 138;
    effect on debt versus equity finance, 43–
    44; and elasticity of demand for corporate
    form of business, 188–89; individual tax
    rate, 35, 91, 138, 175; potential effect on
    total debt, 13; repeal of general utilities
    doctrine, 98, 101–02, 154; and retention
    of corporate equity, 97–98
Tax reform proposals: minimum tax on dis-
    tributions, 15–16, 117, 132, 171–72; to
    reduce tax bias for debt finance, 106–08,
    166–69; Revenue Reconciliation Act of
    1989, 163–64, 170. See also American
    Law Institute corporate tax reform pro-
    posal; Dividend relief; Cash flow tax; Tax
    integration
Tax shelters, 32, 34
Tax system, 1–2; bias in favor of corporate
    debt, 3–4, 19, 27, 31–32, 40–41, 83, 91–
    92, 135, 138–39, 173–74, 176; indexa-
    tion, 202; influence on individual versus
    corporate borrowing, 27, 31–32
Textile mill industry, leverage activity, 71
Titman, Sheridan, 84n
Treasury: and Internal Revenue Code, sec-
    tion 385, 139, 143; reclassification of ad-
    justable rate convertible bond, 144

United Kingdom: advance corporation tax,
    112n; dividend relief from double taxa-
    tion, 160–61

Warren, Alvin, 92n
Wessels, Roberto, 84n
West Germany, dividend relief from double
    taxation, 160–61
Wigmore, Barrie, 155
Windfalls: ALI plan to avoid, 115–18, 126;
    cash flow tax to avoid, 119–25; from divi-
    dend relief, 114–15; reform structure for,
    128–29; from tax integration, 10, 15, 18,
    108–09
Wolfson, Mark A., 19, 83, 95n, 174n, 191n